THE PRICE OF GREATNESS

Also by Jay Cost
*A Republic No More: Big Government and the
Rise of American Political Corruption*

THE
PRICE

OF

GREATNESS

Alexander Hamilton, James Madison, *and the* Creation *of* American Oligarchy

JAY COST

BASIC BOOKS

New York

Basic Books
Hachette Book Group
1290 Avenue of the Americas, New York, NY 10104
www.basicbooks.com

Printed in the United States of America

First Edition: June 2018

Published by Basic Books, an imprint of Perseus Books, LLC, a subsidiary of Hachette Book Group, Inc. The Basic Books name and logo is a trademark of the Hachette Book Group.

The publisher is not responsible for websites (or their content) that are not owned by the publisher.

Print book interior design by Amy Quinn

Library of Congress Cataloging-in-Publication Data
Names: Cost, Jay, author.
Title: The Price of Greatness : Alexander Hamilton, James Madison, and the Creation of American Oligarchy / Jay Cost.
Description: First edition. | New York : Basic Books, [2018] | Includes bibliographical references and index.
Identifiers: LCCN 2017042662| ISBN 9781541697461 (hardcover) | ISBN 9781541697485 (ebook)
Subjects: LCSH: United States—Politics and government—1789–1815. | Madison, James, 1751–1836. | Hamilton, Alexander, 1757–1804.
Classification: LCC E310 .C795 2018 | DDC 973.2/6—dc23
LC record available at https://lccn.loc.gov/2017042662

ISBNs: 978-1-5416-9746-1 (hardcover), 978-1-5416-9748-5 (ebook)

LSC-C

10 9 8 7 6 5 4 3 2 1

This work is dedicated to my parents, John and Lyn Cost

CONTENTS

AUTHOR'S NOTE

For the convenience of the reader, I have altered the spelling, capitalization, and punctuation of historical passages to make them conform to modern conventions. No substantive changes of any sort have been made to direct quotations.

INTRODUCTION

LIKE FASHION, AMERICAN political biography is notoriously faddish. With the exception of a few hardy perennials like Abraham Lincoln and George Washington, historical figures often fall in and out of favor with biographers. Not that long ago, Thomas Jefferson and Andrew Jackson were popular subjects, but interest in them has waned noticeably in recent years. Lately, more attention has been paid to Alexander Hamilton and James Madison—perhaps more so than at any point since their own times. Hamilton was the subject of a widely acclaimed 2004 biography by Ron Chernow, which reintroduced the first secretary of the treasury to Americans and inspired the award-winning Broadway hit *Hamilton*. There will probably never be a musical written about Madison, a quiet, diminutive planter from Virginia, but he has also enjoyed a renaissance and has been the subject of many scholarly treatments in recent years as well as of biographies geared toward a mass audience, including one written by Lynne Cheney, the former second lady of the United States.

This renewed interest in Madison and Hamilton is richly deserved. Too young to lead the country into the Revolutionary War, they were nevertheless among the heroes who helped save the peace. Having ascended to the summit of American politics by the mid-1780s, they were indispensable in framing the Constitution. Remarkably well educated, politically savvy, and possessing the boldness that comes naturally with youth, they helped draft the new government at the Constitutional Convention and then defended it in the *Federalist Papers* and at the Virginia and New York ratifying conventions. These two giants of the early republic are well worth our attention.

Yet despite this recent revival, little has been written about the relationship between Madison and Hamilton. This leaves significant gaps in their stories. Not only were they central actors in the early years of the new republic, but their stories are inseparable. Though they were close allies and even friends in the 1780s, they became bitter rivals in the 1790s. After the project of framing a new government was finally completed, they turned on each other, and their dispute led to the first partisan political divide in our country. What happened? And more important, what does their falling-out tell us about the Constitution, our government, and our politics? More than two hundred years later, these questions continue to linger.

JAMES MADISON JR. was born on March 16, 1751, into a family with a large estate in the Piedmont region of Central Virginia. He went to the College of New Jersey (now Princeton University), where he was instructed by the influential Scottish Presbyterian minister John Witherspoon, a signer of the Declaration of Independence. In 1776 Madison entered the Virginia House of Delegates, where he fell into the orbit of Thomas Jefferson. This was the start of a lifelong friendship and one of the greatest political partnerships in American history.

Alexander Hamilton, the illegitimate child of James Hamilton and Rachel Faucette, was born on the Caribbean island of Nevis on January 11, 1757. Abandoned by his father and orphaned by the death of his mother, his early life was one of hardship and loss. But he was an unusually bright boy, and he landed a job as a clerk at an import-export firm. As a young man, he emigrated to North America and enrolled in King's College (now Columbia University), where he was soon caught up in the fervor of the revolutionary cause. His courage and intellect placed him in the first rank of young recruits, and George Washington hired him as his aide-de-camp.

In the summer of 1782, Hamilton was named a delegate from New York to the Congress of the Confederation, where Madison had been serving since 1780 as a delegate from Virginia. From that point forward, the fate of the one would be inextricably connected to that of the other. They would seem to make for an unlikely duo. Hamilton was a man brimming with confidence and passion. Having bootstrapped himself from a lowly life in the West Indies to a promising career in American politics, he was convinced he was a man of destiny. Madison, on the other hand, was usually underwhelming on first impression. Short and slight, he had a soft voice and an unassuming disposition. But he was widely known to be a dogged, skillful, and pragmatic legislator.

Background and personality aside, the two had much in common. They were both extremely well read. By the time the Constitution was ratified, Hamilton's only equal on matters of public finance was Robert Morris, and Madison's knowledge of political philosophy was rivaled only by John Adams and Jefferson. They were both formidable debaters and writers; they had thought through virtually every public matter and could defend their views with uncommon skill. They also inclined toward arrogance. Convinced of the rectitude of their own beliefs, they were quick to cast aspersions on those who disagreed—including, eventually, one another. But that was still years away, when they entered national politics.

In November 1777, the newly freed colonies adopted a new governing charter, called the Articles of Confederation, which called for just a "firm league of friendship" among the thirteen states, each of which retained its sovereignty. There were no federal courts and no executive branch, and Congress was endowed with little real authority. The result was a national power vacuum, which was filled by state governments looking out for themselves. Madison and Hamilton were determined to fix that.[1]

They would find nothing but frustration in Congress, and they eventually turned their attention to radically revising the terms of government, replacing the Articles of Confederation with a system that actually worked. Their behind-the-scenes politicking was essential in helping organize the Constitutional Convention, which opened on May 25, 1787, in Philadelphia.

As was his habit, Madison came to the meeting better prepared than anybody else. Arriving before the convention began, he and his nationalist allies—those who wanted a strong central government—agreed on a bold new vision: the Virginia Plan, formally introduced by Governor Edmund Randolph but largely Madison's brainchild. It was the culmination of Madison's study of government since his Princeton days. His research had lately been aided by a steady stream of books sent to him by Jefferson, then serving as minister to France. The Virginia Plan was not only a brilliant plan of government; it was also a political masterstroke. By seizing the initiative, Madison and the nationalists dominated the agenda through the early weeks of the convention and oriented the delegates toward the idea of replacing, rather than merely revising, the articles.

Though Hamilton served at the convention as a delegate from New York, his role was limited. Modeled on the British constitution, his plan of government envisioned life tenures for the president and senators—making it too elitist for the convention. Worse for Hamilton, John Lansing and Robert Yates, his fellow delegates from New York, were opposed to a strong national government. Because each state received one vote on all matters, Lansing and Yates overrode Hamilton again and again. He departed the convention on June 30, and though he returned for brief spells, he contributed little thereafter except his signature on the final draft.

Neither Madison nor Hamilton was particularly satisfied with the finished project. The nationalists had to compromise on many points with delegates who opposed centralizing power. Still, the two thought it was the best that could be practically achieved, so they committed themselves to its defense. Their first task was to coauthor a series of essays, published in New York newspapers, laying out the logic behind the Constitution and the case for ratification. The first entry in what would be known as the *Federalist Papers* was published on October 27. Hamilton would compose more than half of the eighty-five essays, and Madison penned twenty-nine. John Jay was originally engaged to assist, but he took ill, so he authored only five articles.

The bulk of the *Federalist Papers* was published prior to the spring of 1788, after which Madison and Hamilton turned to their respective states' ratifying conventions. By the time the proceedings in Virginia and New York began, eight states had already ratified the Constitution, meaning that just one more was needed for it to technically become the law. But for all practical purposes, the assent of Virginia and New York was necessary. Virginia was at that point the most populous state in the union, and although New York was smaller, its central location gave it special importance.

Opposition within each state was fierce. New York governor George Clinton disapproved of the Constitution, and his allies were well represented in the state convention. In Virginia, the charismatic Patrick Henry came out against it, as did George Mason. However, the Constitution had the support of Madison; of Randolph, who had refused to sign it at the Constitutional Convention but now supported ratification; and of George Washington, who did not participate in the ratifying convention but whose influence in Virginia was everywhere felt. Madison was no rhetorical match for the fiery Henry, but the convention decided to debate the Constitution clause by clause, enabling Madison to offer careful, considered arguments. Henry, for all his eloquence, could not mount an effective counterattack, and the convention approved the Constitution by a margin of 89 to 79 on June 25. With New Hampshire having ratified it a few days earlier, there were now ten states on board, creating sufficient pressure on New York that that state approved it as well.

With the Constitution ratified, Washington was the obvious choice for president. He selected Hamilton as secretary of the treasury. Meanwhile, Madison won election to the House of Representatives, despite the best efforts of Henry, whose allies in the state legislature situated Madison's Orange County home in a congressional district that was, on the whole, Anti-Federalist. Madison had to contest the seat against James Monroe—his friend and Jefferson's former pupil—who had voted against ratifying the Constitution. Ultimately, Madison won a comfortable though not overwhelming victory and took his seat in Congress when it opened in New York in the spring of 1789. The first session was largely spent organizing the government, and Madison served as the Washington administration's de facto prime minister. He shepherded through bills to create the cabinet and the courts, funneled the many suggestions for revising the Constitution into the Bill of Rights, and helped craft a national tax plan. Meanwhile, Hamilton was hard at work finalizing the details of his economic program. He submitted his groundbreaking *Report Relative to a Provision for the Public Credit* (commonly called the *Report on Public Credit*) to Congress in January 1790. This was followed in December of that year by *The Second Report on the Further Provision Necessary for Establishing Public Credit,* commonly called the *Report on a National Bank.* In December 1791, he submitted the *Report on the Subject of Manufactures,* commonly called the *Report on Manufactures.*

Taken as a whole, these reports represented Hamilton's ideas on how the new government could forge a national economic marketplace. The first step was the management of the public credit. He called for a full repayment of the national debt to the current holders of public certificates, as well as an assumption of the state debts. Next, he proposed a national bank, modeled on the Bank of England, that would be privately owned but would house public tax revenues and offer loans to the government. Finally, he called on the government to patronize manufacturing, through policies like bounties and protective tariffs, as a way to diversify the American economy. Hamilton's program was highly controversial. The ratification of the Constitution notwithstanding, Americans still remained fearful of an overly powerful central government.

What shocked many was that Madison, one of the premier nationalists of the 1780s, could not abide Hamilton's plan. Although Madison wanted a strong and effective central government, he thought Hamilton's ambition was to invest the moneyed elite with permanent governing power, thereby diluting the authority of the people and ultimately centralizing authority around himself. Madison looked back to the debates of the Constitutional Convention, when Hamilton called Britain's constitutional monarchy the best system in the world. Madison feared that the secretary, having lost that battle at the convention, was now seeking to win the war via public policy. He resolved to thwart what he perceived were dark designs, and in this effort he was soon joined by Jefferson. Their alliance against Hamilton's economic policies would mark the start of party politics in the United States, with Hamilton's Federalist Party facing off against Jefferson and Madison's Republican Party (or, as they are commonly called today, the Democratic-Republican Party).

The Republican-Federalist dispute soon took on a foreign-policy dimension. The French Revolution precipitated a war between Great Britain and the new French Republic, which placed the United States in the middle. The United States had a treaty of alliance with France (or at least with prerevolutionary France), but Great Britain was its primary trading partner. President Washington dispatched John Jay, then serving as chief justice of the Supreme Court, to hammer out an agreement with the British, though he won few concessions. Still, Hamilton vigorously supported the resulting Jay Treaty, writing pamphlets on its behalf. Madison, for his part, struck back by trying to have the House deny the funding necessary to carry the treaty into effect.

By the end of Washington's presidency, American politics had become a morass of hyperbole, backbiting, and paranoia. Vice President Adams, who had not been directly involved in the vitriolic debates of the previous eight years, narrowly defeated Jefferson for the presidency in 1796. He inherited a politically untenable situation. The Republicans lined up against him, and the so-called High Federalists—that is, those Federalists loyal to Hamilton—did not trust him. Intrigues by foreign agents led to a bout of anti-French hysteria, emboldening the prowar wing of the Federalist Party and outraging the Republicans. Adams, however, was committed to neutrality and came to peace terms with France in the Convention of 1800.

Jefferson won his presidential rematch against Adams in 1800, and the Federalists were driven from government, never to return. Tragically, Hamilton was killed in a duel with Vice President Aaron Burr in 1804, robbing his party of its leading intellectual light. Meanwhile, the nation enjoyed several years of peace and prosperity under Republican rule. Jefferson's first presidential term was a success, capped off by the purchase of Louisiana in 1803. But international affairs would dominate his second term, as the United States was caught between the British and the French once more.

Madison succeeded Jefferson to the presidency in 1809, and like his predecessor, he tried to broker a lasting peace. But the effort was to no avail, and the country went to war against Great Britain again, in 1812. Prowar Republicans thought this an opportunity to assert the nation's independence once more, and maybe even to take Canada. But the war was fought to a draw, and in 1814 British soldiers burned the fledgling capital, Washington, DC. The Treaty of Ghent brought peace between the two nations, although with no major concessions from either side. After the war, the Republicans markedly changed course from their previous views, endorsing an aggressive program of national development, which included several old Hamiltonian proposals, such as the Second Bank of the United States and a protective tariff—both of which were signed into law by President Madison himself.

By the time Madison retired to private life in 1817, he seemed to have come full circle. He allied with Hamilton in the 1780s, opposed him in the 1790s, and finally acquiesced to his plan for the nation in the 1810s. Madison and Jefferson had won the political battle when they defeated the Federalists in 1800. However, Hamilton's ideas on economics and finance would dominate the remainder of the nineteenth century, having been implemented by none other than Madison himself.

These are the undisputed facts of the changing relationship between Hamilton and Madison, but an acceptable theory that connects all these episodes has remained elusive. Instead, historians are inclined to offer partial accounts—favoring either Madison or Hamilton, often at the expense of the other. Pro-Hamilton writers claim that Madison's turn against Hamilton was tantamount to "denying an earlier version of himself," which he did under "ideological strain." Madison saw the old world he knew—one dominated by the landed gentry of Virginia—slipping away, to be replaced by a commercial class stationed in New York. He responded by trying to "inhibit government from undertaking a range of things one does not approve of." Though pro-Madison historians tend not to be so pointed in their critiques of Hamilton, they suggest that Hamilton's commitment to popular government was somehow disingenuous. This academic debate has a parallel in the present-day political divide too. Today, Republicans are more likely to favor Madison for his praise of limited government, whereas Democrats are apt to think highly of Hamilton, not least because of his status as an immigrant and his antislavery attitudes. It has not always been so—Hamilton was until recently a hero of business-minded Republicans—but the general point stands. Madison and Hamilton are often seen to represent opposing views of the kind of nation the United States was, is, and should be.[2]

In this sense, both sides of the argument are right: Madison and Hamilton did and still do represent different visions for the country. But it is only by studying them together, and by tracking the making and then the dissolution of their friendship, that we can fully understand those visions, how they relate, and why they still matter today.

MADISON AND HAMILTON belonged to a political movement in the 1780s that generally cohered around three basic principles. The first was a commitment to a liberal government, which emphasized the protection of individual rights. As Jefferson argued in the Declaration of Independence, "governments are instituted among men" to secure certain "unalienable rights," including life, liberty, and the pursuit of happiness. The Virginia Declaration of Rights, authored by Mason, added the protection of property to the list. This view of the ends of government was heavily influenced by the writings of English philosopher John Locke.[3]

Second, they were part of the tradition of republicanism, or self-government. As Cicero put it, "*res publica, res populi*" (the commonwealth is the concern of a people), who are "associated with one another through agreement on law and community of interest." Liberty, in the republican conception, has less to do with protecting property and more to do with the proper construction of the state. Citizens in a republic are free because they are governed by laws that they themselves have a hand in making and not by the whims of an arbitrary sovereign. Typically, republics were thought to be unstable—easily corrupted from their proper form into a tyranny (misrule by a king), oligarchy (misrule by the rich), or ochlocracy (misrule by the mob). Philosophers had concluded that a secure government required mixing the republican principle of majority rule with some other form, like monarchy, to create a balance between factions of society as a bulwark against decay. Montesquieu, a French philosopher and historian who was widely read in the United States at the time, had argued in *The Spirit of the Laws* that Great Britain—which balanced the democratically elected House of Commons against the aristocratic House of Lords and a hereditary sovereign—was the one system in the modern world founded on the spirit of liberty. The Founders, however, had rejected the mixing of classes or estates in government and sought to found a stable republic solely on the principle of majority rule.[4]

Third, they were nationalists, arguing that the thirteen states had to bind themselves more firmly together if the ideals of liberalism and republicanism were to be secured. This view was more practical than moral, as it involved a question of how to achieve the shared principles of liberalism and republicanism. It was also much more controversial. Though most Federalists and Anti-Federalists agreed in general on liberalism and republicanism, they disagreed on the nature of the union. The Anti-Federalists, having just thrown off the shackles of a distant government in the Revolution, were not too keen on sanctioning another one. Plus, the Federalists were arguing against the conventional view of republicanism, which held that a smaller republic was preferable, because the citizenry would be more homogeneous and better able to keep an eye on their representatives. Nevertheless, the miserable experiences of the 1780s—an impotent national Congress combined with selfish and often illiberal states—had convinced most Americans that a firmer union was necessary.[5]

Liberalism, republicanism, and nationalism were broad categories, and it was up to each statesman to figure out for himself how they should be blended together. As such, it was typical for the Founders to disagree, if not on the big principles then at least on the finer points. Even Jefferson and Madison—whose friendship and political alliance endured for half a century—had respectful but sharp disagreements about the permanence of the Constitution and the role of the masses in government. Meanwhile, Hamilton and Madison agreed on enough points to align in the 1780s, but they always had vast disagreements, which came to the forefront in the 1790s.[6]

It is not my intention to elaborate the full scope of their political thought, as that would be an unwieldy task; rather, I will emphasize certain themes within each view that help account for their complicated relationship. Hamilton's program emphasized what I call *national vigor*. He thought it necessary to develop the country's commercial strength to bind the country together and strengthen its ability to rival foreign powers. In *Federalist* 11 he described this vision as "one great American System" that "would baffle all the combinations of European jealousy to restrain our growth." This meant establishing a reliable currency, encouraging the expansion of credit, and promoting economic diversification. These policies admittedly rewarded the wealthy, but he had a bigger purpose in mind. He wished to turn the wealthy into mediators of the general welfare—dispensing benefits to them in the short run but ultimately reorienting their self-interests to the national interest. Hamilton's vision of government was not "of, by and for rich people," as some critics have said, but rather a public-private partnership between the wealthy and the state, for the benefit of all Americans. The quintessential example of Hamilton's approach was the Bank of the United States—mostly owned by private investors but holding federal tax revenues and serving as a lender for the government. Yes, the wealthy would profit from their ownership of the stock, but a well-run bank promised benefits that would flow throughout the whole economy.[7]

Madison's views, on the other hand, emphasized what I call *republican balance*. He believed the government had to behave like a neutral judge, fairly dispensing policy benefits and burdens according to the merits of each case. As such, he thought Hamilton's policies were too one-sided in their favoritism to the wealthy. The rest of the nation should derive some immediate benefits too. He also worried about the potential for Hamiltonian mediation to corrupt republican government. He perceived a dangerous dynamism inherent in the secretary's use of the moneyed class to promote the general welfare. Institutions like the Bank of the United States are not a one-way street: the government can employ it for the public good, but the bank's directors and stockholders can leverage its special status for their own purposes, to enrich themselves at the public's expense or even to take control of economic policy. In the parlance of classical republicanism, this is corruption, as the government begins to look like an oligarchy—rule by and for the rich at the expense of the national interest. Madison looked warily at the experience of Great Britain, which had empowered private corporations like the East India and the South Sea Companies to execute national economic policy, only to see those private corporations come to wield political influence in Parliament and wreak economic havoc when their schemes failed. He feared the same dangers from Hamilton's system.

As it turned out, both were right, each in his own way. Hamilton's economic plan was brilliant and has rightly been praised for establishing the financial foundation for the Industrial Revolution in the United States. He borrowed the best ideas from the great European finance ministers of the 1700s and reimagined them for the American context. His plan for the national and state debts created a stable currency for the first time since the Revolution. The Bank of the United States kept tax revenues secure and was always ready to lend money to the government as the need arose. Moreover, it facilitated economic development by responsibly extending credit throughout the private sector. And though Hamilton's program to protect American manufacturing was too controversial for the 1790s, it eventually came to form the basis of the nation's industrial policy.

Even so, the criticisms Madison leveled against Hamilton had merit. The secretary's program was egregiously one-sided, offering few direct benefits to common people, most of whom were farmers. Moreover, Hamilton's policies did in practice breed corruption, in that they intermingled popular sovereignty with oligarchy. He wanted to redirect the interests of the moneyed class toward the needs of the nation, and he succeeded, but the relationship was dynamic, as Madison had feared. The wealthy effectively captured the government, at least in crucial instances. The protracted fight in 1790 over the assumption of state debts was in large part due to the defiance of wealthy speculators, who risked the national credit to reap a windfall profit. The Panic of 1792 was a product of speculative frenzy by this same group, whose key players had been in or were closely connected to the new government. Ultimately, they forced Hamilton to, in effect, buy them off with federal tax dollars.

The key lesson from the Madison-Hamilton battle is not that one was right and the other wrong, but that their feud represents a clash of fundamental American values. The Constitution was premised on liberalism, republicanism, and nationalism—on the supposition that only a stronger, more prosperous union of the states would protect individual rights and secure self-government. But after the Constitution was ratified in 1789, the principles of republicanism and nationalism came into conflict. It seemed as though the country could become a strong and mighty nation, or it could remain a true republic, but it could not be both. Hamilton was the advocate of a vigorous nationalism, while Madison defended the principles of republicanism—and the tension inherent to these principles turned the old friends into bitter enemies.

Hamilton died in 1804, but his death did not bring an end to this conflict of values. Jefferson and Madison had their own ideal of national development, a vision that emphasized small farms as the backbone of a commercially vibrant nation. This was more in keeping with strict republican probity, but it did not do enough to keep the nation independent of the European powers. After years of futile efforts to vindicate US neutrality through peaceful means, the country returned to war with Great Britain in 1812. However, the United States was in no condition to wage such a conflict, and it was lucky to sign a peace treaty in 1815 that ceded no territory or rights to Great Britain. By war's end, it was clear to many that the old Jeffersonian vision for the nation was insufficient.

After the war, Madison and his Republican allies resolved to strengthen the nation's economic foundations, and they embraced Hamilton's old strategy of mediation. This was not simply a rote repetition of the old Hamiltonian system but an expansion and broadening of it. Whereas Hamilton had privileged the wealthy few, the Republicans invited all kinds of economic factions to receive benefits from the government. So the Second Bank of the United States would have branches dispersed all across the country rather than concentrated in the northeast. Industrial protection would take the form of tariffs that benefited whole sectors of the economy rather than bounties or cash payments to a handful of firms. And an ambitious program of internal improvement would benefit many locales by directly connecting the country together via a network of roads and canals. In sum, the postwar Republican program was an effort to finally reconcile Hamiltonian nationalism with Madisonian republicanism.

Yet this hybrid of Hamiltonian economics and Madisonian civics was just as dangerous to republicanism as the Hamiltonian original. Once again, oligarchy began to creep into the republic, as the directors and stockholders of the Second Bank of the United States misused their public authority to line their own pockets and influence the course of public policy. Even more dangerous, this Hamiltonian-Madisonian synthesis gave rise to a kind of mob rule, or what Madison called *majoritarian factionalism,* via federal tax policy. A diverse array of small economic factions eventually realized that they could combine into a legislative majority to manipulate the tariff rates for their own benefit, at the expense of the good of the nation. This produced the first great constitutional crisis of the young republic in 1832–1833, when South Carolina declared the Tariff of 1828 null and void.

And so the battle between Madison and Hamilton was not merely a clash of personalities but, rather, a durable conflict between nationalism and republicanism, two values at the very heart of the American creed. The Preamble to the Constitution proclaims:

> We, the people of the United States, in order to form a more perfect Union, establish justice, insure domestic tranquility, provide for the common defense, promote the general welfare, and secure the blessings of liberty to ourselves and our posterity, do ordain and establish this Constitution for the United States of America.

This single, forceful sentence introduces a Constitution grounded in the principles of liberalism, republicanism, and nationalism. The thirteen states were to form a single nation, governed by the people for their own benefit, under the condition that certain rights cannot be abrogated. These three values, inextricably linked, serve as the foundation upon which our Constitution was framed. But as the quarrels between Madison and Hamilton illustrate, republicanism and nationalism are also in conflict with one another—in their day and in our own, as we shall see. Here then is a paradox at the heart of the Constitution. Just as a circle cannot be squared, our nationalist ambitions cannot always be reconciled to our republican scruples.[8]

1

THE GREAT DESIDERATUM

JAMES MADISON WAS arguably the most important political philosopher of the Founding era. Only John Adams and Thomas Jefferson come close to rivaling him, and neither was present at the Constitutional Convention to influence the proceedings. Madison's political thought drew liberally from a wide variety of traditions—the classical republicanism of Polybius and Cicero, the modern republicanism of Machiavelli and James Harrington, the liberalism of John Locke, the Scottish Enlightenment thinking of David Hume and Adam Smith, and the opposition ideology of Lord Bolingbroke. He used these as tools to craft his own, unique system of politics.[1]

Yet in his day and our own, Madison has often been charged with inconsistency, and not just because of his feud with Alexander Hamilton. At times, Madison's positions seemed to vacillate on the scope of federal power, the extent of state sovereignty, the role of political parties, and the proper way to understand the Constitution. There is some merit to the accusation of inconsistency, which contemporary scholars often call the "Madison Problem," but to linger on these discrepancies is to misunderstand the purpose to which Madison dedicated his public life. He never devoted his energies to publishing a systematic treatise of politics. Instead, most of his political thought comes down to us through speeches, letters, notes, and anonymous essays meant to influence the public discourse. Though he grappled with the big questions that engage philosophers, his interests were never far from the contemporary matters of politics. He was not sitting atop an ivory tower, laying down timeless truths that warriors in the political arena would dismiss as idle considerations. He himself was in that arena, fighting to defend and advance his core values amid a changing array of opponents and circumstances. Rather than criticize Madison for inconsistency, it is much more profitable to determine why he changed some views but not others, which values were central to his political identity and which were not.[2]

When Madison took his seat at the Constitutional Convention in May 1787, he was already a veteran of American politics. His many years of studying political philosophy, combined with a decade of service in legislative councils, had turned him into a wise and able statesman, though he was just thirty-six years old. The next thirteen months would be the most consequential of his career. Between the spring of 1787 and the summer of 1788, he helped draft the Constitution in Philadelphia, wrote twenty-nine of the essays that became known as the *Federalist Papers,* and defended the new government at the Virginia ratifying convention.

In Madison's writings from this period, a phrase recurs several times: the "great desideratum in government." The word "desideratum"—antiquated today, though more common in the eighteenth-century lexicon—means something essential or necessary. So Madison was interested in the one quality that government must have above all others. In an essay he penned to organize his thoughts for the Constitutional Convention, he argued that the great desideratum in government was to make it "sufficiently neutral" toward all parts of society that it could prevent one part of the nation "from invading the rights of another," without becoming an interest of its own, "adverse to that of the whole society." In a letter to George Washington from around the same time, Madison wrote that the "great desideratum" was to find a "disinterested and dispassionate umpire." In other words, Madison sought the provision of impartial justice—without regard to economic, religious, or social standing—primarily for "the security of property and public safety."[3]

The problem with justice, as Hume put it, is that "the frailty or perverseness of our nature" is such that man "is seduced from his great and important" interest in justice "by the allurement of present, though often very frivolous temptations." In *Federalist* 10, Madison drew on Hume to outline the various ways that people split into factions, or groups "united and actuated by some common impulse of passion, or of interest, adversed to the rights of other citizens, or to the permanent and aggregate interests of the community." He blamed factionalism on different opinions on religion and government, loyalty to some leaders over others, and above all "the various and unequal distribution of property." This last, he felt, fuels all sorts of economic factions—creditors, debtors, farming, manufacturing, shipping, and commercial. And in those rare instances when "no substantial occasion presents itself" for humanity to divide into factions, "the most frivolous and fanciful distinctions" will suffice—people will divide into factions just because that's what they tend to do.[4]

Madison believed that "the regulation of these various and interfering interests forms the principal task of modern legislation," a job that he felt would grow more burdensome over time. Eventually, human populations outstrip nature's capacity to provide for them. In due course, "the proportion of those who will labor under all the hardships of life, and secretly sigh for a more equal distribution of its blessings" will increase, perhaps even outnumbering "those who are placed above the feelings of indigence." Once the destitute reach a certain proportion of society, they may come to threaten the rights of property and the public tranquility. This was not a problem that yet afflicted the United States. But Madison wished to frame a system "to last for the ages," and he was determined not to "lose sight of the changes which ages will produce." Thus, it was incumbent upon a republican government to maintain a durable balance among such bitterly opposed factions.[5]

Having established the need for some fair-minded umpire, Madison's next question was where to find one. Since the time of Aristotle, republican theorists had generally agreed that a mixed form of government—which blended the principle of majority rule with an aristocracy, monarchy, or both—was the most stable, as it balanced different social classes against one another. Many republicans, including Adams and Hamilton, pointed to the British constitution of the eighteenth century as the best the modern world had produced, establishing a system whereby the sovereign ruled jointly with Parliament. But Madison strongly disagreed with this notion. In theory, a king or a class of nobles could serve as the neutral umpires that society needed, arbitrating fairly among social factions, but in practice a "hereditary or self-appointed authority" is a "precarious security" for justice. The king may support the noxious designs of one faction or even unite against everybody in pursuit of his own selfish ends. In Madison's view, those "who have swayed the British Scepter" had been "detestable pictures of tyranny and cruelty."[6]

Therefore, a republic must "be derived from the great body of the society, not from . . . a favored class of it." Yet Madison was also wary of the masses. The people are not a repository of special wisdom; rather, "there can be no doubt that there are subjects to which the capacities of the bulk of mankind are unequal." Moreover, although the people are virtuous to some extent—for otherwise "no form of government can render us secure"—they are easily tempted by their interests or passions. And in a simple democracy, there is nothing to stop a selfish or headstrong majority from committing injustices. Suppose, for instance, the government is considering a law "concerning private debts." Any plan would inevitably place creditors on one side and debtors on the other. "Justice ought to hold the balance between them. Yet the parties are and must be themselves the judges; and the most numerous party, or, in other words, the most powerful faction must be expected to prevail." Or suppose the government is debating protective tariffs to stimulate domestic industry. Such a question "would be differently decided by the landed and the manufacturing classes; and probably by neither, with a sole regard to justice and the public good." What about distributing the tax burden? That task must be undertaken with "the most exact impartiality, yet there is perhaps no legislative act in which greater opportunity and temptation are given to a predominant party, to trample on the rules of justice. Every shilling with which they overburden the inferior number, is a shilling saved to their own pockets."[7]

Madison was working within the broad stream of republican political thought—trying to identify the system of government that would best supply the impartial justice that a republic requires. Breaking with past precedent, he argued that monarchies or aristocracies are no bulwark for justice, as they can devolve into tyranny or oligarchy. Yet he also held that a straightforward democratic system could lead to what the classic theorists might call *ochlocracy,* and to what he called *majority factionalism.*

Having rejected the classic solutions to creating a durable republic, Madison proffered an ingenious alternative, placing the onus for impartiality on well-organized political conflict. The people, and only the people, have total authority—consistent with his view of republicanism—but they rule a government intentionally designed to promote "equilibrium in the interests and the passions of the society itself." His primary mechanism for accomplishing this task is commonly called the *extended republic.* The conventional wisdom in his day was that republics must be small so that the citizens would have relatively homogeneous views, but he thought diversity was the key to success. "A greater variety of parties and interests" makes it "less probable that a majority will have a common motive to invade the rights of others," and if such a motive exists, "it will be more difficult for all who feel it . . . to act in unison with each other." The extended republic, he considered, "was the only defense against the inconveniences of democracy consistent with the democratic form of government."[8]

As such, Madison's Virginia Plan created a powerful but quite diverse national government. It proposed two chambers of Congress, both of which would be apportioned according to population. It authorized Congress to legislate in all cases where it deems the states are "incompetent" or the "harmony of the United States" hangs in the balance. It gave Congress the power to veto state laws that, in its judgment, contradict "the articles of union." No longer would "the states . . . pursue their particular interests in opposition to the general interest." Instead, the veto would give the national government the power to "control the centrifugal tendency of the states," which threatened to "destroy the order and harmony of the political system." And because many factions would occupy a stronghold in the diverse national government, he believed it could be trusted to wield these powers responsibly.[9]

Madison also suggested a number of supplemental features to further mitigate the dangers of majority factions. He thought a Senate term ranging from six to nine years was "by no means too long," for it would "give to the government that stability which was everywhere called for," by insulating senators to "withstand the occasional impetuosities" of public opinion. Moreover, the Virginia Plan called for members of the Senate to be nominated by the state legislatures and confirmed by the House rather than directly elected by the people. He also recommended a council of revision, made up of the president and members of the judiciary, "as a check to precipitate, to unjust, and to unconstitutional laws," though a supermajority in Congress would possess the authority to override its decisions.[10]

Under the guidance of this "well constructed union," Madison thought that the virtue and wisdom of the people could be fully revealed. The principle of representation would elevate to the government "fit characters" who could "refine and enlarge the public views." The extended republic would prevent impassioned or self-interested factions from gaining control of the government. And the separation of powers would provide "auxiliary precautions" to further protect against mischief. All of this would slow the tempo of deliberation down, so that, through an "intercourse of sentiments" among the citizenry, "public opinion" could become settled upon sound principles of justice and the true needs of the community. Though he was suspicious of momentary flights of public passion, he believed that free government depended upon the "cold, considerate, and cautious" opinions of the people.[11]

REPUBLICAN BALANCE WAS at the core of Madison's constitutional thinking, and it also informed his views on public policy. As his ideal state carefully calibrated the interests of one faction of society against those of all the others, he naturally thought public policy had to do likewise. After all, the product of the complicated processes of government is policy—and because he wanted to create a balanced governing process, he thought policy had to be balanced as well.

This helps explain why Madison was such an effective legislative leader. He viewed the task of the legislature as akin to that of a court—to calmly evaluate the various proposals and select those that most closely conform to the principles of justice and the needs of the whole nation. "What," he asked, "are many of the most important acts of legislation, but so many judicial determinations, not indeed concerning the rights of single persons, but concerning the rights of large bodies of citizens?" Though Madison always endeavored to do right by his own constituents, he also saw himself as a national statesman, and he usually endeavored to broker a final compromise that was good for the nation and reasonably fair for all parties.[12]

The first prominent example of this approach was Madison's effort to enact a national impost, or a tax upon imports, in the early 1780s. The Articles of Confederation did not give Congress the power to lay and collect taxes. Instead, Congress depended upon requisitions from the states, and because these had not been forthcoming in sufficient amounts, Congress was unable to pay its bills. As a work-around, Madison and his nationalist allies, including Hamilton, drafted an impost to be enacted individually by the thirteen states. To lure them into implementing the plan, Madison helped design an intricate logroll (a legislative maneuver that builds a majority coalition by giving enough legislators a parochial or local incentive to support it) that offered policy benefits in exchange for adopting the tax. The items intended to coax Virginia were assumption by the national government of state debts and the abatement of unpaid requisitions due to Congress from the war-ravaged states. Meanwhile, to attract the small states, Madison proposed that large states like Virginia cede their claims on western territory to the national government. Thanks to his guidance, the impost would offer something for every state, and the nation as a whole would be better off too.[13]

Congress stripped away the benefit for Virginia, which disheartened Madison but did not dissuade him from arguing the merits of the impost. Instead, he still hoped to get the proposal through the Old Dominion. In April 1783 he wrote a letter to Edmund Randolph that highlighted his conception of republican statesmanship: "If a few enlightened and disinterested members would step forward in each legislature as advocates for the necessary plans, I see with so much force the considerations that might be urged, that my hopes would still prevail." Ultimately the impost failed, and the national government fell even further into disarray. Nevertheless, the effort to enact the impost was one of Madison's most consequential endeavors during his time in the Confederation Congress and an example of how he approached public policy.[14]

Madison continued to strive for policy balance after the Constitution was ratified. One of the top priorities of the new government was to finally raise revenue via excise taxes and tariffs on imported goods. Naturally, every member of Congress wished to shift as much of the tax burden as possible off his own constituents, but Madison was keen on producing a final tax package that equitably distributed the burdens of maintaining the government. Consider, for instance, his defense of a duty on salt. He argued on the House floor, "In order to determine whether a tax on salt is just or unjust, we must consider it as part of a system, and judge of the operation of this system as if it was but a single article; if this is found to be unequal it is also unjust." The West made greater use of salt and would thus pay more in tax, but "the equilibrium is restored when you find this almost the only tax they will have to pay." He took a similar position regarding the duty on molasses: that tax affected the North more than the South, but the overall system was fair because the tax on sugar burdened the South more than the North. In short, his posture during the tax debate of 1789—during which he persistently battled against the demands of various cliques in

Congress and endeavored to build a bill that was fair to all—was similar to his position during the impost fight of 1782–1783.[15]

IF MADISON SAW balanced public policy as a republican virtue, he also often saw one-sided policy as a vice. He believed that republics, as a general rule, should not play favorites, and he worried about the unintended consequences of such one-sidedness. He was particularly concerned about monopolies, licenses, charters, or any exclusive grant of privilege from the state to some individual or faction. He feared that such policies could alter the careful balance of political power in a republic.

Usually we think of public policy as dispensing benefits or burdens, not power, which is assigned to the three branches according to the Constitution. But Congress has discretion to distribute power as it sees fit in some cases. Consider, for instance, the rather uncontroversial copyright clause in the Constitution. "To promote the progress of science and useful arts," Congress may grant "for limited times to authors and inventors the exclusive right to their respective writings and discoveries." This empowers Congress to grant authors or inventors licenses—that is, monopolistic authority over what they create—at least for a time.[16]

The notion that government had the right to dispense licenses, charters, patents, and exclusive rights dated back to long before the Constitution, and it often covered a much wider array of policies than books or inventions. For instance, the British East India Company was created in 1600 by Queen Elizabeth I via a royal charter that gave the company exclusive rights to the Indian trade. Elizabeth thus created a public-private partnership. The company stockholders would enjoy the immediate profits, but the nation as a whole would benefit from the expansion of commerce. The powers conferred by the state to the company were vast. Along with the Bank of England, it was central to the English economy in the 1700s and took charge of the civil administration of India.

Placing such authority in private hands worried Madison. His system of government was premised on carefully ordering political power throughout society, so he was wary of legislation that might tamper with the balance he was looking to create. In an unpublished essay written around 1820, he admitted that although monopolies are "in certain cases useful, (they) ought to be granted with caution." They may "produce more evil than good" by giving factions a public sanction to commit "local injustice and oppression" by "laws and regulations." By their very nature monopolies bless certain factions characterized by their ownership of "different sorts of property" and holding "animosities" toward other factions; the favored factions may then use the benefits as a tool for "oppression" that was either legal or very hard to combat through the legal process.[17]

Madison's first significant encounter with a monopoly gone bad was the church of Virginia. In 1619, the Virginia House of Burgesses established the Church of England as the official church of the colony. A religious revival in the 1730s and 1740s—often referred to as the First Great Awakening—led to the growth of other Protestant congregations, such as the Baptists and Presbyterians, but these other congregations faced legal restrictions and sometimes persecution. That situation did not sit well amid the growing revolutionary sentiment sweeping the colony by the 1770s.

Madison was particularly outraged by the heavy-handedness of the government. In a letter to his college friend William Bradford in January 1774, he argued, "Ecclesiastical establishments tend to great ignorance and corruption." In April, he followed up on this theme in another missive to Bradford in which he complained about the church's efforts to resist reform. He noted that the clergy, who were sponsored by the state, were flexing their political muscle to protect their privileges and to disempower those "dissenters" who "rob[bed] them of the goodwill of the people and [might] in time endanger their livings and security." Not only does granting an exclusive license create the possibility for abuse, but it can also impede the government's ability to reform the terms of the original deal. In other words, when a state bestows wealth or prestige upon some group, the group can employ those resources to protect and extend its privileges. This was what Madison noticed in the case of the church. Using their elevated station—which ultimately was a grant of privilege from the government itself—the clergy worked from purely selfish motives to prevent the government from reforming the church for the good of all.[18]

A similar dynamic contributed to the Boston Tea Party. The East India Company had by that point become a central cog in the British economic machine, and many of its stockholders had won election to the House of Commons, where they looked for ways to aid the company. By the 1770s, the company was struggling financially and asked Parliament for a £1 million loan. Because the interests of the company and the government were so intertwined, Lord North, the British prime minister, granted the request. He also allowed the company to sell its surplus product directly to North America, circumventing colonial tea merchants. Fatefully, North expected that because the price of tea would be lower if the merchants were no longer serving as middlemen, the colonists would accept a tax on the tea. But he miscalculated: a coalition of merchants and revolutionaries dumped a shipment of India's finest into Boston Harbor.

These cautionary tales showed Madison how a republic can be corrupted by some types of public policy. In his understanding, a republic is supposed to govern for the good of all, which requires that political power be distributed in a way that creates a balance among factions. In these cases, the exclusive grant of a license disrupted that balance, making the government more responsive to the needs of the monopolists than the public at large.

Madison still recognized that monopolies are often useful, as illustrated by the text of the copyright clause: to encourage the arts and sciences, it is necessary to give inventors and authors exclusive control over the fruits of their labors. So Madison had a set of practical rules for when and how to grant such privileges. Above all, he held that monopolies clearly had to be in the public interest and that they should not be indefinite. Recognizing that at their core exclusive licenses are a gift from the government to some private faction, he thought it crucial that the terms of the agreement be beneficial for the government. Plus, he usually recommended some kind of buyout clause to enable the government to effectively cancel the contract by paying off the private party.[19]

Above all, Madison thought that because the power to grant exclusive contracts is so potentially dangerous, it should be explicitly authorized by the Constitution, not inferred from vague clauses in the governing instrument. This was the ground on which he objected to Hamilton's Bank of the United States in 1791, a stance that has long earned him the charge of inconsistency. But in fact, Madison had taken the same position a decade earlier. In 1781 Robert Morris proposed that the Congress of the Confederation charter a Bank of North America. Though Madison generally supported Morris and usually advocated a relatively broad reading of the powers granted to Congress under the Articles of Confederation, he thought Morris's proposal lacked constitutional sanction. Accordingly, he endeavored to strip the provision of public incorporation from the initial legislation. When that failed, he voted for the final bill, which did not actually incorporate the bank but authorized Morris to proceed. When Morris began taking subscriptions in December, public enthusiasm for the endeavor was underwhelming, prompting the financier to return to Congress to ask it to make good on its earlier promise of incorporation. Madison agreed, albeit reluctantly. In a lengthy note on the subject in January 1782 to Edmund Pendleton, he explained that he had been placed in a "dilemma." Something had to be done to solve the nation's financial problems, especially because payments to the army were at risk, but because the Pennsylvania legislature had adjourned, there was no alternative but for Congress to incorporate Morris's bank. Madison concluded, "As this is a tacit admission of a defect of power I hope it will be an antidote against the poisonous tendency of precedents of usurpation."[20]

UNBALANCED PUBLIC POLICY could threaten Madisonian republicanism in another way too: by creating conflicts of interest within representative government. One-sided policy, favoring one faction over all the others, should face a struggle to be enacted in a democratically elected Congress, at least in theory. But members of Congress are human beings, just like their constituents, and have their own ambitions, interests, and desires. If policies under debate benefit factions that members of Congress happen to be part of, members will have a conflict between their own interests and their duty to their constituents. Maybe they will do the right thing and vote with their constituents, but maybe they will not. And if they do not, then the republican balance Madison was seeking will have been corrupted, for in that instance, it is not the people who rule but, rather, the factions that legislators happen to be aligned with.

In other words, the efficacy of representative government cannot be taken for granted. Putting aside the question of whether the many or the few should rule, the fact is that the actual ruling is done by representatives of these classes, representatives who themselves are prone to the same flaws as all people. Economists call this the *principal-agent problem:* the principals (in this case, the voters) elect agents (their representatives) to do their business in government, but it can be difficult for the principals to monitor the agents to ensure they are doing the job they are supposed to.

Madison obviously had no formal training in modern economics, but he grasped this problem on a philosophical level. In *Federalist* 10, he argued that a "scheme of representation" is superior to direct democracy because it can elevate statesmen who "possess the most attractive merit" and thus is better able to realize the public good than if the people were to govern directly. But having been in various legislative bodies for over a decade by that point, he had a realistic view of the kinds of people who actually serve in government. He knew that "representative appointments" were sought not only for the "public good" but also out of "ambition" and "self interest." Unfortunately, those animated by such "base and selfish" motives are the "most industrious" and the "most successful in pursuing their object." Thus, though representative government can refine public opinion by passing it "through the medium of a chosen body of citizens, whose wisdom may best discern the true interest of their country," it also creates the potential for conflicts of interest, as legislators can sacrifice the general welfare to their own passions.[21]

This paradox endangers Madison's republican balance, although in a different way than does the threat from charters, licenses, and investments. In those cases, power has formally been transferred, via the law itself, to groups that subsequently abuse their authority. Here, although the distribution of power remains nominally republican—the people elect their representatives, just as always—power has *effectively* been transferred, as representatives exercise their authority not on the people's behalf but for themselves and their accomplices. This informal corruption can be very dangerous to republican government, for its beneficiaries hold a kind of unwritten trust, protected by a quiet alliance in the halls of power. Though the people retain the technical prerogative to elect their representatives, a governing cabal effectively nullifies this right.

In *Federalist* 51 Madison argued that the Constitution's elaborate system of checks and balances would combat this problem by setting self-interested politicians against one another. "Ambition must be made to counteract ambition," he famously asserted, so that "the interest of the man" is "connected with the constitutional rights of the place." Though representative government can control the excesses of human nature, it too must be controlled, for "what is government itself, but the greatest of all reflections on human nature?" Separation of powers acts on politicians in government in the same way that the extended republic acts on social factions: both force a grand clash of interests in which no single person or group is the dominant party, increasing the likelihood that the ultimate compromise advances the general welfare.[22]

Of course, Madison did not think that the Constitution would cure this disease altogether. As he noted in *Federalist* 55, "A degree of depravity in mankind . . . requires a certain degree of circumspection and distrust. So there are other qualities in human nature, which justify a certain portion of esteem and confidence. Republican government presupposes the existence of these qualities in a higher degree than any other form." No constitution can alter mankind's inherently selfish nature. At best, it can only structure the rules of the game to minimize the chances that such selfishness will destroy republicanism. After that, the friends of good government must rely upon a stock of "fit" characters who possess sufficient "wisdom . . . patriotism and love of justice" to vindicate the public interest through the course of everyday politics.[23]

Madison was such a character, and his commitment to the nation's experiment in self-government was exemplary. During his time in public office, he exhibited a strict ethos of public propriety. As he wrote in his "Autobiography," it was his policy "never to deal in [public] property, lands, debts, contracts and money, while a member of the body, whose proceedings might influence these transactions." There is no indication that he ever traded his public authority for private profit, and given his money struggles late in life, he paid a price for fidelity to this principle.[24]

Moreover, he could typically be counted an implacable foe of any scheme in which politicians sacrificed the general welfare for their own gain. This usually meant opposition to land or debt speculators, who had friends in Congress happy to work on their behalf. In his private letters, this seemingly mild-mannered statesman dripped contempt for the "stockjobbers," the "landjobbers," and the politicians they bought off. A decade before he was battling the stockjobbers whom he thought were benefiting illicitly from Hamilton's financial program, he fought with equal determination the landjobbers looking to gain windfall profits from the disbursement of the western territory. The issue in the early 1780s had to do with the borders of the thirteen former colonies. Roughly half of them had clearly defined boundaries; the other half could lay claim to some portion of lands to the west, thanks to their original royal charters. Virginia claimed more land than any other colony, and its claims were the strongest of the lot.[25]

This discrepancy created a severe problem. Companies were created in "four-sided" states to purchase titles in "three-sided" states from Native Americans, who had paltry or nonexistent claims to the land. These titles had no standing in the three-sided states but were legal tender in the four-sided ones. By 1779 Virginia had declared such contracts null and void, established a land office of its own, and promised to use its surplus territory to pay the bonuses owed to Virginia veterans. In the background were the first stirrings of the divide between large and small states that would feature at the Constitutional Convention in 1787. The four-sided states had no room to grow and stood to make no money from land sales, so they were jealous of the three-sided states, and not without reason. Why should royal charters granted by a sovereign the states had just overthrown play any role in determining who was to benefit from the sale of public land? Meanwhile, the three-sided states had an equally good reason to disregard their rivals, which had sanctioned the purchase of illegitimate titles from the Native Americans.[26]

Madison stepped into the fray in September 1780. With Joseph Jones, a member of Congress from Virginia and good friend of Jefferson's, he proposed that Georgia, North Carolina, and Virginia cede a portion of their western territories to a "common fund," out of which would be created new states, with the unceded western land to be used as bounties for war veterans. However, "all purchases and deeds from any Indian or Indians . . . which have been or shall be made for the use of any private person . . . shall be deemed and taken as absolutely void." This was a quintessentially Madisonian proposal. For starters, he was thinking about more than the parochial interests of Virginia, taking instead a broad view of the country's well-being. At the same time, there was to be no special exemption for the landjobbers and their cronies in government, who had hoped that Congress would eventually validate their dubious contracts. On this point, Madison was steadfast.[27]

When Congress struck the item invalidating Native American purchases from the package, Madison intuited that this was the handiwork of the speculators. He commented to Jones that the motivation was "gratifying private interest at the public expense." Still, the resolution passed the next month, and though Madison's worry about the landjobbers eased to some extent, his sardonic view of them did not change. In November, he wrote to Jones, "I do not believe there is any serious design in Congress to gratify the avidity of land mongers, but the best security for their virtue in this respect will be to keep it out of their power."[28]

Madison was right to remain suspicious. In response to the resolution, Connecticut, New York, and Virginia all ceded their lands.

Virginia did so on the condition that the claims of out-of-state companies would not be validated. But the "land mongers" were not deterred. Congress sent the cession proposals to a committee that was sympathetic to the interests of the speculators, and in October 1781 Madison fretted to Pendleton that though Virginia had made "every opposition and remonstrance," there was "little hope of arresting any aggression upon Virginia which depends solely on the inclination of Congress." Congress did not accept Virginia's cession, though it nevertheless turned down the committee's recommendation that it reject the cession outright. Eventually, a committee less sympathetic to the speculators took up the offer and produced a compromise whereby Congress would stop just short of explicitly rejecting the claims of the speculators and would not guarantee Virginia the land it claimed southeast of the Ohio River. Congress approved the compromise in September 1783, and Virginia accepted it in 1784, after Madison had left Congress.[29]

The establishment of a common fund for the western territory was an enormous step forward in the development of a truly national identity, and Madison deserves credit for helping bring it about. But note that the land speculators were so intent on reaping a payday for themselves that they antagonized the three-sided states and weakened the union. This is a perfect illustration of Hume's warnings about human beings: it is in their true interests to behave equitably, but they are often tempted by the lure of immediate self-gratification. It is dangerous for the public good for factions to have loyal agents in the government, and wise statesmen have to be on the lookout for such corruption. By the time Madison took his seat in the First Congress, this was a lesson he had learned well.

2

ONE GREAT AMERICAN SYSTEM

JUST BEHIND THE Metropolitan Museum of Art in New York City stands an impressive granite sculpture of Alexander Hamilton, depicted in the colonial era while he was in service as George Washington's aide-de-camp. A small dedication at the base of the monument reads that it was presented by Hamilton's son, John Church Hamilton, in 1880. John Church, who was just a boy when his father died, committed much of his adulthood to the maintenance of Hamilton's memory, writing a multivolume biography that still serves as a basic framework for scholars. The statue itself was dedicated just two years before John Church died, aged eighty-nine.

John Church's lifelong dedication to his father's memory is a touching manifestation of a son's love. It also speaks to the profound effect that Hamilton had on the people around him. In his day, he inspired deep loyalty and adulation among many. The opposite is no doubt true as well, for John Church's strenuous efforts were in part intended to repair Alexander's reputation, which sank posthumously during the populist waves of the Jeffersonian and

Jacksonian eras. During that time, Hamilton's sterling contributions to the Founding were overlooked and he was dismissed as a crass elitist, a friend to crooked speculators, and even a monarchist.

As late as the 1960s, admirers of Hamilton still found themselves on defense against the traditional Jeffersonian caricature. In recent decades, however, his reputation has experienced a marked turnaround among historians and among the general public. On the whole, this has been a welcome development, although modern defenders of Hamilton often fall into the sort of overwrought hero worship he inspired in his own day. They are too quick to cast Hamilton as the farsighted protagonist of American economic greatness, against the myopic agrarianism of Thomas Jefferson or the cunning opportunism of James Madison. In correcting the misstatements and misunderstandings perpetuated by the Jeffersonians of yore, they overlook or underestimate many of the problems inherent to Hamilton's political philosophy.

A temperate view of Hamilton's career must reject the overused categories of Federalist hero and Republican villain and instead recognize the deep similarities between Hamilton and Madison. Both of them dedicated their careers to reconciling the principles of liberalism, republicanism, and nationalism inherent to the American creed. Both proffered ingenious theories of government that endeavored to accomplish this task. And both fell short of the mark.

Not coincidentally, Madison and Hamilton started from the same philosophical place. They were both strongly influenced by David Hume's writings on human nature—particularly the relationship between reason and passion in governing individual behavior. In *A Treatise of Human Nature,* Hume argued that "reason is, and ought only to be the slave of the passions, and can never pretend to any other office than to serve and obey them." Similarly, Hamilton held that "nothing is more fallacious than to expect to produce any valuable or permanent results, in political projects, by relying merely on the reason of men. Men are rather reasoning tha[n] reasonable animals for the most part governed by the impulse of passion." Madison and Hamilton were also persuaded by Hume that a stable government must corral those passions, which lead inevitably to what Madison called "the violence of faction." In an unpublished essay from 1795 defending his economic program, Hamilton averred that faction is "the natural disease of popular governments."[1]

Madison and Hamilton agreed that reining in those passions required a stronger central authority. The states had proven themselves incapable of serving the public interest, so power had to be transferred to a new, national government. A main point of difference between the two was how this authority should be constituted. In a daylong speech introducing his plan of government to the Constitutional Convention, Hamilton argued, "In every community where industry is encouraged, there will be a division of it into the few and the many. Hence, separate interests will arise. There will be debtors and creditors, etc." The task of republican government was to organize these factions so "that each may defend itself against the other." All of this sounded distinctly Madisonian, but Hamilton diverged from his friend on the sufficiency of the extended republic, which he did not believe offered enough protection against the danger of mob rule. As he wrote in his notes for the address, "A democratic assembly is to be checked by a democratic senate, and both these by a democratic chief magistrate. The end will not be answered—the means will not be equal to the object. It will, therefore, be feeble and inefficient."[2]

In contrast, Hamilton proffered a more traditional notion of mixed government. He praised the "proper adjustment" the British had made to the principle of majority rule. It was "the best model the world ever produced," in part because a permanent position for the few constituted a check upon the excesses of the many. His system of government basically imported the British constitution to the New World, minus its hereditary aspects. Senators would enjoy life tenure based on good behavior and would be appointed by an electoral college, whose members would be chosen by the people. The president would also enjoy life tenure and would be separated from the people by *two* electoral colleges. Only the House would be directly elected by the people, and its members would serve three-year terms.[3]

Hamilton believed that this approach would not only protect the rights of the minority but would also better advance the interests of the whole nation. Because the upper echelons of the government would be insulated from the public, exceptional leaders who rose to its lofty ranks would be free from the demands of electoral politics to serve the greater good. In this way, the British had it right. "Their House of Lords is a most noble institution," he argued. "Having nothing to hope for by a change, and a sufficient interest by means of their property, in being faithful to the national interest, they form a permanent barrier against every pernicious innovation, whether attempted on the part of the Crown or the Commons." He thought that the executive could serve as another bulwark against destructive impulses, and he held that "the English model was the only good one on this subject." The British monarch possessed a "hereditary interest" that was "interwoven with that of the nation." Thus, the king was all but incorruptible. Foreign nations could never hope to bribe him, and domestic factions had little sway over him. Instead, he was free to "answer the purpose of the institution."[4]

Having separated the few from the many, Hamilton further suggested empowering the governing elite to direct the affairs of state via "influence"—or, in contemporary parlance, patronage: the distribution of jobs, emoluments, honors, and other private benefits. He believed that men were driven by their passions—for wealth, esteem, glory—and he felt that the government had to "avail itself of those passions, in order to make them subservient to the public good—for these ever induce us to action."[5]

On this issue, Hamilton again followed Hume, who argued that the patronage distributed by the Crown maintained the balance of the British system. Because the Crown had, in effect, purchased the support of members of Parliament, "the House of Commons stretches not its power, because such an usurpation would be contrary to the interest of the majority of its members." Hume thought that keeping Parliament in check was "necessary to the preservation of [Britain's] mixed government" and that therefore the patronage offered by the Crown served the greater good.[6]

Similarly, Hamilton thought that executive-directed patronage could orient the interests of politicians to the cause of the new government. In his view, one of the problems with the Articles of Confederation was that the "dispensations of honors and emoluments of office" were left entirely to the states, thereby encouraging men to attend to parochial considerations. If the new executive branch could distribute benefits, it could reorient them toward the national interest. It would be ideal, he acknowledged, if there were enough farsighted statesmen in government not to have recourse to such bribery. Alas, such men are always in short supply, and "a reliance on pure patriotism had been the source of many of our errors." He did not relish this tool, but he concluded, "We must in some degree, submit to the inconvenience."[7]

To be sure, Hamilton only supported the use of influence insofar as it could advance the good of the nation. He held in contempt politicians who used their public station solely to enrich themselves. A decade before the Constitutional Convention, for instance, he had noticed that the price of flour had doubled in advance of the French fleet's arrival, and he suspected that Samuel Chase—a member of the Confederation Congress and a future Supreme Court justice—had quietly disclosed Congress's plan to purchase flour in anticipation of the reinforcements so that he could corner the market. This was an example of corruption for no greater purpose, and it prompted a stern rebuke from the future treasury secretary.[8]

Hamilton's views on influence foreshadowed his later political battle with Madison and Jefferson. In Great Britain, patronage from the Crown had been a tool employed by Prime Minister Robert Walpole to implement a modern financial system. Walpole's administration had drawn heated rebukes from polemicists like Lord Bolingbroke and the pseudonymous authors of *Cato's Letters,* who believed that his efforts were undermining the independence of Parliament. In the 1790s, Madison and Jefferson would frame their opposition to Hamilton along the same lines. Jefferson, for instance, recalled that Hamilton celebrated the British system not in spite of its "corruption" but because of it. "Purge it of its corruption," Jefferson recalled Hamilton saying, "and it would become an *impracticable* government. As it stands at present, with all its supposed defects, it is the most perfect government which ever existed." Jefferson and Madison believed this was evidence that Hamilton wished to destroy the new republic and replace it with a British-style monarchy. But they misunderstood the treasury secretary. Like Hume, Hamilton believed that "corruption," or influence, was essential to republican statecraft. The British had used patronage to balance power between Crown and Commons, and Hamilton thought it could establish the supremacy of the federal government over the querulous, irresponsible states.[9]

THESE IDEAS SET Hamilton far apart from most of his contemporaries, but he thought such extreme measures necessary to counteract the centrifugal tendencies of the Articles of Confederation. The fear of disunion deeply troubled him throughout the 1780s. His early *Federalist* essays, particularly 6, 7, and 8, read like jeremiads against the dangers of continued state supremacy. In *Federalist* 6 he predicted that "if these States should either be wholly disunited, or only united in partial confederacies," they would have "frequent and violent contests with each other" because "men are ambitious, vindictive, and rapacious" and that if they were governed by "independent, unconnected sovereignties," they would find causes to war upon each other. The problem was endemic to human nature, and Hamilton ran through a long history of European conflicts to convince his fellow Americans that they should expect no better of themselves or their leaders.[10]

In *Federalist* 7 Hamilton outlined the many ways Americans might be turned against one another. "Unsettled claims" over "the vast tract of unsettled territory within the boundaries of the United States" could offer "an ample theatre for hostile pretensions." Commerce could serve as "another fruitful source of contention," as each state would inevitably implement a "system of commercial policy peculiar to itself . . . which would beget discontent." Another cause for concern could be the inability "to agree upon a rule of apportionment" of the public debt that would be "satisfactory to all." And if states could not agree to pay whatever share was agreed

to, then delinquent states would inspire "complaints, recriminations, and quarrels" from the other states. Laws that violated public
contracts—like the extreme debt-relief measures enacted by Rhode
Island—could be a cause for disunion, for they would "amount to
aggressions on the rights of those states whose citizens are injured
by them." Finally, he fretted about "jarring alliances" between individual states and European powers, which could cause the New
World to become "entangled in all the pernicious labyrinths of European politics and wars."[11]

In *Federalist* 8 Hamilton brought this parade of horrible pos-
sibilities to a grisly conclusion by predicting that the inevitable
outcome of such rivalries would be "desultory and predatory" war,
leading to permanent military establishments. "Plunder and devas-
tations ever march in the train of irregulars," he proclaimed darkly.
The terrors created by roving bands of poorly trained, unpaid soldiers eventually induce all nations, even those "most attached to
liberty," to sacrifice "their civil and political rights" for the sake of
security. "To be more safe, they at length become willing to run the
risk of being less free" and thus sanction "standing armies." This
was a potent fear in the minds of eighteenth-century republicans,
who believed that a standing army "elevates the importance of the
soldier, and proportionably degrades the condition of the citizen."[12]

These dire prophecies were of a piece with Hamilton's political
philosophy. What the country needed was a strong central authority
that channeled the individual passions of men to the common good.
The existing conditions could not long persist, he feared. Sooner
or later the bonds of brotherhood forged during the Revolutionary
War would loosen, the states would turn against one another, and in
time republican government would be trampled under the marching boots of standing armies. Such a retrogression had to be fore-
stalled, and his plan of government—elitist as it may have seemed
to his contemporaries—was created with this purpose in mind.

FOR HAMILTON, FORGING a stronger union was more than solely a
constitutional project. It also had to be advanced by public policies,
particularly those that dealt with matters of economics. A farsighted

system that governed finance and commerce, he believed, could join the interests of otherwise disparate factions in American society into a shared quest for greater prosperity. This would facilitate economic growth, promote domestic tranquility, and engender international respect.

"The importance of the Union, in a commercial light," was the subject of *Federalist* 11, an essay that anticipated Hamilton's work as secretary of treasury. In it, he noted that "the adventurous spirit" of "the commercial character of America" had made Europe intent on "depriving us, as far as possible, of an active commerce" and "clipping the wings by which we might soar to a dangerous greatness." But the choice was America's to make. "Under a vigorous national government, the natural strength and resources of the country, directed to a common interest, would baffle all the combinations of European jealousy to restrain our growth." If the government would facilitate "an unrestrained intercourse between the states," all citizens would benefit "by an interchange of their respective productions. . . . The veins of commerce in every part will be replenished, and will acquire additional motion and vigor from a free circulation of the commodities of every part." He christened this vision "one great American system."[13]

Hamilton amplified this argument in *Federalist* 12, where he claimed that "the prosperity of commerce" was the "most productive source of national wealth," for it "multipl[ies] the means of gratification" and "vivif[ies] and invigorate[s] the channels of industry." In this way, it could promote harmony among the many factions of the nation. "The assiduous merchant, the laborious husbandman, the active mechanic, and the industrious manufacturer" all have an interest in their own welfare, and the promotion of commerce could bring them together in the quest for enrichment. Even the "often-agitated question, between agriculture and commerce," long marked by frequent "rivalships," could be resolved by commerce, showing these otherwise disparate groups "that their interests are intimately blended and interwoven."[14]

When the country ratified the Constitution, it took the first step toward erecting Hamilton's single "great American system."

He believed it was then the task of the new government to advance this project via its commercial program—a heavy burden that would fall mostly on his shoulders. The Confederation Congress had left public finance in a state of total disarray. The great financier Robert Morris had had to beg, borrow, and steal to finance the Revolutionary War, as the states had refused to pay their share of the costs. The peace did not bring an end to their stinginess, and all through the 1780s the nation's credit standing steadily worsened. Hamilton would therefore face a formidable challenge, yet it was also an unprecedented opportunity to design public policy as he saw fit. He modeled himself after the great architects of European finance, especially Jacques Necker and Walpole. Necker, who served as finance minister to Louis XVI, reshaped the entire French economy, while Walpole's policies had transformed Great Britain into a world power. Hamilton would find in these consequential men not only policy ideas he could adapt to the American situation but also the inspiration for turning the Treasury Department into the mainspring of the new government.[15]

Hamilton's approach to commercial policy paralleled his view of patronage. Just as influence was useful to yoke the interests of politicians to the national government, wise commercial policy could engender loyalty among the wealthy to the Constitution. This, he believed, was of primary importance. Though land was plentiful, the young country was desperately cash poor. Liquid assets were becoming increasingly concentrated in the hands of a small class of merchants and financiers who, he knew, would be betting on the nation's future, one way or the other. He wanted to court the rich with favorable policy, for if their interests aligned with those of the United States, they would bet on the nation's success. And if they believed the new Constitution would succeed, they would loan the government money at reasonable rates of interest and eventually invest in private development, generating the commercial prosperity he thought essential.

Hamilton therefore wished to transform the moneyed class into mediators of the public good. The wealthy few would directly benefit from commercial policy in the short term; however, by

reorienting their financial interests to the interests of the new government, the secretary would make them instruments of his economic agenda. He was confident that if given the opportunity to
serve their country in this way, the rich would rise to the occasion.
Like many Founders, including Jefferson and Madison, Hamilton
believed in a natural aristocracy, a select group whose God-given
talents qualified them to lead others. But unlike Jefferson and Madison, Hamilton tended to assume that the rich had already demonstrated that they were members of this elite. His high esteem for
the wealthy contributed enormously to the partisan vitriol of the
1790s and was the ultimate cause of many mistakes he made in
government. Over the course of his tenure at the Treasury Department, he would exhibit a shocking naïveté regarding the greed and
small-mindedness of the speculative class, which attached itself like
a barnacle to his administration. They were not the natural aristo-
crats he assumed them to be. Many were just crooks who abused
his misplaced trust.[16]

HAMILTON'S FIRST ECONOMIC priority was to create a uniform
national currency. During the 1780s, there was little specie (that
is, metal coins) in circulation. Continental dollars, national debt
certificates, and state debt certificates were the main forms of cash.
The problem was that all of these depended upon faith in the government, which was sorely lacking. In fact, people expected the
government to devalue the currency by printing more and to fail to
honor its debt obligations. Therefore these different papers traded
at varying discounts, inhibiting the development of a national economic marketplace, which was a prerequisite for commercial prosperity. The solution, in Hamilton's judgment, was for the national
government to promise a full repayment of the public debt. If people had confidence in the government, debt certificates could be
reliably employed as money throughout the country.[17]

Hamilton submitted the *Report on Public Credit* to Congress in
the winter of 1790. In it, he argued that a "properly funded debt . . .
answers most of the purposes of money." So long as the public debt

was an "object of confidence," it could be used by individuals to make purchases and pay private debts. Hamilton believed that a sound and stable currency would have far-reaching implications, extending trade, promoting agriculture and manufacturing, lowering the interest rate for borrowing money, and increasing the value of land. As he famously put it, "The proper funding of the present debt will render it a national blessing." Given that the debt was increasingly concentrated in the hands of wealthy speculators in the eastern cities, funding it would generate windfall profits for that narrow faction, but he considered it worth it in the long run. Though his program would substantially increase the value of their holdings, it would eventually redound to the good of the whole nation.[18]

Hamilton's debt plan had two major components. First, he called for repayment of existing federal certificates mostly at face value. Foreign creditors would have their obligations repaid at precisely the terms for which the debt was originally contracted. As for holders of the domestic debt, he proposed a reduction in the interest rate from 6 to 4 percent in exchange for options on western land, to be paid to the current holders of the securities. He would also use revenue from the post office to create what was called a *sinking fund,* or money set aside for the purpose of paying off the principal of the debt.

Second, he called for the federal government to assume the debts of the thirteen states. Though there was a compelling reason for tending to the national debt right away—namely, securing the creditworthiness of the new government—the state debts were not a direct concern of the national government under the Constitution's federated system. Nevertheless, he argued vigorously that the secondary benefits justified assumption. He claimed that it would cut down on intergovernmental competition for tax revenue, increase the efficiency of taxation (by making it easier to tax items that moved through the stream of interstate commerce on the national level), alleviate the burden on states that were less able to pay their debts, and avoid potential blowback against the nation's credit from disappointed owners of state paper.

Most notably, he asserted that assumption would facilitate national unity. "If all the public creditors receive their dues from one source," he argued, "their interest will be the same," united "in the support of the fiscal arrangements of the government." On the other hand, the perpetuation of the state debts would create "distinct interests, drawing different ways" and would "be likely to give place to mutual jealousy and opposition." This claim was strongly reminiscent of his argument at the Constitutional Convention that patronage could channel individual passions toward a single, national government instead of a multiplicity of state governments. Here, Hamilton argued that federalizing all public debts would give creditors a stake in the success of the Constitution that would supersede their loyalty to the individual states.[19]

Having developed a monetary foundation for commercial prosperity, Hamilton went on in the *Report on a National Bank,* submitted to Congress in December 1790, to show how the government might jump-start the economy. His proposed Bank of the United States would be a public-private enterprise. The government would own a minority stake in the bank and deposit its tax revenues there, but otherwise the bank would be privately owned and managed. Such an institution would provide two direct benefits for the government. First, it would lend "greater facility to the government in obtaining pecuniary aids, especially in sudden emergencies." During the Revolutionary War, Congress had often struggled to raise funds, for there was no financial system akin to what we take for granted today. Hamilton held that a nationally chartered bank would always be available in a pinch to supply cash at reasonable rates of interest. Moreover, the bank, by offering loans to the public, would "facilitat[e] the payment of taxes."[20]

Visionary that he was, Hamilton saw something even bigger in the proposal: a good bank could be vital for national commerce. He argued in the *Report* that gold and silver, "when they are employed merely as the instruments of exchange and alienation, have not been improperly denominated dead stock." However, when specie is deposited in banks with good credit, they can circulate their own notes throughout the economy, effectively creating "a far greater sum than the actual quantum of their capital in gold and silver." Hamilton was talking about what today is commonly called *fractional-reserve banking,* whereby a bank's deposits amount to only a fraction of the loans it makes. Premised on the idea that not every depositor would withdraw all of his or her deposits at once, fractional-reserve banking had become widely employed by the major European banks in the eighteenth century. Hamilton believed that by creating such a bank in the United States, the government could inject a massive infusion of capital into the fledgling economy.[21]

Moreover, Hamilton believed that a public-private bank could rechannel the self-interests of the wealthy toward the good of the nation. In 1780, he had written a letter to James Duane, a New York politician, arguing that the nation's currency woes could be traced to the fact that men of wealth did not have faith in the government. What was required was a "joint basis of public and private credit," which could only be conjoined under a national bank. Such an institution would allow members of the moneyed class to acquire "the whole or part of the profits" and thus would give them "an immediate interest to hold" the credit of the government. His model was the Bank of England, which "unites public authority and faith with private credit," enabling Great Britain to acquire "sufficient funds to carry on her wars." In a letter from around the same time, he similarly claimed that a bank could link "the interests of the state in an intimate connation with those of the rich individuals belonging to it," turning "the wealth and influence of both into a commercial channel for mutual benefit, which must afford advantages not to be estimated."[22]

Hamilton had ardently supported Morris's Bank of North America, and the two men corresponded frequently throughout the 1780s. Ultimately, that institution lacked the necessary backing to accomplish the grand purposes Hamilton had in mind. But as secretary of the treasury, he could rectify that. His proposed bank would have an initial capitalization of $10 million. Shares would be sold to the public for $400 apiece; 25 percent was to be paid up front, and just 25 percent of the up-front money had to be paid in specie. The rest was deliverable in the form of government debt certificates. The result was that for just $25 in hard currency, one would receive a *scrip,* or a guaranteed option to own a share of bank stock. Thus, creditors who just a few short months earlier may have owned debt from South Carolina or Connecticut had transferred that credit to the new federal government and now had an option to cash it in for a piece of the Bank of the United States. At long last, here was the opportunity for the "joint basis of public and private credit" that he had sought for a decade, with the loyalty of the wealthy now firmly attached to the Constitution.[23]

The bank passed quickly through Congress in the winter of 1791, but President Washington hesitated at signing it into law, questioning its constitutionality. The president solicited opinions on the matter from Attorney General Edmund Randolph, Secretary of State Jefferson, and Hamilton. Hamilton's argument hinged upon the idea that the bank was constitutional under the necessary and proper clause. Though chartering a bank was not a specifically enumerated power, it would aid in certain tasks that the Constitution did bestow upon Congress, such as the regulation of the currency. His argument ultimately persuaded Washington, though Hamilton's main ambition behind the bank—the promotion of national unity through economic prosperity—was not an enumerated power of Congress. By using commercial policy to establish the preeminence of the federal government, the secretary was in effect outflanking the Anti-Federalists who had sought at the Constitutional Convention to preserve state power.[24]

His debt and banking proposals having created a solid financial groundwork for commerce, Hamilton next turned to the need for economic diversification. The *Report on Manufactures,* submitted to Congress in December 1791, proposed a farsighted system of industrial protection to promote manufacturing. Hamilton's tariff recommendations were passed by Congress, but his main instrument of protection was bounties, direct subsidies to select industries. The legislature could not abide this. Accordingly, the trade policy of the United States, as a general rule, did not begin offering protection to industries until after the War of 1812. And when it did, the emphasis was on indirect subsidies like tariffs rather than direct payoffs like bounties.[25]

The timing of the *Report on Manufactures* was not propitious. By the time it was presented, dissatisfaction with Hamilton's program had developed into an organized political opposition. There was also little by way of popular demand for such a system, as the United States was still almost entirely agricultural in 1791. Still, by arguing for industrial protection in a nation of farmers, Hamilton offered his most emphatic statement yet about the potential for commercial development to harmonize the disparate forces in society. He wrote, "The trade of a country which is both manufacturing and agricultural will be more lucrative and prosperous, than that of a country which is merely agricultural." He predicted a number of specific advantages, like encouraging division of labor, increasing the use of machinery, promoting immigration to fill a growing number of factory jobs, and facilitating new opportunities to develop personal talents.[26]

Hamilton anticipated that the agricultural class would complain about the unfairness of his program, acknowledging that "there is a degree of prejudice against bounties from an appearance of giving away the public money, without an immediate consideration, and from a supposition, that they serve to enrich particular classes, at the expense of the community." This "temporary expense," he assured his readers, would be "more than compensated, by an increase of industry and wealth, by an augmentation of resources and independence, and by the circumstance of eventual cheapness." His program would not only strengthen the nation at large, but it would also aid agriculture—eventually. A diversified economy with a robust manufacturing sector would provide "a more certain and steady demand for the surplus produce of the soil," protecting American farmers from fluctuations in the world markets, which "is of the first consequence."[27]

Hamilton's system of protection was therefore of a piece with his broader agenda to use the moneyed class as a mediator for the public good. Capital owners would enjoy a direct and immediate reward from the government, which, by encouraging their enterprises, would assist all citizens in due course. And his strategy of mediation was similar to his advocacy of patronage. In general, he believed that the government should deploy select benefits to important social, political, and economic actors in order to bind their private interests to public purposes. Honorary titles, sinecures, debt repayment, bank stock, protective bounties—all of these were Hamiltonian efforts to corral the passions of men for the sake of the national interest.[28]

In his own time and for generations thereafter, Hamilton's views were misunderstood as monarchical or oligarchic. Jeffersonians cast him as a man whose secret desire was to undo the Revolution of 1776 and restore a government run by and for the wealthy. Hamilton's political thinking was undoubtedly elitist. He had great faith in men of natural talent and comparatively little confidence in the masses. But he was well within the revolutionary tradition that joined liberalism, republicanism, and nationalism. His methods may have come off as "high toned" to his critics, but his goal was to secure a stable, vigorous, and free republic in the United States. His system was far from perfect, but his intentions were earnest, and his positive contributions to the American experiment in self-government were enormous.

In Madison, Hamilton found a wise and crafty ally during the 1780s. Their partnership was premised on several shared values. Both believed that people were easily led astray by selfish interests that undermined the cause of good government. Both felt that this human frailty had primarily manifested itself through the parochialism of the state governments. Both held that the cure for this ailment was to invest the national government with greater power.

But Madisonian balance and Hamiltonian vigor diverged thereafter. Madison believed that government had to be a kind of neutral umpire, arbitrating dispassionately among the competing claims of social and economic factions. Hamilton, on the other hand, thought government should function more like a head coach. Just as a coach starts some players and benches others to maximize the team's chance of victory, Hamilton intended to favor some factions over others based on their usefulness to the national good. Accordingly, he crafted a system of government that provided space for a natural aristocracy to govern free of electoral politics, supported the use of patronage in the practice of statecraft, and designed commercial policy that plied the wealthy with special benefits. So long as the political debate was about the impotence of the Articles of Confederation, this disagreement was merely academic. But after the project of establishing the new Constitution was settled, the two allies would quickly become bitter enemies. Madison simply could not abide Hamilton's unrelenting partiality toward the rich, and he worried that the secretary's policies were corrupting power relations in the republic.

The coming clash would baffle the two antagonists and set the tone for partisan vitriol over the course of the next decade—and in retrospect, it prefigured contemporary American politics. Hamilton's economic policies have a lot in common with the general bent of twenty-first-century political economy in the United States. His specific proposals, such as a public-private bank and a system of industrial protection, are not utilized anymore. Policy makers now rely on the Federal Reserve and generally think free trade is ideal for economic development. But Hamilton's basic goals—economic diversification and growth—as well as his belief that the government can and should help achieve them are in line with present-day views. Madison's theories on economics and society, by contrast, are antiquated. He envisioned a future in which mankind's endeavors could not keep up with its propensity to procreate—which is exactly the opposite of what has occurred. Indeed, agricultural productivity has continued to grow to the present day, despite the fact that fewer people and less land are involved in farming.

And yet on the question of politics, Madison was often more farsighted than Hamilton. Not in every way, of course: Madison was a slaveholder who denied African Americans their God-given rights, and Hamilton was a member of the New York Manumission Society. But Madison's ideal of an impartial government that treats all citizens in a balanced manner is much closer to our own views than Hamilton's unabashed favoritism to the wealthy. And though Madison was hardly a democrat by contemporary standards, he had more esteem than Hamilton for the sovereignty of public opinion, which anticipates the modern conceit that politics should be in the hands of the people at large.[29]

Modern America, then, is an amalgam of Hamilton's economic priorities and Madison's political scruples. The United States did not come to this hybrid view immediately or easily. Instead, their philosophies of government would have to compete with one another and then be tested by the realities of politics, economics, and world affairs. The first test arrived almost as soon as the Constitution was ratified.

3

DOING FULL JUSTICE

THE YEAR 1789 was a time of civic unity. George Washington was unanimously chosen by the Electoral College to be the nation's first president. His dealings with Congress were cordial, establishing sound precedents for interbranch relations that endure to the present day. For its part, Congress adopted the Bill of Rights, organized both the judicial branch and the major cabinet departments, and finally implemented a national tax. For those who had lived through the tumult of the prior fifteen years, the harmony of that year must have been an enormous relief.

But it was not to last very long. The public debt had been a divisive issue under the Articles of Confederation, and when the new Congress began deliberating on how to pay the nation's bills in the winter of 1790, disagreements again became intense. Surprisingly, Alexander Hamilton and James Madison—who had worked together on debt issues in the 1780s—would find themselves on opposite sides this time around. The divide puzzled both men, neither of whom could ever provide a fair and accurate account of what exactly had happened. In private, Hamilton would accuse Madison of being a fool, a liar, a man of bad character. Madison, for his part, would see in Hamilton an irrepressible elitism.

It is indeed unusual that two friends and colleagues could be driven so far apart in such a short period of time. But looking at it today—with the benefit of historical perspective—it appears less surprising. There were, in fact, early indications of the tensions between Hamiltonian vigor and Madisonian balance that portended the feud of the 1790s.

For one thing, their differences can be found on a close reading of the *Federalist* papers. In *Federalist* 10 Madison argued that a large sphere of governance would help prevent one party from abusing the rights or interests of another or of the whole. Though Hamilton was certainly sensitive to the importance of justice (which he discussed in his prior *Federalist* essays on the problems of disunion), in *Federalist* 11 he reached beyond the inherent defensiveness of *Federalist* 10 and envisioned the possibility of grand coordination among all groups in a shared quest for ever-increasing economic prosperity. The two goals are not necessarily in conflict with one another, but they are not necessarily in concert either. A vigorous nation may not always be a just one, and a just republic may not be very vigorous.

In other situations, their disagreements were more manifest, usually arising when the interests of the wealthy were at stake. In 1782 Madison and Hamilton were serving in the Confederation Congress, which was beset with all manner of financial problems, mostly owing to the fact that it was not empowered under the Articles of Confederation to levy any kind of tax. That year, Congress decided to depreciate the currency, raising the question of what the exchange ratio should be for redemption of the old currency. Hamilton advocated that it be set around 100:1, a generous ratio given the circumstances—favorable to speculators who had begun acquiring the old notes on the cheap, in many cases after they had stopped circulating through the economy. He wanted to court the allegiance of these moneyed elites and believed that this exchange rate "would multiply the advocates for federal funds for discharging the public debts, and tend to cement the Union." Madison objected to Hamilton's proposal and preferred a ratio of approximately 150:1, less generous to the speculators. Madison figured that they had bought the old currency in expectation of windfall profits from the government and that the Confederation Congress was under no obligation to honor the notes at Hamilton's rate. Instead, Madison wanted a credit for the old redemptions "as equity might require," a phrase that is consistent with his general emphasis on fairness among all factions of society.[1]

The two remained on good terms during the first year under the Constitution, but in September there was another hint of their coming dispute. Madison opposed a motion in the House of Representatives from Thomas Scott of Pennsylvania, a Hamilton ally, to locate the new capital near "the center of wealth, population, and extent of territory." Madison objected to considering wealth "in determining the place where the seat of government ought to be." Government is meant for the "citizens at large," who by right should have "equal facility to communicate with it." At the time, this turned out to be a small matter. Madison's objection carried the day, and the final location of the capital would be rolled into the Compromise of 1790, which also settled the lingering dispute over public debt. But the issue was nevertheless loaded with symbolism. In this statement, Madison anticipated a major objection to Hamilton's policy program, which in its immediate effects would not supply the "equal facility . . . due to all ranks" of society.[2]

Still, these minor differences aside, the political questions of the 1780s usually did not separate Madison and Hamilton. That changed when Hamilton submitted the *Report on Public Credit* to Congress in January 1790. He followed that up with the *Report on a National Bank* in December of the same year and then the *Report on Manufactures* in December 1791. These three documents were Hamilton's effort to translate the principles of national vigor into public policy, and they dominated the political conversation for the remainder of President Washington's first term. This was when the latent dispute between Madison and Hamilton finally became active, for Hamilton's efforts to invigorate national development struck Madison as profoundly unfair. And with that, their old spirit of respectful collegiality devolved into a rancorous political brawl.

THE *REPORT ON Public Credit* called for repayment of the national debt to its current holders and for federal assumption of the state debts. It was a bold agenda, but Hamilton could be excused for expecting support from Madison, who had backed an early version of Hamilton's assumption plan during the impost fight in the early 1780s and had endorsed a repayment plan for the national debt in 1783 that was basically the same as the one in the *Report on Public Credit.*

Moreover, Madison was at that point more tolerant of public debt than Thomas Jefferson. A few months before Hamilton released the *Report on Public Credit,* Jefferson had written Madison that because "the earth belongs in usufruct to the living . . . no man can, by natural right, oblige the lands he occupied, or the persons who succeed him in that occupation, to the payment of debts contracted by him." Jefferson took this as a maxim that bound not only individuals but whole societies. Accordingly, "no generation can contract debts greater than may be paid during the course of its own existence." Eventually Madison would offer a more Jeffersonian view, but in this case he expressed a milder opinion in his response to Jefferson. He wrote that "debts may be incurred for purposes which interest the unborn, as well as the living," such as "repelling a conquest, the evils of which descend through many generations." He also noted that the benefits from "the present debt of the United States," incurred largely because of the war, were "principally for the benefit of the posterity."[3]

Nevertheless, a wide gulf separated Madison and Hamilton on the matter of the national debt. One of Madison's main objections to the *Report on Public Credit* was Hamilton's seeming lack of interest in paying down the principal. Madison told Edmund Randolph that under Hamilton's plan, it would take "40 or 50 years" to extinguish the debt, "which considering intermediate probabilities, amounts to a perpetuity." Hamilton was drawn to the idea of a permanent debt, thanks to the experience of Great Britain during the eighteenth century. Its national debt had created a foundation for public credit, which enabled it to finance wars on the European continent. But Madison had long been a skeptic of such financial innovations. In 1779, before he entered the Confederation Congress, he had worried about "public credit sinking under the weight of an enormous debt." Speaking in Congress in 1790, he called for a "simple, unembarrassed" system of repayment, and he hoped to "shorten the duration of the debt as much as possible."[4]

Madison also opposed Hamilton's plan to fund the national debt because it violated his commitment to an equitable distribution of the burdens and benefits of government. In particular, Madison believed the secretary was giving too much to the moneyed class that had been speculating in the debt and not enough to the war veterans to whom it had initially been issued.

After the war, veterans were paid not in hard currency but in debt certificates, commonly known as Pierce Notes. Desperately in need of cash, they began selling these government IOUs in 1784, flooding the market. Speculators took full advantage of the rock-bottom prices and snatched up the Pierce Notes for ten to fifteen cents on the dollar, betting that the government would eventually redeem some portion of the obligation. In November 1788 Pierce Notes were trading for about eighteen cents on the dollar, but as rumors of Hamilton's funding plan began to spread through the major financial centers, their prices rose quickly. By December 1789, right before Hamilton submitted the *Report on Public Credit,* they were trading at roughly fifty cents on the dollar, as financiers eagerly anticipated windfall profits from Hamilton's funding plan.[5]

Though Madison had supported a full funding of the national debt in the early 1780s, he had done so before the speculators had acquired so many debt certificates. The more recent developments had deeply offended his sense of fair play. He did not like it when the land speculators tried to get the Confederation to validate their dubious titles in the 1780s, and he did not like the idea of debt speculators reaping such a bounty in 1790. That this was coming at the expense of Revolutionary War veterans only made him angrier. The soldiers had now been mistreated twice: first when the Confederation government paid them for their service with low-grade paper, and again now when Hamilton proposed, in effect, to pay their wages to the speculators. The fact that the price of Pierce Notes increased so quickly just prior to the publication of the *Report on Public Credit* further suggests that investors were trading on inside information.

Unlike some of Hamilton's opponents, who proposed a major haircut as an alternative, Madison had no desire to default on the debt. "No logic, no magic, in my opinion, can diminish the force of the obligation," he stated flatly. The question was who should receive the payment. Hamilton called for the entire sum to go to current holders of the debt, which privileged the speculators over the soldiers. Madison's view was that both the veterans and the speculators had legitimate claims. Veterans could rightfully complain because they had "never really been paid," which was doubly offensive because they had suffered a "singular hardship" for a military service that could "never be forgotten." Now was the time for the government to satisfy the "stipulated and expected" value that had been promised. Moreover, he thought paying back the soldiers would improve public credit, showing that the government would honor the promises it had once made. At the same time, the speculators had taken a real risk by purchasing the debt, and repayment "is but the just reward of that risk: That as they hold the public promise, they have an undeniable demand on the public faith." It was also necessary for the government to pay them, as "that [is] the best foundation of public credit."[6]

The veterans and the speculators were locked in a zero-sum game; a win for one group would necessarily mean a loss for the other. So, Madison proposed a fifty-fifty compromise. To the current holders of the debt, Madison would grant "the highest price which has prevailed in the market," or about fifty cents on the dollar. The other half would go to the original holders. "This will not do perfect justice," he admitted, "but it will do more real justice, and perform more of the public faith than any other expedient proposed." The present holders of the debt "will have a profit that cannot be reasonably complained of," and "the original sufferers will not be fully indemnified, but they will receive, from their country, a tribute due to their merits."[7]

Madison's main speech in defense of his plan, given on the House floor on February 11, 1790, was a pristine application of his political theory. He laid out the broad principles of justice that should govern the distribution of debt payments and then proceeded to apply them in a sober manner. Shorn of the broader context, his proposal seemed eminently reasonable. And yet it was voted down—overwhelmingly so. The opposition stung him, and on February 14 he fulminated to Jefferson that though he was "aware of the difficulties of the plan," he thought they "might be removed by one-half the exertion that will be used to collect and color them." This caustic reaction was typical of the private Madison, when he was losing a political debate and felt his sense of fairness violated.[8]

The truth is that Madison's alternative funding plan went down to defeat because it was a bad idea, and his colleagues knew it. So committed was he to the principle of distributive fairness that he was blinded to the long-term consequences of his scheme. By dividing repayment equally between the speculators and the veterans, he was effectively sanctioning a breach of the debt contract, which would have had wide-ranging ill effects. In the *Report on Public Credit,* Hamilton explained that in such a situation, the value of all certificates would plummet, as investors would begin to doubt "the chance of the continuance of [the] profit." This would result in a real loss of national wealth, raise the borrowing costs of the government, and perhaps freeze the debt market altogether. On top of that, how would the government of 1790 actually go about locating the veterans who originally held the certificates? It simply did not have the money, manpower, or expertise to undertake this kind of project.[9]

Still, Madison had a fair point. It is shocking to compare the shoddy treatment of Revolutionary War veterans to the behavior toward those who served in later conflicts, especially given that the Revolutionary War was one of the deadliest struggles in American history. Still, the United States in 1790 simply could not afford the policy balance that Madison was calling for. The country had to make a choice, and though privileging the speculators over the veterans may have left a bad taste in the mouth, Hamilton was right to do so. If ever the country hoped to be wealthy enough to provide justice for all parties, it had to encourage the rich to invest in the nation, which meant fostering confidence in government debt and thus showing partiality to the speculators.[10]

THE FIGHT OVER funding the national debt was quite brief. Hamilton's *Report on Public Credit* was submitted to Congress on January 9, 1790. Madison made the case for his alternative in speeches on the House floor on February 11 and 18, and his proposal was voted down on February 22; Congress then moved on to debate the federal assumption of state debts. In all, the whole affair lasted just over six weeks. In contrast, the debate over assuming the state debts dragged on for more than five months, from mid-February until early August. It was the first acrimonious political battle of the new government, in no small part because Madison had a much stronger argument on assumption than he had had on funding.

Hamilton's economic case for assuming the state debts in the *Report on Public Credit* was mostly indirect. The federal government did not need to involve itself in the debts of the states, but he thought assumption would streamline taxation and redirect the loyalty of public creditors toward the national government, which was essential to his overall project. In most respects, his thinking was persuasive, but the context is important to understand Madison's opposition.

Madison, who had supported an assumption plan while serving in the Confederation Congress, still believed that "the principle" of assumption was "in favor of the United States," given that much of the state debts had been accumulated fighting the Revolutionary War. It was not right for some states to have paid more than others for what had been a common struggle. Nevertheless, he objected to Hamilton's plan on several grounds.

First, Madison believed that assumption had to be accomplished with "the great object of doing full justice," which he felt Hamilton's plan failed to do. When Madison supported assumption in 1781–1782, no state had made much headway in paying off its debts, so a simple assumption would have been reasonably equitable. But not in 1790. The Revolution had been over for nearly a decade when Hamilton issued the *Report on Public Credit,* and states had made unequal progress in paying their creditors back. Maryland, Virginia, North Carolina, and Georgia had paid off a large portion of their obligations, but Connecticut, Massachusetts, and South Carolina were still deep in the red. A simple assumption of the debts as they stood in 1790 would therefore have punished the states that had repaid their creditors. Madison and his allies thought it proper to wait until after the completion of the final settlement of accounts, which was already in process and was expected in the next year or two. This master tabulation would determine the contributions that each state had made to the Revolutionary cause and credit them if their expenditures were greater than their share of the entire cost. By proposing to assume the state debts prior to the completion of the final settlement of accounts, Hamilton was in effect guessing that when that tabulation was completed, the indebted states would be found to have been, on net, creditor states. On the other hand, states that had paid off their debts were expecting a big bounty from the final settlement, but they would gain relatively little under Hamilton's plan to assume the debts right away.[11]

Moreover, there were doubts as to when or if the final settlement would be completed. The state accounts were messy, and controversy had arisen over what were and were not war-related expenditures. And if assumption were to take place before the final settlement was completed, what guarantee was there that the creditor states that had paid most of their debts would receive full remuneration? In a pointed letter to Edmund Pendleton in March 1790, Madison noted that "Virginia will not be less a creditor on the final settlement . . . but this may *possibly* never take place. It will *probably* be at some distance." He was right to be skeptical. With their debts assumed by the national government, why would Connecticut and Massachusetts ever agree to the increased taxes necessary to reimburse Virginia and North Carolina?[12]

Additionally, Hamilton's assumption plan was quite extravagant, with an initial price tag of $25 million (the final payout was closer to $21 million). Albert Gallatin, the brilliant Swiss-born politician and ally of Madison and Jefferson, argued in 1796 that assuming the state debts before the final settlement had led to an "additional and unnecessary" increase in the national debt. According to Gallatin, if Hamilton had waited until the final settlement of accounts, the national government could have brought the states to the same level of equity for $10.9 million less. Considering that the total debt at the end of 1790 was just $71.1 million, this was a substantial difference. Hamilton thought this additional burden was worth it, as it shifted the loyalties of the moneyed class from the states to the federal government, but for Madison and his allies, this was a big price to pay.[13]

Madison was also bothered once more by the frenzy of speculative activity going on in New York, where the government was located during the First Congress. As speculators were bidding up the price of Pierce Notes, they were also dispatching agents southward, especially to the Carolinas, to snatch up any state debts they could get their hands on from public creditors who were not in the know. Madison was well aware of this—his boarding house at 19 Maiden Lane was just a short walk to 68 Wall Street, where the New York Stock Exchange would be founded in 1792—and while in New York he complained to Jefferson about the "eternal buzz" of "the gamblers." He found this sort of behavior patently offensive, and with good reason. New York financiers knew what was happening weeks or even months before many southern creditors, which gave the former the ability to effectively defraud the latter.[14]

Finally, Hamilton's plan to assume the state debts in 1790 differed markedly from the approach that Madison had helped draft in the early 1780s. In that plan assumption was just one part of a broader package designed to incentivize the thirteen states to adopt the impost. It was intended to lure the debt-ridden states, but the impost deal also included a land cession and a tax abatement for war-torn states. Hamilton's *Report on Public Credit* did not have any such balance. It was instead a transfer of wealth from the national coffers to the debtor states. Madison could not abide this. As he argued on the House floor, "The plan will give as much dissatisfaction and work as much injustice to a majority of the states as a non-assumption may disappoint the citizens of Massachusetts."[15]

Madison found few allies to oppose Hamilton's plan to fund the national debt, but he had more success in stopping the assumption of state debts. Starting with a base of Anti-Federalists who feared that assumption was the first step toward obliterating state sovereignty, he then recruited members who, like himself, approved of it in certain circumstances but thought Hamilton's proposal needed substantial modifications. Madison also found allies among those members who had speculated in land using depreciated state paper; Hamilton's assumption plan would raise the value of those certificates and undermine their schemes. Madison won over most southern congressmen and about half of the northern members— just enough to defeat assumption in the spring. The advocates of assumption were shocked but undeterred, and the fight dragged on into the summer. Finally a compromise was hammered out, with Jefferson serving as mediator, whereby in exchange for assumption before final settlement, the capital city would be placed on the Potomac River, states that had paid down their debts would receive a bonus, and the rules governing the settlement of accounts would be loosened. This deal, often referred to as the Great Compromise, swung a handful of members whose districts bordered the Potomac, creating a very narrow coalition in its favor, though Madison remained opposed until the bitter end.[16]

Hamilton had the better argument on funding the national debt, but the debate on assuming the state debts was a much closer call. The national debt had to be tended to immediately, but the state debts were not a top priority of the federal government. So why not wait until the final settlement of accounts? That could have ensured that the states were treated fairly in the final package, and, as Gallatin argued, it could have saved the federal government quite a bit of money.

Moreover, assumption led to unforeseen negative consequences. Though Hamilton had hoped that it would help bind the union together, in fact the unfairness of the plan set the states apart from one another and led to talk of disunion. Furthermore, Hamilton was too optimistic about the taxing power of the new government. Though the economics were as he said—the federal government was better able to tax items as they moved through the stream of commerce—there was widespread opposition to internal taxes throughout the 1790s. Discontent over domestic taxation led to the Whiskey Rebellion and facilitated the triumph of Jefferson over John Adams in 1800 on an antitax platform.[17]

The funding battle had showed the limits of Madison's republican balance, but the fight over assumption illustrated the limits of Hamilton's national vigor. In his efforts to develop the national economy, Hamilton placed too small a premium on fairness. Binding the nation together into a firmer union and facilitating national development through commerce and finance were laudable goals, but the means toward these ends were important too. Maybe Madison overemphasized the importance of balance in a republic, but it is certainly important, for practical as well as for moral reasons. Hamilton needed to get his proposal passed through a popularly elected House of Representatives, yet assumption gave direct benefits to a few states at the expense of the many. Why did he expect legislators to blithely assent to a raw deal for their constituents? He badly miscalculated congressional sentiment, and in so doing he inadvertently fomented political opposition to his agenda and even to his position as treasury secretary.

IN DECEMBER 1790 Hamilton submitted his plan to charter a national bank to Congress, which approved it the following February. The initial public offering for the Bank of the United States began in July 1791, and the bank opened for business in Philadelphia on December 12, 1791. It was the culmination of years of research and politicking by the young secretary.[18]

Madison had long been a skeptic of national banks, and during the House debate he opposed Hamilton's proposal on several grounds. To start with, Madison thought the specifics of the plan were tilted toward eastern speculators rather than the public at large. He told his colleagues that "the profits will be so great that the government ought to receive a very considerable sum for granting the charter," or in other words a kind of bonus, but Hamilton's proposal included no such measure. Instead, the benefits of the plan were "unequal between the public and the institution in favor of the institution."[19]

Moreover, the bank would accept subscriptions beginning just a few weeks after the law was enacted, leaving little time for people around the country to purchase stock. News took much longer to travel in 1791 than it does today, and Madison believed that people far from New York would not have a fair chance to own a stake in the bank. He considered that "an exclusion of those remote from the government, in favor of those near enough to take advantage of the opportunity." He was right. Subscriptions to the bank sold out so quickly that a secondary market soon opened up, where bank scrips traded for much more than their face value.[20]

Madison also worried about the way an institution like the bank—mostly owned by private investors but blessed with a public charter and holding federal tax revenue—might corrupt the delicate power relations that republican government must maintain. "The power of granting charters," he warned, "is a great and important power." By concentrating economic authority in the hands of just a few stockholders and managers, the government was creating the potential for abuse. "Public affairs in Europe" had shown that such a public-private corporation had the potential to become a "powerful machine . . . competent to effect objects on principles, in a great measure independent of the people." This was a backdoor to oligarchy, or rule by the rich, who could use the financial might of the institution to wield political power.[21]

Just as with the Bank of North America, Madison believed that Hamilton's bank required specific sanction from the people, via the instrument of government itself. But this view seemed to contradict his discussion of the Constitution's necessary and proper clause in *Federalist* 44. There he defended the authority of Congress to make "all laws . . . necessary and proper for carrying into execution" the enumerated powers. An explicit enumeration of all powers, he had argued, would be a "chimerical task," for it would require "a complete digest of laws on every subject to which the Constitution relates." Instead, he had asserted that the Constitution distinguishes between the "general powers," which were enumerated, and the "means of attaining the object of the general power," which were implied by the necessary and proper clause. In his defense of the bank's constitutionality, Hamilton relied on this very notion. He argued to President Washington that the government may rightfully employ the bank "as an instrument or means of carrying into execution any of the specific powers" under the Constitution. Because the bank facilitated Congress's enumerated powers to regulate the currency and collect taxes, it was constitutional—just as Madison had earlier seemed to argue.[22]

However, Madison believed that the Constitution had to be read in light of its republican origins. Years later, he explained that "the divergence between" himself and Hamilton "took place—from his . . . wishing to administer the government . . . into what he thought it ought to be; while, on my part, I endeavored to make it conform to the Constitution as understood by the Convention that produced and recommended it, and particularly the state conventions that *adopted* it." Significantly in his view, the Constitutional Convention had considered granting Congress the power to issue charters, but the delegates had voted against it. Moreover, the delegates at the ratifying conventions did not conceive that the Constitution sanctioned such an authority. Therefore, the Constitution did not sanction it.[23]

Yet Madison did not always adhere strictly to the dictates of the ratifying conventions. After all, the conventions had proposed a raft of amendments to the Constitution, some intended to protect civil liberties, others to limit the scope of federal power. In whittling these suggestions down to the Bill of Rights, Madison systematically excluded those that expressly reined in the authority of the new government. Furthermore, Madison was often prepared to read between the lines of the Constitution when it suited his policy goals. In 1789, for instance, he recommended that the government patronize a scientific expedition to Baffin Bay to study magnetic theory. He told Congress, "If there is any considerable probability that the projected voyage would be successful, or throw any valuable light on the discovery of longitude, it certainly comports with the honor and dignity of government to give it their countenance and support." There is no explicit constitutional sanction for such an expenditure, and it is not at all clear that the ratifying conventions would have supported such a spending power. Madison also favored chartering a national university in 1796. The government was offered stock in the Potomac Company as an endowment, so establishing a national university in Washington, DC, would simply be a matter of chartering a body to receive donations. Madison presented to the House a memorial in support of the new institution, but action on it was postponed by a vote of 37 to 36. Again, justifying such an action required a fairly broad interpretation of implied powers, which may or may not have passed muster with the ratifying conventions. Most famously, as secretary of state, Madison helped Jefferson purchase Louisiana from the French in 1803, even though there was no explicit sanction in the Constitution for such an acquisition. Years later, John Quincy Adams called this "an assumption of implied power greater in itself and more comprehensive in its consequences" than any that had gone before it. This may have been an overstatement, but not by much.[24]

These positions seemed to be in tension with Madison's argument that the bank would violate the original intentions of the ratifying conventions, but it is important to appreciate his anxiety over the ability of such institutions to corrupt republican government. To appreciate this, contrast Hamilton's bank to a national university. The latter could never become a "powerful machine . . . independent of the people," as a national bank could. Its purpose would be the acquisition of knowledge and the education of the citizenry, which were always in the public interest. But corporations like the bank concentrated wealth and political power in private hands, creating the potential for oligarchy. Though intended to serve the public interest, they need not operate on behalf of it and in prior instances had proven they could become detrimental to the public interest. That the bank would incidentally aid the government in accomplishing some of its essential functions was, in his opinion, insufficient justification.[25]

At the end of his career in government, Madison changed his mind on the matter of a national bank, and as president he signed the charter for the Second Bank of the United States. Contrary to his dire warnings in 1791, the Bank of the United States had been an exemplary steward of the economy through the course of its twenty-year charter, and the nation sorely missed it during the War of 1812. Madison's concerns about corruption, as it turned out, were unfounded in the case of Hamilton's bank—but *not* in the case of the Second Bank of the United States. Though it facilitated economic growth in the 1820s, its early years were marked by rampant corruption, and during its final years it became the very sort of political machine that Madison had feared. In this way, both Madison and Hamilton were right. A national bank was necessary for the development of the young nation, but it was also a threat to its republican character.

THE FIGHTS OVER funding, assumption, and the bank were exhausting. Funding opened a wide political rift between Madison and Hamilton. Assumption dragged on for months and split Congress in two. Though the bank was quickly approved by Congress, it divided Washington's cabinet, as Secretary of State Jefferson and Attorney General Randolph opposed Hamilton's plan. By the time Hamilton unveiled his *Report on Manufactures* in December 1791, he had little forward momentum remaining. Congress never seriously considered a program of bounties for industries, which was the central protective element of the plan, and the secretary would soon find himself on the defense against a campaign to oust him from office, quietly orchestrated by Madison and Jefferson.

Still, the *Report on Manufactures* highlighted the widening philosophical and policy divide between Hamilton and Madison. By making a thorough justification for industrial protection in an agricultural nation, Hamilton offered his most emphatic statement yet about the potential for commercial development to harmonize the disparate forces in society. Meanwhile, Madison's opposition furnished another case study of how his notion of fairness informed his policy views.

Madison considered himself a supporter of free trade, believing that "if industry and labor are left to take their own course, they will generally be directed to those objects which are the most productive." Nevertheless, he was not a hardliner. He admitted that industrial protection made sense in certain situations, such as during wartime or as a way to encourage other nations, especially Great Britain, to sign a treaty of commerce with the United States. He was also willing to admit some modest forms of industrial protection as *political* circumstances required. During the effort to enact the Tariff of 1789, for instance, he agreed to grandfather considerations for industries that had received state support under the Articles of Confederation.[26]

More than anything else, Madison could not abide the unfairness of Hamilton's program. In Madison's view, government had to be studiously neutral in its treatment of different sectors of the economy and regions of the nation: benefits or burdens to one class of the citizenry should be balanced by a similar regard for all the others. Hamilton's protective scheme simply did not do that. A few months after the *Report on Manufactures* was submitted to Congress, Madison wrote a scathing indictment of it for the *National Gazette,* the newspaper edited by his friend Philip Freneau to oppose Hamilton's policies. In Madison's view, "a *just* government" is one that "*impartially* secures to every man, whatever is his *own*." But he felt that Hamilton's protective policy—with its "arbitrary restrictions, exemptions, and monopolies" denying citizens the "free use of their faculties, and free choice of their occupations"— obliterated this notion. Madison fumed that it was unjust for the government to "oppress one species of property and reward another species."[27]

Madison also registered constitutional objections to Hamilton's program of bounties. The secretary justified his system by recourse to the general welfare clause, which grants to Congress the authority to "provide for the common defense and the general welfare." Madison told Pendleton that if the government "can do whatever in their *discretion* can be *done by money,* and will promote the *general welfare,*" then the concept of limited power has lost all meaning, replaced by an unlimited authority for Congress to do as it pleases. It is difficult, once again, to reconcile Madison's opposition to protective bounties with his support for other measures, like the funding of scientific expeditions. But if the Constitution is understood as a document whose purpose is to maintain a fair and balanced government, his positions make more sense. A scientific expedition would promote knowledge, which benefits all of society; by contrast, in Madison's view, a protective bounty would enrich some at the expense of the rest.[28]

Industrial protection was not a major point of debate in the 1790s. Hamilton just did not have the political capital to force the issue, and most members of Congress hailed from agricultural districts. Still, the *Report on Manufactures* was a harbinger of things to come. The United States soon enough embarked on a century-long course of industrial protection, starting with the Tariff of 1816, signed into law by none other than President Madison. By that point, he had come to appreciate the need for the government to have a more direct stake in promoting a stronger manufacturing base. But that did not mean he was originally incorrect that protectionism was a danger to his theory of balance. By the time of his death in 1836, the tariff had become the means by which certain sectors of the country could enrich themselves at the expense of others.

A COMPARISON OF the views of Hamilton and Madison from this period indicates that Hamilton had a better understanding of the national economy and its needs. Funding the national debt, assuming the state debts, and chartering a national bank all turned out to be beneficial for the nation. And though the main points of Hamilton's protective plan were rejected, the principles embedded in the *Report on Manufactures* were adopted by subsequent generations of policy makers. Take all these policies together, and Hamilton does look like an American Walpole or Neckar—a farsighted visionary who performed an enormous service to his country.[29]

Yet this conclusion overlooks the nuances of Madison's critiques. Madison supported a full repayment of the national debt and some sort of equalization among the state debts. He opposed the Bank of the United States mainly on constitutional and prudential grounds, believing such an institution could be useful but was also risky and so had to be treated with delicacy. And though he opposed Hamilton's program of bounties, he had been willing to compromise on the general issue of protection. In other words, the two were not that far apart on the specific policy debates. Madison's consistent objection during this period was that Hamilton's policies were too one-sided, an eminently fair point.

Moreover, Madison's critique points to legitimate problems with the strategy of mediation, even if Hamilton's intentions were above reproach and his execution sound. Madison believed that vague sentences in the Constitution did not give the government license to play favorites, and that doing so anyway could be extremely dangerous to the republican quality of the regime. Hamilton rejected that view, and he had good reasons for doing so, but what was there to prevent the strategy of mediation from being abused in the future? Just because Hamilton endeavored to use mediation prudently in 1790–1792 did not mean that politicians later on would do so too. Hamilton's approach to governance, in other words, implicitly assumed that a certain class of statesman, a "natural aristocracy," in the parlance of the age, would be ready to helm the ship of state. Yet history has shown that such noble characters have often been unavailable, and sometimes even unwanted by a mass public.

A final matter was especially troubling to Madison during the debates over Hamilton's plan. If it primarily benefited the commercial class, why was so much of it enacted by the new government? After all, the Constitution, whose ink was barely dry in 1790, called for a government of the people, by the people, and for the people. As Madison argued during the assumption battle, he did not think the people actually supported the initiative. "If we could ascertain the opinions of our constituents," he argued, "I believe we should find [that] four fifths of the citizens of the United States [would be] against the assumption . . . [and] that those who would be for an assumption would not amount to one-fifth." So why did so many representatives support Hamilton's assumption plan and, more generally, the rest of the secretary's program? Madison concluded that too many members of Congress had been speculating in government funds and had personal financial stakes in the success of the secretary's system. These conflicts of interest were tempting officials to sacrifice the public good to enrich themselves, thereby corrupting the new republic.[30]

4

THE TOOL AND THE TYRANT

IN THE WINTER of 1791, Thomas Jefferson wrote a letter to Philip Freneau, an old friend of James Madison's from Princeton, offering him a job as a clerk in the State Department. "The salary indeed is very low," Jefferson explained, "but also it gives so little to do as not to interfere with any other calling the person may choose." The "calling" that Jefferson and Madison had in mind was a newspaper, opposing the financial policies of the administration and their main architect, Treasury Secretary Alexander Hamilton.[1]

This was an extraordinary development. Madison and Hamilton had been colleagues and even friends just sixteen months earlier. Now they were bitter political foes. Madison was not a vengeful man. During his career in politics up to that point, he had worked with people on issues where he had common ground, even if they disagreed on other matters. He had his enemies, to be sure—Patrick Henry at the top of the list—but he was not the sort to take political disagreements so personally. What explains the change?

Madison hinted at the reason for his new posture in an essay for the *National Gazette,* the paper that Freneau would come to edit. "Public opinion sets bounds to every government," he wrote, "and is the real sovereign in every free one." This was a typical view among eighteenth-century American republicans, but Madison went on to worry that public opinion in an "extensive" republic could struggle to exercise its proper authority. It was harder to "ascertain" and was more easily "counterfeited," and citizens in such a nation may feel "more insignificant." This anxiety contrasted markedly with his confidence in *Federalist* 10, where he argued that the main danger to a republic was a majority that ruled against the interests of the public. Self-interested minorities, he had claimed in that essay, were not a primary concern in a government built on the rule of the people, for they could easily be dispatched by the "republican principle, which enables the majority to defeat its sinister views by regular vote." But in the *National Gazette,* he fretted about such majorities *failing* to cohere, thereby leaving sinister minorities to rule in the people's place.[2]

This new anxiety is critical to understanding Madison's sudden, aggressive turn against Hamilton. His determination to force the secretary out of the government was, in his own mind, an effort to remove from the halls of power a minority clique, supposedly helmed by Hamilton, that was abusing public authority. The secretary, Madison believed, was using his economic program to exploit conflicts of interests among public officials, inducing them to support his policies at the expense of the general welfare. His alleged goal was to redesign the American republic to look more like the British system.

The charge that Hamilton was secretly orchestrating the activities of elites and public officials as a prelude to monarchy is not convincing in retrospect. Though the secretary had long been partial to the British government, he had no intention of transforming the republican character of the United States. By his own reckoning, his system was designed with just and proper purposes in mind: to reorient the passions of selfish men toward the new government, for the sake of invigorating the whole nation. He was wholly innocent of this incendiary accusation.

Still, Madison's critique, stripped of hyperbole, had merit. By dispensing benefits so one-sidedly to the wealthy, Hamilton's strategy of mediation activated conflicts of interest among public officials, undermining the republican quality of the government. Many high-ranking government officials were heavily invested in public securities, even as they were voting on how public debt should be handled. During the assumption battle of 1790, the speculators hijacked the debate, refusing to fund the national debt unless Madison and his allies gave in on assumption. Then, in 1791–1792, speculators close to Hamilton leveraged their inside information in an effort to corner the public-securities market, precipitating a panic that Hamilton was forced to ease by offering what was basically a bailout. In these cases, the moneyed class acquired effective control over the government, directing public affairs for its own ends rather than for the good of all. While Madison was wrong to identify Hamilton as the leader of this clique, he was right to see it as a corrupting influence in the young republic.

THOUGH MADISON ABIDED by a strict personal ethos against private dealings on any matter over which he held a public trust, many members of the government did not have such ethical qualms. They regularly mixed the quest for private profit with the duty of public service. Land speculation had been a main avenue for such activity for some time prior to the ratification of the Constitution. At the time, the national and state governments held vast tracts of unoccupied territory and were disposing of it in a variety of ways. Thus the potential for conflicts of interest among public officials was quite real: they were tempted to legislate in ways that lined their own pockets or to act on tips from fellow officials about the course of action the government was set to take. Madison himself had to deal with these problems while serving in the Confederation Congress in the early 1780s.[3]

The Constitution and the powerful national government it created provided financiers with a vast array of new, exciting opportunities, especially for speculation in the public debt. William Maclay, a senator from Pennsylvania and a dyspeptic critic of Hamilton, wrote in his diary that the "new Constitution raised a singular ferment. . . . Every one ill at ease in his finances; every one out at elbows in his circumstances; every ambitious man, every one desirous of a shortcut to wealth and honors" was excited about what "could be wrought to their purposes, either in the funds of speculation it would afford, the offices it would create, or the jobs to be obtained under it." Soon enough, the public debt—both national and state—was concentrated in the hands of a very small number of people, typically in the major cities of the East. Many members of Congress—including Elbridge Gerry of Massachusetts, Oliver Ellsworth of Connecticut, Thomas Fitzsimons and Robert Morris of Pennsylvania, and Philip Schuyler and Rufus King of New York—had extensive holdings, often running into five figures (a large sum for the age). In general, owners of the public debt voted strongly in favor of Hamilton's economic plans, whereas nonowners opposed it.[4]

Leadership positions in the Bank of the United States also went to many current and previous members of Congress. Roughly half of the bank's first board had held, was holding, or would hold an eminent position in government. The rest of the board was mostly made up of important businessmen who owned vast sums of public securities. The same was true of the Society for Establishing Useful Manufactures (SEUM). The brainchild of Hamilton and Tench Coxe, assistant secretary of the treasury, this private company fit hand in glove with Hamilton's *Report on Manufactures*. Its purpose was to build labor-saving innovations, such as mills and distilleries, as a template for industrial development throughout the whole country. The board drew heavily from the New York speculative class and included William Duer, who preceded Coxe as assistant treasury secretary, and Alexander Macomb.[5]

There were other, more informal points of connection between the moneyed class and the government. Senator Maclay filled his diaries with stories of the "Hamilton galley" coming to watch the House debates on assumption and suggested that the geographical proximity of the speculators to the First Congress enabled them to exert undue influence. Speculators also personally sidled up to members of Congress and high government officials to extract information from them before it became public knowledge. The crafty speculator and former apothecary general Andrew Craigie was noted for this. During the winter of 1789–1790, he lodged with six New England congressmen, including Ellsworth. In his private correspondence, Craigie was blunt about his motivations: "I know no way of making safe speculations but by being associated with people who from their official situation know all the present and can aid future arrangements either for or against the funds." Craigie, in fact, was so well connected that he knew of the famed Compromise of 1790 almost as soon as the deal was struck.[6]

Their wide-ranging networks enabled some officials and their friends to leverage inside information for personal enrichment during the early years of the new government. Shortly after Hamilton submitted his *Report on Public Credit,* Maclay determined that members of Congress were employing their advanced knowledge to establish a "system of speculation" whereby they sent representatives to the South to buy state debts from public creditors not in the know. Senator Benjamin Hawkins told Maclay that he had "passed two expresses with very large sums of money on their way to North Carolina for purposes of speculation in certificates." Maclay also identified Representative Jeremiah Wadsworth of Connecticut as a major speculator and fretted that "the members of Congress are deeper in this business than any others," with Duer ultimately coordinating the endeavors. In July 1790, Maclay met with Charles Pettit, who had been appointed as Pennsylvania's agent to settle accounts with the national government. But Pettit did not talk about the logistics of final settlement; rather, he seemed to be acting "as an agent for the public creditors. . . . He teased me to tell him who were the principal holders of certificates in Boston, Newport, New York, etc.," Maclay wrote, "declaring that he wished to correspond with them, and unite with them in the common cause."[7]

Maclay was onto something, for there were many speculative schemes afoot in the winter of 1789–1790. Craigie flatly stated that members of Congress initially delayed acting on Hamilton's funding plan "because their private arrangements [were] not in readiness for speculation." Yet no gambit was as daring as the one put together by Duer. During his career in government, he regularly used his public offices as a gateway to personal profit. Hamilton's decision to name Duer assistant secretary of the treasury was fateful, for though he was qualified for the job, he was morally unfit to wield such power.[8]

The participants in Duer's debt-buying scheme at one point included businessman William Constable, Craigie, Duer, Gouverneur Morris (a delegate to the Constitutional Convention), Senator Robert Morris, Postmaster General Samuel Osgood, Wadsworth, and perhaps King. The first version of the plan, developed sometime in 1788, was to purchase a portion of the foreign debt that soon had to be repaid to France. Gouverneur Morris went to France for this purpose, carrying a letter of introduction from Madison to Jefferson, who was at the time minister to France. Writing in secret code, Madison told Jefferson, "I am a stranger to the errand on which [Gouverneur] Morris goes to Europe. It relates I presume to the affairs of [Robert] Morris which are still much deranged." As it turned out, the French were not interested in the terms the Americans were willing to offer, so the speculators moved on to the Netherlands with a scheme to sell the Dutch a portion of the domestic debt of the United States.[9]

Duer's plan also involved speculation in state debts. Gouverneur Morris and Robert Morris were working with Constable on this endeavor as early as the spring of 1789 in expectation that assumption would be included in Hamilton's system. Meanwhile, Duer and Constable signed a memorandum of agreement to borrow on the domestic debt they had purchased in order to acquire state debts. Craigie was actively purchasing state debts too, and he may have been brought into the Duer circle for this purpose. One estimate of the value of this speculation is $5.4 million, a very significant amount for 1789.[10]

The critical elements in Duer's machinations were advanced knowledge of Hamilton's funding plan and a general reputation for being in the know. If the cabal knew about the funding proposal before the current owners of the debt did, it could buy the debt at very low prices. Then it could use its members' stature in government to convince foreign purchasers that it knew what the eventual plan would be, enabling it to sell the debt at a tidy profit. This made Duer the integral partner. By July 1789 Craigie thought that though Duer might not be stationed at the treasury, "he will no doubt be well provided for and have great influence which will be of importance." As it turned out, Duer was named assistant secretary and played an important role in drafting the *Report on Public Credit*. Simultaneously, he was essentially trying to set up the first international banking syndicate based in America, one that could compete with the great financiers of Europe.[11]

THE SCHEMES OF the Duer syndicate were probably the most audacious of this period, but there were many more mundane efforts by officials to use their public station to enrich themselves. What do these tell us about the early republic?

A Hamiltonian view on government would justify this mix of business and politics as being similar to the patronage that he had argued should be dispensed by the executive branch—an unseemly but necessary feature of statecraft. He knew better than anybody that the speculators were going to bet on the new government, one way or the other, and he needed to do everything he could to make sure they were bullish about its prospects. Duer and his associates were trading on insider information and taking advantage of unsuspecting creditors, but their actions helped cement the bond between the moneyed elite and the new government. Their activities were regrettable, but the result was ultimately for the greater good.

Madison did not see matters in this light. In the first place, he denied that Hamilton's program ultimately advanced the public good. Moreover, he thought that conflicts of interest among public officials were a danger that a republic had to guard against, not a tool to advance the public interest. He saw the speculative frenzy as a sign that the balance of power in the government was shifting from the people to the moneyed elite. There had been no formal alteration to the character of the republic, no law passed that dispossessed the people from their right to rule, but a change was nevertheless underway. Though the public retained nominal control over the government, real power was increasingly held by the speculators by virtue of the fact that so many members of Congress were counted among their number. And now, Madison feared, this clique was entrenching itself within the government permanently.

Was Madison simply complaining about the unseemliness of "influence," or did he have a legitimate point, that the speculators were subverting the public good? Importantly, the self-interests of governmental officials could not have been the decisive factor in most matters that came before the legislature in the early years of the new government. Madison's alternative plan for funding the national debt went down to an overwhelming defeat, the Bank of the United States was broadly approved, and Congress never took up Hamilton's system of bounties. A 1793 effort to censure Hamilton, led by Representative William Branch Giles but supported by Madison and Jefferson, was based on a flimsy case and should have lost on the merits, regardless of the speculative endeavors of the political class. In all of these cases, even if those members who were voting their self-interests had abstained, the results would have been the same.[12]

Yet when it came to the question of assumption, congressional speculation played a crucial role. The vote on this measure was exceedingly close, and the narrow difference was due to a split in the delegations of New York and Pennsylvania and the uniform support of New Jersey's members. None of these states stood to gain much from assumption, but many of their representatives were heavily invested in government certificates, which implies that the speculative motive carried weight. This by itself was not evidence of corruption, as opposed to Hamiltonian influence; it all depended on whether the ultimate measure was good for the country or not. However, when we consider the *lengths* to which some advocates of assumption were willing to go—placing the credit of the young nation at risk for their payday—we can identify an instance of corruption. Their vehemence was contrary to the public welfare and thus justified Madison's complaints.

THE LONG-STANDING CONSENSUS on the Compromise of 1790 is that it was a regional logroll. Northerners secured Hamilton's assumption plan, and Southerners secured the location of the capital on the Potomac River rather than in Pennsylvania or New York. The main evidence in support of this conclusion comes from Jefferson, who recorded in his diary that he brokered a meeting between Hamilton and Madison around June 20, 1790, at which the deal was struck.

And yet this narrative is not without problems. To start with, neither Hamilton or Madison framed the bargain in this way; only Jefferson did. And by his own admission, Jefferson was only noddingly familiar with the disagreement, having recently taken his position as secretary of state. Moreover, the main deal on the location of the capital was hammered out between the Pennsylvania and Virginia delegations *prior* to June 20. Additionally, Hamilton had little sway with either delegation, and it is not clear that they would have felt bound by the terms he had struck. Madison, meanwhile, was a member of the House, but the main fight over the capital had been in the Senate, so it is uncertain how influential he could have been. Moreover, the final deal on assumption included considerations for those states, such as Virginia, that had paid off their debts.[13]

The consensus view also tends to take a cynical view of Madison's motives, specifically, that his main agenda was to extort the Potomac River location from the Hamiltonians, placing the good of the nation at risk to win a prize for his home state. This overly simple conclusion ignores the wealth of documentary evidence to the contrary that is contained in the *Papers of James Madison*. Madison was acutely aware of the speculative frenzy occurring around assumption, which was a crucial factor in his behavior in the spring and summer of 1790. He had good reasons for this suspicion.[14]

Without disputing the traditional account, a thorough reexamination of the evidence suggests that Jefferson's story is incomplete. No doubt, regional interests were at play, but there was more going on. The fight over assumption struck a very deep chord in

Madison's mind. He was quite disturbed by the conflicts of interest at work on assumption and believed they threatened the republican quality of the government.

As noted previously, there was broad support for some kind of assumption of the state debts. Hamilton claimed that assumption would bind the state creditors to the nation and facilitate the payment of all public debt, as the federal government had better means to accomplish this than the states. Anti-Federalists, who were skeptical of central authority, did not buy those arguments, but many of them were from southern states, which generally believed that they had paid more than their share for the war and thus were eager to receive some kind of remuneration.

The real debate came down to the timing of the assumption, whether it should occur before or after the final settlement of accounts. If it happened before final settlement, it would please Hamiltonian nationalists, who thought it was good to transform state prejudices into support for the national government, and benefit states that had accumulated large amounts of debt. Losers under this plan would be the states who had already paid back a large share of their debts, and doubted that they would ever receive a proper credit for their wartime contributions, and the Anti-Federalists, who thought the cost of Hamilton's assumption was too big a price to pay for national unity.

Both sides had reasonable claims, and a judgment on Hamilton's assumption based solely on the merits was a genuinely close call. Madison, in general, shared Hamilton's desire to place the national government in a position superior to the states. However, he objected to the unfairness of the proposal. He believed that Virginia, along with a majority of the other states, was made worse off by the plan, so he sought to modify it during the House debate throughout the spring. His efforts were initially successful, as Hamilton's version of the measure was narrowly voted down in April 1790.

This was, at any rate, the public dimension of the debate. But there were machinations going on behind the scenes, for many politicians had been speculating in land or debt and had a personal stake in the outcome of assumption. Land speculators would be better off if assumption did not happen immediately. Assumption would increase the value of state debt certificates, which land speculators had been using to make their purchases and thus wanted to keep as cheap as possible. But a large, mostly northern group of legislators had bet that the policies of the new government would increase the price of public debts. They very much wanted assumption to happen, the sooner the better. By holding assumption at bay, Madison was denying them an enormous windfall.

Madison did not know the details of the many speculative schemes afoot in 1790, but he certainly grasped that something was up. In fact, the speculators themselves tipped their hand to him. On February 17, 1790—the day before he addressed the House on his alternative plan to fund the national debt—he received a pseudonymous letter from someone calling himself "Foreigner." In trying to persuade Madison to change his position on funding the national debt, Foreigner offered crucial details of the Duer syndicate's plans. Foreigner told Madison that "certain agents offered to contract with Hollanders to furnish a large amount of the domestic debt of the United States." The Dutch were "taught to believe, from what they supposed unquestionable authority" that "the debt was subject to no new liquidation . . . and that the assignees stood on a footing not less eligible than the original claimant." In other words, the Duer syndicate had assured the Dutch that they could buy domestic debt with confidence that the new government would make a full repayment to its current holders. But now Madison was proposing that half of that payment go to the original holders of the debt, which would upend their whole scheme. Foreigner noted that the Dutch investors "are principally the same persons to whom we are indebted for foreign loans," and then darkly speculated about the way American faith would be seen in Europe if Madison's plan was implemented. The author took a personal shot at Madison as well, for having supposedly flip-flopped on the issue of the debt: "In what light must you be viewed by foreigners when they compare your address of 1783 with the principles you advanced in support of your amendment?"[15]

The most likely author of this letter was Duer himself. Having been in the government for some time, he was familiar with Madison's position regarding the debt in 1783. He would have known the details of the funding plan and Madison's opposition to it. And he would have known the details of the scheme to sell domestic debt to the Dutch. Moreover, the author of the letter unreasonably believed that he could persuade Madison in this way, and Duer was known for his overconfident disposition. It is of course possible that somebody else in the group—perhaps Constable or Craigie—penned the letter, but that is less likely. If Duer did write it, it was yet another example of his tendency to mix public duties with private interests, for here was the assistant secretary of the treasury trying to talk a member of Congress out of a proposal that would be bad for his personal interests.

The Foreigner letter could only have solidified Madison's opposition. It was too clever by half, for in its defense of Hamilton's funding plan, it admitted the existence of a cabal that had so far been kept secret. Who, Madison must have wondered, were the "certain agents" furnishing the Dutch with "a large amount of the domestic debt?" Who instructed the Dutch "to believe" on "unquestionable authority" that the domestic debt was "equally binding upon the government as the foreign?" The only people in a position to do so would have been those in and around the government.[16]

As the House moved on to the matter of assumption, Madison sensed a force acting from behind the scenes. From the early days of that debate, he had noticed a strange demand from the advocates of the measure: assumption of the state debts *had* to be coupled to funding the national debt, such that if the one did not pass, then neither would the other. In a March 3 House debate with Theodore Sedgwick and Gerry—both from Massachusetts and both deeply involved in speculation—Madison noted that such a linkage had not been sought during the debate over the public debt in the 1780s. He commented that he "was sorry to hear gentlemen declare, that an affirmative decision of the question of assumption was an essential preliminary to the success of the great business of providing for the support of public credit." It did not make sense to him to conjoin the two, "either by the practice of members on other occasions, or on principles of justice or policy." Rather, he thought that there was a "real distinction . . . between the debts" and that they should be adjudicated accordingly.[17]

Madison's point was fair, for though Hamilton's *Report on Public Credit* proposed funding the national debt and assuming the state debts, the justifications given for each were notably different. Funding the national debt was an essential task that had to be done with deliberate speed, especially for the portion owed to foreign creditors. All major factions agreed that it was a top priority to implement proper measures as quickly as possible for their satisfaction; otherwise, the national credit would be jeopardized. Meanwhile, the benefits to the nation from assumption were secondary and hardly of immediate concern. Not only that, but the debate over assumption was not about its merits per se; rather, the question was whether it should happen before the final settlement of accounts. What Madison's opponents were doing, in his judgment, was holding repayment of the national debt hostage, saying, Give us the assumption of state debts *right away,* or we will damage the national credit. As he wrote in July to James Monroe, who was at that point practicing law in Virginia, "It seems, indeed, as if the friends of the measure were determined to risk everything rather than suffer that finally to fail."[18]

It was not just the opponents of assumption who were distressed by these threats. Fitzsimons, a supporter of Hamilton's program who had actually introduced the assumption resolutions to the House in February, commented to Coxe in April, "While I lament the probable consequences, I cannot but condemn the conduct of some of the supporters of the measure. They have pressed it without discretion and really so as to disgust some who gave into it more with a view to the national accommodation than from the conviction of justice or necessity of it."[19]

What could possibly possess the advocates of assumption to practice this kind of brinksmanship? Madison hinted at his view in a letter to Edmund Randolph in May. "The zealots for the assumption of the state debts," he wrote, "keep back in hope of alarming the zealots for the federal debt. . . . Motives are felt I suspect which will account for the perseverance." The last line of this passage is worth exploring in detail. In the *Vices of the Political System of the United States,* written before the Constitutional Convention in 1787, Madison argued that legislators were motivated by three concerns: political ambition, personal interest, and the public good. Which of these three motives did Madison "suspect" would explain the "perseverance" of the assumption advocates?[20]

One obvious reason to advocate assumption was the interests of the debtor states, a motive that could be seen as a type of ambition. Those who wished to further their careers in state politics were induced to press for assumption, even going so far as to threaten dire consequences if it was not delivered. They may also have genuinely prioritized the welfare of their states above that of the whole nation. Such motives were certainly in play, but Madison doubted their sufficiency. The three states that would benefit substantially from assumption were Connecticut, Massachusetts, and South Carolina, but Madison had hardly noticed a great agitation in those state governments. In a speech on the House floor on April 22, he asked, "What evidence have we that there will be any great disappointment or discontents from a non-assumption?" Very little, he concluded. "The legislature of Massachusetts" had been "apprised that this matter was under consideration, and yet there has been no declaration from them. . . . On the contrary, it would appear from the measures they have taken to provide for the payment of their state debt." Most of the other states had been silent. The only legislature that had made "any declaration on the subject" was South Carolina.[21]

Even if those states were in a hurry to have their debts assumed, their members hardly accounted for the scope of the coalition of "zealots." As Madison wrote to Monroe on April 17, "The eastern members talk a strange language on the subject" of assumption, namely, that it was a requisite for funding the national debt and even for preserving the union. Which eastern members did he have in mind? Certainly those from Connecticut and Massachusetts, whose motives could—at least in part—be explained by state parochialism. But as Madison noted in an April 13 letter to Henry Lee,

"Massachusetts and South Carolina with their allies of Connecticut and New York are too zealous to be arrested in their pursuit, unless by the force of an adverse majority." The parochial interests of New York were barely at stake in assumption. The Empire State was not one of the major indebted states, which is why its House delegation split on the final vote. So why were the proponents from New York so worked up?[22]

And what about the Pennsylvania delegation? In several diary entries, Maclay noted a similar ardor among assumption's advocates in the state, even as its congressional delegation was also split on the matter. On February 22, 1790, he wrote of a meeting for the Pennsylvania delegation, "The ostensible reason was to consult on the adoption of the state debts, but the fact to tell us that they were predetermined to do it. [Robert] Morris swore 'By G— it must be done!' and [Representative George] Clymer, strange to tell, expatiated on the growing grandeur of Pennsylvania if it was done. . . . These appeared strange words to me coming from that quarter." Strange words, indeed. Pennsylvania, like New York, would not reap much from assumption. So why did it have to be done?[23]

If political ambition could not account for the zealotry Madison observed, then neither could solicitation for the general welfare. One could adopt the perfectly legitimate Hamiltonian position that assumption of the state debts was necessary to cement the union. However, these "eastern members" took matters much further than that. They demanded an *immediate* assumption, before final settlement, or else they would block funding of the national debt. There was no way to justify such strict terms by pointing to the national welfare. Despite its craft and guile, even the Foreigner letter admitted this point by implication. The Dutch had been the nation's foreign creditors during the war, they were expecting a complete repayment, and it was essential that the United States make full and speedy provision for that expectation. Refusing to fund the national debt would have done enormous damage to the union that Hamilton was endeavoring to strengthen.

If public spiritedness could not explain this insistence, and political ambition explained at best a portion, what then was left? In

Madison's view, the only remaining motive was personal interest. Many public officials had a large financial stake in seeing assumption through to completion as soon as possible. Duer and his cronies had not simply sold national debt certificates to the Dutch. They had also gone searching for state debts that they could snatch up from unsuspecting sellers. They were not alone—according to Craigie, members of Congress had suspended debate on assumption so they could buy state paper before its holders knew any better. More than a few had borrowed money to do so. And why not? The momentum in the winter of 1789–1790 was with Hamilton. Assumption seemed like a sure thing, so what was the danger of buying state debts on margin? But Madison surprised them. As a result of his efforts, assumption went down to defeat in the House on April 16, 29 to 32. This was a disastrous blow for the speculators. Facing significant losses, and perhaps debtor's prison, they elected to hold the funding plan hostage until assumption was passed and the government gave them the windfall they demanded.[24]

So resolute were some of the speculators that they even hamstrung the secretary's debt proposals in the Senate, where his agenda was otherwise greeted much more favorably. To keep costs in line, Hamilton's *Report on Public Credit* had proposed reducing the rate of interest on the domestic portion of the national debt from 6 percent to 4 percent. But this raised the ire of Robert Morris, Schuyler, and King—all of them were strong supporters of Hamilton, but they were also heavily invested in domestic debt and so demanded the full repayment. They ultimately forced Hamilton to agree to a compromise whereby the principal on the debt would be paid at 6 percent interest but the overdue interest would be repaid at 3 percent.[25]

Madison rebuked the speculators in the House directly during a debate on April 22. Wadsworth warned that without assumption, there would be "a general clamor through all the eastern states against the national government." This prompted a response from Madison that was carefully phrased so as not to offend the honor of the gentleman from Connecticut but nevertheless made perfectly clear that the gentleman from Virginia knew what was really going on. He recommended to Wadsworth and his allies that they "no longer assume a pre-eminence over us in the nationality of their motives." He asked them to "forbear those frequent assertions, that if the state debts are not provided for, the federal debts shall also go unprovided for . . . that the union will be endangered." He hoped instead that they would allow "patriotism and every other noble and generous motive" to induce them to "establish public credit by a due provision for the public engagements."[26]

For his part, Maclay was characteristically blunt in his diagnosis. On June 6, he wrote in his diary that the assumption plan was "the basis on which speculation has built all her castles." Members of Congress had resolved to "load the ass; make the beast of burden bear to the utmost of its abilities." On July 17, he wrote of a "general belief that the assumption was forced on us to favor the views of speculation," but he added, "Nor have the members themselves kept their hands clean from this dirty work. . . . From henceforth we may consider speculation as congressional employment." Though Jefferson helped broker the final compromise on assumption, he ultimately reached a similar conclusion. Writing in his diary a few years later, he claimed that the eastern members who threatened the dissolution of the union "were the principal gamblers in these scenes."[27]

As the spring of 1790 wore on, Madison's correspondence with his allies registered growing alarm over assumption. He expressed a guarded optimism in April, after he narrowly defeated the measure, yet his confidence waned as the weeks wore on and its zealots refused to yield. He concluded a May 25 letter to Virginia governor Beverley Randolph with the warning, "We had flattered ourselves that the project of assuming the state debts was laid aside, at least for the present session . . . but the zeal and perseverance as well as the number of its advocates, require that we should not be too sanguine in our calculations." Two days later, he wrote his brother Ambrose that "the project of assuming the state debts is revived and likely to employ further time. I hope we shall be able to defeat it, but the advocates for it are inconceivably persevering as well as formidable in point of numbers." On June 17 he indicated the impending defeat of his position in a letter to Monroe. Assumption, he averred, "still hangs" on Congress and had "benumbed the whole revenue business." The advocates of assumption were so insistent on holding up funding that Madison suspected it would "yet be unavoidable to admit the evil in some qualified shape." What else could he do? The funding plan had to be implemented, if not for the domestic portion of the national debt then certainly for the part held by international creditors—but the assumption partisans would have it no other way.[28]

Meanwhile, Hamilton was at his wit's end. The opposition to assumption seemed too firm to break, and his allies were threatening to ruin the national credit. Jefferson recounted running into Hamilton toward the end of the spring:

> Going to the President's one day I met Hamilton as I approached the door. His look was somber, haggard, and dejected beyond description. Even his dress uncouth and neglected. He asked to speak with me. We stood in the street near the door. He opened the subject of the assumption of the state debts, the necessity of it in the general fiscal arrangement and it's indispensable necessity towards a preservation of the union: and particularly of the New England states, who had made great expenditures during the war, on expeditions which tho' of their own undertaking were for the common cause: that they considered the assumption of these by the Union so just, and it's denial so palpably injurious, that they would make it a sine qua non of a continuance of the Union. That as to his own part, if he had not credit enough to carry such a measure as that, he could be of no use, and was determined to resign.

At Jefferson's invitation, Madison and Hamilton met at his residence for dinner around June 20 to broker a deal. The final compromise added extra federal payments to states that had paid down their debts and extended the time for states to submit claims for the final settlement of accounts; as a result, in Madison's words, "in a pecuniary light, the assumption is no longer of much consequence to Virginia." Additionally, the capital would be placed on the Potomac River, after a temporary stint in Philadelphia. This was later called the Great Compromise of 1790.[29]

Even with these concessions to Virginia, Madison was still thoroughly disgusted with the final measure. As he told Monroe in late July, the compromise was far from a triumph; rather, it was "an unavoidable evil, and *possibly* not the worst side of the dilemma." Note Madison's hyperbolic use of italics. The alternative to the compromise was the ruin of the national credit and possibly the dissolution of the union, so it was certainly not the "worst side of the dilemma." But he was signaling how supremely disappointed he was with the whole affair. In his judgment, the vehemence of the speculators had made it necessary for him to accept a measure that he thought was bad for the country. The deal at Jefferson's residence only sweetened what remained, for him, a very bitter pill. In the end, he agreed only to cease his active opposition, not to vote for the final package.[30]

As for Hamilton, he had inadvertently predicted the whole debacle in the *Report on Public Credit.* "Should the state creditors stand upon a less eligible footing than the others," he warned, "it is unnatural to expect they would see with pleasure a provision for them. The influence which their dissatisfaction might have, could not but operate injuriously, both for the creditors, and the credit, of the United States." This is exactly what happened. With advance warning of the assumption plan, the moneyed class plunged relentlessly into speculation in state certificates under the bullish expectation that the measure would pass speedily. However, they underestimated the breadth of the opposition and especially Madison's facility in organizing it on the House floor. Left with no alternatives but assumption or enormous losses, the speculators joined with debtor states to insist on either immediate assumption or national ruin.[31]

BY THE END of 1791, the main elements of Hamilton's financial program had been implemented by Congress. Yet the task of management had just begun. Hamilton had created what he hoped would be a symbiotic relationship between the moneyed class and the government. The wealthy would make a profit from investing in public endeavors, and the government would have easy access to cheap credit. Moving forward, it would fall upon Hamilton to make sure that the relationship would continue to be mutually beneficial. This was easier said than done. From the summer of 1791 through the winter of 1792, a group of speculators—which again included the irrepressible Duer—would abuse the implicit authority the government had entrusted to them, sacrificing the public interest for their own personal gain.

Hamilton's system was an enormous boon for public creditors. Each provision of the system—the funding of the national debt, the assumption of the state debts, and the chartering of the bank—was good for them in and of itself. But these measures compounded one another so that those who happened to hold public securities prior to 1790 received an enormous bounty. State and federal paper were trading well below face value before 1790, so when the government offered a full repayment for all public certificates, it granted windfall profits to the holders of public debt, state and national. This bounty was compounded by the terms of the new Bank of the United States, whose stock became available for purchase in the spring of 1791. To acquire a share of the bank, an investor only had to make a down payment of 25 percent, and only 25 percent of the down payment had to be made in hard cash; the remaining 75 percent could be paid in debt certificates, making the once-cheap paper all the more valuable.[32]

As a matter of dollars and cents, Uncle Sam has handed out substantially larger bounties to the wealthy over the years. Yet this one was special. Given that these benefits were being distributed as a consequence of a financial system that was being created from scratch, public creditors were not simply reaping an economic reward; they were being given political power. Hamilton was betting that wealthy creditors could be used to secure the government's finances, which implicitly meant that the government was now obliged to keep them reasonably happy. Prices would have to be kept stable, so the government—in particular Hamilton and his

Treasury Department—would have to monitor the market and would have to intervene to maintain stability.

Investors easily grasped the unspoken deal Hamilton was offering them. Subscriptions to the bank were filled shortly after they were opened to the public, and a secondary market for scrips quickly blossomed. Madison, appalled by the spreading frenzy, wrote to Jefferson in the summer of 1791, "It seems admitted on all hands now that the plan of the institution gives a moral certainty of gain to the subscribers with scarce a physical possibility of loss." Demand for the bounty was virtually limitless, and the prices for scrips kept going up. In August 1791, Henry Lee wrote to Madison and described the frenzy he witnessed as "one continued scene of stock gambling; agriculture, commerce, and even the fair sex relinquished, to make way for unremitted exertion in this favorite pursuit."[33]

Naturally Duer was involved in the scramble, having resigned from the Treasury Department the previous spring, just as the assumption battle was reaching a fever pitch. Hamilton had accepted the resignation "with regret" but had added tellingly, "I confess, too, that *upon reflection* I cannot help thinking you have decided rightly." The secretary never should have hired Duer in the first place, and he seems to have been relieved that his friend had elected to depart. But Hamilton's troubles with Duer were far from over. Having been integral in helping design this new architecture of finance, Duer was well positioned to make the most of his extensive knowledge.[34]

By early August, scrips were trading for roughly $300 apiece, though their face value was just $100. This was unsustainable, and on August 11 the upward momentum stalled, and then prices began to fall back. King told Hamilton that the mania had to do with rumors of the secretary's opinions. "It can scarcely be believed that these gentlemen have any foundation for their assertions, but the fact will suggest to you the utmost caution on this subject." Hamilton responded by telling King that he thought the proper price for a scrip was $195, arguing that "a bubble connected with my operations is of all the enemies I have to fear, in my judgment, the most formidable."[35]

Hamilton also reached out to Duer, who he suspected was caught up in the mania. He told him of the rumors swirling around that Duer was in league with Constable to inflate "the balloon as fast as possible" by making "fictitious purchases in order to take in the credulous and ignorant." Hamilton warned Duer that he was too "sanguine," saying, "You ought to be aware of it yourself, and to be on your guard against the propensity." Yet Hamilton nevertheless provided him with almost the same information he gave King. He wrote that the "real value" of a scrip was "about 190" and that he hoped that Duer would be "able to support it" at that level.[36]

It is striking to contrast Hamilton's willingness to share inside information with King and Duer with his response to Henry Lee just twenty months earlier. In December 1789 Lee had written Hamilton asking for a tip about his financial plan, but Hamilton had rebuffed him, citing the desire to avoid even the "suspicion" of "an impropriety." Now Hamilton was providing Duer and King, two of the most prominent speculators in the whole country, with precisely that kind of information.[37]

And Hamilton went even further. On August 15, he asked William Seton, president of the Bank of New York, to purchase $150,000 worth of debt on behalf of the trustees of the sinking fund, which had been established to use post-office revenue to retire the national debt. Privately, Hamilton explained to Seton that the purpose of this purchase was to stabilize the market "to keep the stock from falling too low in case the embarrassments of the dealers should lead to sacrifices; whence you will infer that it is not my wish that the purchases should be below the prescribed limits." Hamilton added, "If there are any gentlemen who support the *funds* and others who *depress* them, I shall be pleased that your purchases may aid the *former*. This in great confidence."[38]

The stated purpose of the sinking fund was to help pay off the national debt, not to prop up the debt market by buying from speculators. But Hamilton's financial program was premised upon the debt functioning as currency, which required a stable market. A crash would have been calamitous, so he had no choice but to take these dramatic steps. Through his communications to Duer and

King, and then his instructions to Seton to buy from the speculators, he had established what is known as a *put,* signaling that there
was a minimum price for securities that, if breached, would bring
the government in as a buyer to restore confidence. Federal Reserve
chairmen Alan Greenspan and Ben Bernanke offered similar puts
during their respective tenures, responding to various financial
panics by lowering interest rates.[39]

The problem with such maneuvers is their moral hazard. If investors know that the government will bail them out if their investments go bad, they will be more likely to take risky bets. In fact,
this seems to have been exactly what happened with Duer. In all
probability, Duer made a killing from the whole affair, having sold
at a higher price than he had bought. In addition, he now had a
sense of what Hamilton's floor price was. Little wonder that Duer,
whom Hamilton rightly pegged as too optimistic, entered the fray
once again. In December 1791, Duer and Macomb formed a private partnership for "making speculations in the debt of the United
States." This was the basis of an ambitious partnership that would
come to be known as the Six Percent Club, named after a certain
type of government debt, and that included Constable as well as
the other major investors in the SEUM. To begin, they agitated for
the creation of a new state bank, primarily as a way to depress the
value of the Bank of New York so they could snatch up its shares.
This acquisition, in turn, financed their effort to corner the market
on the 6 percents by July 1792, just prior to the due date for the
next installment on payments for bank scrips. That way, the club
could either charge exorbitant prices for the 6 percents that were
necessary to pay for the next installment on bank scrips or acquire
the scrips on the cheap. Duer and Macomb plunged into the ven-
ture with vigor, exhausting every possible line of credit, going so far
as to borrow from shopkeepers and widows. A new bubble inflated
and spread into other areas of financial activity.[40]

Hamilton viewed this new round of irrational exuberance with
concern, writing Seton, "These extravagant sallies of speculation do
injury to the government and to the whole system of public credit,
by disgusting all sober citizens and giving a wild air to every thing."

Once again, the secretary was caught in a trap of his own making. He was dependent upon the moneyed class to keep the price of government securities at or near par value, and the current mania endangered the stability he needed to maintain.[41]

Soon enough, through the intervention of the Treasury Department, investors discovered that Duer had exhausted all available lines of credit. Duer had been lax in settling his old accounts from his time at the Treasury Department, and Oliver Wolcott Jr., the Treasury's comptroller, had made repeated requests to Duer to repay the money he owed. On March 12 Wolcott told the federal district attorney of New York to instruct Duer to make payment, but Duer was unable to do so. When word of Duer's inability to pay hit the street, the prices for all manner of public securities began to sink. Duer soon wound up in debtor's prison, as did Macomb. The nation's first financial panic was on, as owners of public debt—no longer certain about its true value—unloaded their holdings, sending the price spiraling downward and creating even more confusion. Hamilton instructed Seton to use the sinking fund to purchase even more public securities, prevailed upon other banks to offer short-term loans, and organized financiers in New York to act as lenders of last resort to keep the crisis from spreading further. This time, the secretary's plan worked, perhaps because the panic finished Duer and Macomb off for good, and nobody else was so bullish as to try such a reckless maneuver.[42]

But Hamilton's work was not yet complete. Duer was in charge of the secretary's pet project, the SEUM, and had borrowed from it for his speculative endeavors. Hamilton privately encouraged Duer to give "peculiar regard" to repaying the SEUM, but Duer was ruined. So Hamilton asked Seton for a $10,000 loan from the Bank of New York for the SEUM, adding, "To you my dear sir I will not scruple to say *in confidence* that the Bank of New York shall suffer no diminution of its *pecuniary faculties* from any accommodations it may afford to the Society in question. I feel my reputation much concerned in its welfare." This was an extraordinary request, for Hamilton was not a private citizen asking for a loan. He was the secretary of the treasury, and he offered no pledge of personal security or collateral. He merely promised "no diminution of . . . *pecuniary faculties*"—a promise that carried weight because of his public office.[43]

MADISON UNDERSTOOD THESE events as representing the corruption of republican government. He knew that the self-interest of politicians was a danger to republicanism, as it induced them to use their public authority for their own enrichment rather than for the greater good. And he had seen such misbehavior firsthand during the debate of the early 1780s over the fate of the western lands. He saw something similar at work a decade later. The government was too cozy with the public creditors and had sacrificed the general welfare to the interests of this particular faction.

This was the downside of Hamilton's strategy of mediation. The secretary was offering bounties to the financial class of the young republic, and because that class had so many agents within or close to the government, he had activated conflicts of interest that were detrimental to the public interest. This is the main reason that Madison—and eventually Jefferson—was so angered by the events leading to the Compromise of 1790. Madison was not, in theory, averse to the assumption of state debts. He just thought it was unfair. When the measure was defeated, that should have been the end of it. Or, at least, its fate should not have been tied to the fate of funding. Madison connected the "zealotry" of the assumption forces—not just in continuing to push for assumption but in linking it to funding the national debt—as an indication that the creditor class had gained too much power in the government. He was not alone in this regard. Jefferson later came to hold this view, as did Albert Gallatin. And Maclay—who rarely spoke with Madison—had the same opinion.

The Panic of 1792 further illustrated to Madison and his colleagues the dangers of mediation. Hamilton has been praised for his handling of the crisis, especially his adroit use of the sinking fund to stabilize the market, and rightly so. But it is important to remember why he wound up having to do so in the first place. The secretary had transformed public debt into the foundation of the nation's financial system because, as he argued in the *Report on Public Credit,* a "properly funded debt . . . answers most of the purposes of money." This eminently sensible approach gave the wealthy a direct stake in the government and helped improve the circulation of currency throughout the economy. Nevertheless, by pinning the system on public certificates, the government effectively endowed the main holders of that paper with power over the economy. There was little that could be done to stop them from misusing this authority for their own material gain, at the expense of the public interest. Indeed, when faced with an imminent collapse in the price of public certificates, Hamilton twice responded with public bailouts. The secretary harnessed the speculators to the government, as he had intended, but he also yoked the government to the speculators. Because of Hamilton's program, the owners of the public certificates had become, in the parlance of twenty-first-century politics, "too big to fail," so Hamilton was obliged to save them.[44]

In the summer of 1792, as the mania was under way, Madison complained to Jefferson that the government had been captured by a gang of "stockjobbers" who had become "the praetorian band of the government—at once its tool and its tyrant; bribed by its largesses, and overawing it, by clamors and combinations." Jefferson, a man well versed in the history of the Roman Republic, must have been struck by this assertion. The Praetorian Guard of Rome was the group of elite soldiers who protected the emperor, yet because of their close proximity to him, they were in effect able to wield power over him. By casting the speculators in the same terms, Madison was suggesting that their rarefied economic position gave them power over the government.[45]

Madison elaborated on this idea in many essays written for the *National Gazette* in 1791–1792. He suggested that the republic had come to operate "by corrupt influence." Hamilton's system had ensnared the private motives of members of government; overcome with "avidity," they had transformed into "an army of interested partisans . . . whose active combinations" had seized control of the state from the people. In so doing, they had created a "real domination of the few, under an apparent authority of the many." In another essay, he identified this faction as "the antirepublican party," which, though "weaker in point of numbers," is strong with "men of influence, particularly of moneyed." This was one of the first contemporary accounts of party conflict in the United States, and Madison cast it as a battle between the people and the moneyed class for control over the reins of power.[46]

Madison believed that the ultimate intention behind this power grab was to change the character of the government from a republic to "a monarchy bottomed on corruption," as Jefferson put it, with Hamilton at the helm. Madison assailed "those who favor measures" that pamper "the spirit of speculation," "who promote unnecessary accumulations of the debt," "who avow or betray principles of monarchy and aristocracy," and "who espouse a system of measures more accommodated to the depraved examples of those hereditary forms." Each of these points was linked to the next in Madison's mind. The British Crown had maintained its independence despite the potential supremacy of the House of Commons through the disbursement of influence, which in effect bought off members of Parliament to vote the way the king wanted, regardless of what their constituents might prefer. Madison perceived a similar process at work in the United States: members of Congress were voting based on their private interests rather than on the interests of their constituents. He then inferred that this must have been due to a similar intention, that the leaders of the moneyed clique, above all Hamilton, were using the public debt to manipulate the private interests of legislators so that the leaders of the clique could rule in place of the people, just as the king did. Peddling influence, as Madison believed Hamilton was doing, was the "high road to monarchy," even if the people still retained an "apparent liberty."[47]

Hamilton's speech outlining his British-style plan for government at the Constitutional Convention was clearly on Madison's mind during this period. In another essay, he admitted, "In all political societies different interests and parties arise out of the nature of things, and the great art of politicians lies in making them checks and balances to each other." But his opponents wished to increase

such "natural distinctions by favoring an inequality of property"
and to "add to them artificial distinctions, by establishing kings,
and nobles, and plebeians" so that there would be "more checks to
oppose each other . . . and maintain the equilibrium." If Hamilton's
defense of the constitutionality of the Bank of the United States
had thrown *Federalist* 44 back at Madison, Madison was now re-
turning the favor, for this essay evoked, negatively, Hamilton's case
at the convention for separating the few from the many.[48]

Was Hamilton a secret monarchist, as Madison alleged? Certainly not. Modern scholars have found no evidence that Hamilton
wanted to impose a monarchy upon the United States. Moreover,
the historical record is clear that Hamilton never profited from his
economic program, and in fact his personal finances were in terrible
shape by the time he left government. Nor was he dispensing information to build a secret faction with himself at the helm. Insofar
as details of the funding plan were known in certain quarters, it
was not because Hamilton was intentionally tipping off his friends.
The secretary's bent was easily inferred by associates like Constable,
Craigie, and especially Duer, all of whom were eager to profit from
advance knowledge. Hamilton should have chosen his allies with
more discretion, but that is not—or not merely—what he was being criticized for.[49]

The false accusation against Hamilton was one of the most
consequential errors of Madison's career, and not just because he
maligned a great Founding Father and an erstwhile friend and
colleague. Madison fundamentally misdiagnosed the threat facing the nation. He feared an incipient monarchy with Hamilton
as would-be king. He should have feared not a monarchy but an
oligarchy—which in fact Hamilton was struggling, desperately at
times, to constrain. If we take at face value Jefferson's record of his
encounter with Hamilton just prior to the Great Compromise, we
do not see a man about to take personal control over the government. Instead, Jefferson was describing a man at the end of his rope.
Unable to constrain the various forces that had been unleashed in
the young republic, he pleaded with Jefferson to intervene for the
good of the nation. A similar picture presented itself during the

Panic of 1792. Hamilton was not encouraging Duer and Macomb. Instead, he was actively discouraging them and was later forced to bend the rules to clean up their mess.

No doubt, Madison had misjudged Hamilton's intentions, but Hamilton had misjudged the honor and virtue of the wealthy, including many people he called friends. He placed too much faith in the capacity of the "proprietors of land . . . merchants and members of the learned professions" to act as a "credit to human nature" and rechannel their endeavors toward the general welfare. He also overestimated his own ability to lead such a clique, to guide it in ways that never harmed the national interest. At several crucial moments, the speculative faction broke free from his control and inverted the relationship that the secretary thought he had developed—placing the government in hock to private interests, just as Madison had feared would happen.[50]

Fortunately, the material damage from this corruption was decidedly limited. The advocates of assumption may have been willing to risk the nation's credit for a payout, but Madison and his allies were prepared to yield and thus kept the worst from happening. The broader effects on the economy of the Panic of 1792 were quite muted, thanks in no small part to Hamilton's expert management. Ironically, though Madison and Hamilton were on the opposite sides of the issues during this period, they were both intent on protecting the good of the nation against speculative excess.

The real lesson from these experiences was that Hamilton's approach to governance was flawed in important respects. The secretary's plan to use the public creditors as mediators of the general welfare transferred political power from the people to the rich, who then tried to abuse their station for private enrichment. They were largely unsuccessful, but not for lack of trying. Hamilton's effort to develop the national economy had placed the republican character of the new government under threat, and there was no guarantee that the advocates of good government would always be able to defend the public interest against the rich and powerful who threatened it.

5

VEXATIONS AND
SPOLIATION

By THE TIME George Washington took the oath of office for his second term, two political parties had come into being. By and large, their differences came down to their views on Alexander Hamilton's economic program. The Republicans were led first by James Madison and later by Thomas Jefferson and included Senators James Monroe, William Branch Giles, Aaron Burr, and Albert Gallatin. The Federalists tended to be of two types. Presidents Washington and John Adams generally held Federalist views, although they disdained party politics and were guided by their own internal compasses. The more energetic partisans were the loyalists of Hamilton, often known as the High Federalists, including Senator Rufus King, Secretary of State Timothy Pickering, and Charles Cotesworth Pinckney, minister to France.

Domestic policy initially split the two sides during Washington's first term, but disagreement over foreign affairs drove them further apart during his second. Great Britain and the French Republic went to war in 1793, a matter of great import to the United States. Though Great Britain was the nation's main trading partner,

France had been its partner in liberation during the Revolutionary War. What was to be done? The Federalists favored a tighter alliance with Great Britain; the Republicans thought this was foolhardy. In part the disagreement had to do with the heavy symbolism inherent in the Anglo-French conflict. The Federalists held that Great Britain was a country worth emulating, but the Republicans believed that it was a cesspool of corruption. In contrast, the Republicans applauded the French for disposing of their monarchy, whereas the Federalists were shocked at the brutality that French radicalism had unleashed.

Yet the symbolism of the European conflict cannot fully account for the venomous partisanship of this debate. In truth, the fight over foreign policy was also a battle over what sort of nation the United States would become. And the available options ran parallel to those presented during the fight over Hamiltonian finance.

Little wonder, then, that Madison and Hamilton found themselves on opposite sides once more. Madison's foreign-policy views formed in part from his theories on economics and society. He believed that a competition for increasingly scarce resources would eventually set people against one another and would be dangerous for republican government. He believed this process had already begun to weaken Europe, especially Great Britain, but believed that the United States, as an economically independent and virtuous republic, was stronger. Why then should the New World cower before the Old? Madison believed it should drive a hard bargain to secure its neutral rights.

Hamilton's views were just the opposite. Prioritizing the need for economic development and diversification, he sought to bind the country together by emulating the policies of the famed British minister Robert Walpole. To that end, Hamilton believed that the best move for the United States was to maintain trade relations with Great Britain, for they provided the tax revenue that fueled Hamilton's engine of public finance. The worst possible decision would be to provoke a conflict with the former motherland, for it was much more advanced economically than the United States and substantially stronger militarily.

The battle over foreign policy was thus another venue of the larger philosophical conflict that Madison and the Republicans waged against Hamilton and the Federalists in the 1790s, a war that came to define the first party system in the United States. Their views on Britain and France were not directly related to their positions on debt, banking, and industrial protection, but their positions on domestic and foreign matters all flowed from the same assumptions about the nature of the American experiment, and so they fought over foreign affairs just as viciously as they battled over economic matters.

GREAT BRITAIN AND the French Republic maintained an uneasy peace through 1792. France's territorial ambitions became increasingly manifest, as many in the new government thought it should extend to its "natural" boundary beyond the Rhine River. By December, the Dutch were actively requesting Britain's aid under the terms of a preexisting alliance, and Prime Minister William Pitt the Younger was ready to answer the call. The government began to enlist twenty thousand sailors and halted grain shipments to France, which responded by recalling its ministers. The execution of Louis XVI on January 21 set the two nations inextricably against one another, and the French Republic declared war against Great Britain on February 3, 1793.

The difficult position of the United States was complicated by the ambiguity of the Constitution regarding foreign affairs. The president held vast discretion in this realm, but it was not unlimited. The Senate had the authority to advise and consent on treaties, and a decision to declare war belonged to the Congress as a whole. But who was empowered to decide what an existing treaty obligated the United States to do? There was no clear answer to that question, and as has so often been the case throughout the history of our nation, power flowed toward the branch that acted most decisively. In this case, it was President Washington who issued what was quickly called the Neutrality Proclamation, although the statement did not actually include the word. On April 22 Washington announced, "The duty and interest of the United States require, that they should with sincerity and good faith adopt and pursue a conduct friendly and impartial to the belligerent powers."[1]

Madison was extremely disappointed in this. He wrote to Jefferson on June 19 that the administration had made a "most unfortunate error" in disregarding "the stipulated duties to France" and expressing "indifference to the cause of liberty." He also thought it unconstitutional to make the president "the organ of the disposition, the duty, and the interest of the nation in relation to war and peace." But Washington had made his declaration after consultation with his entire cabinet, which unanimously supported it—even Jefferson, an ardent believer in the French Revolution. As he responded to Madison on June 29, "The declaration of the *disposition* of the U.S. can hardly be called illegal." His own concern was that the proclamation was "premature." He would have preferred that Washington hold back and extract from George Hammond, the British minister to the United States, "the broadest neutral privileges."[2]

On the same day that Jefferson expressed qualified support of the proclamation to Madison, the *Gazette of the United States* published the first of seven essays that Hamilton would pen in its defense. Writing under the nom de plume "Pacificus," Hamilton made a vigorous case not only for the legality of the proclamation itself but also for the refusal to aid the French cause. Hamilton argued that the Constitution invested the executive power in the president, subject only to "exceptions and qualifications," which should be "construed strictly—and ought to be extended no further than is essential to their execution." As such, the executive branch is rightly the "interpreter of the national treaties" in circumstances such as the one the nation then faced. Though Hamilton admitted that a posture of neutrality was technically contrary to the terms of the treaty of alliance with the French, the proclamation was still legitimate, for the treaty was primarily "defensive in its principle," and France had been on the offensive in the European theater. Moreover, the United States did not have the means to support France without ruining itself, and the capacity to assist is "a *condition* of our obligation." Furthermore, "military stipulations," such as those included in the treaty, related only to the "ordinary case of foreign war," not to revolutions like that occurring in France. And though American citizens no doubt felt a sense of gratitude toward France for its assistance during the Revolution, a neutral course was in the United States' interests. At any rate, American empathy for the French cause had to be tempered by "the melancholy catastrophe of Louis XVI," whose execution was more a matter of "political expediency, rather than of real criminality." The United States should feel no need to participate in the "angry and vindictive passions" that led to the late ruler's demise.[3]

The Pacificus essays illustrate Hamilton's brilliance as well as his brashness. His arguments were thoroughly reasoned, and Hamilton recognized long before the Republicans did that a vicious bloodlust was helping fuel the French Revolution. But in the context of that particular political moment, they represented a classic case of overselling. Washington's proclamation was reached by the consensus of his ideologically diverse cabinet and was narrowly drafted to accomplish its intended purpose, without needlessly offending anybody. But Hamilton's defense gave a decidedly Federalist gloss to it. Rather than, as Jefferson told Madison, arguing that the proclamation was simply a statement of the disposition of the nation, Hamilton instead claimed that the president had virtually unlimited discretion to interpret treaties and even to abrogate clauses if the necessity should arise—exactly the sort of high-handedness that had aroused Anti-Federalist opposition during the ratification debates in 1788. Not content to leave matters at that, Hamilton then delivered a lengthy indictment of French conduct, which—though certainly not without merit—was bound to alienate many of his fellow citizens, who felt genuine sympathy toward the cause of *Liberté, Equalité, Fraternité*. The essays were also peppered with cheap shots at the Republicans, accusing them of placing the French Revolution ahead of American interests.[4]

Jefferson was thoroughly distressed by the Pacificus essays. Not only was Hamilton disclosing secret cabinet deliberations, but he was also twisting the limited argument of the proclamation to promote Federalist constitutional views and a pro-British foreign policy. "Nobody answers him," Jefferson complained to Madison, "and his doctrine will therefore be taken for confessed." The secretary of state pleaded with his friend to draft a public response. "For god's sake, my dear sir, take up your pen, select the most striking heresies, and cut him to pieces in the face of the public." But Madison was disinclined to do so. He knew that Hamilton could unleash a torrent of written words with ease and that a war of letters could go on indefinitely. Moreover, he wrote to Jefferson, he had a decided "distaste to the subject," an aversion compounded by the "excessive heat" of the summer of 1793. Ultimately, however, Madison relented.[5]

It was not until August 24 that the first of Madison's four essays was published in the *Gazette of the United States,* under the pseudonym "Helvidius." These were hardly Madison's best work. Whereas Hamilton's Pacificus essays exhibited a kind of swashbuckling bravado, Madison's Helvidius responses were labored and pedantic. He mostly avoided discussing either the merits of the proclamation itself or the bigger foreign-policy questions surrounding it and instead stuck to the question of constitutional authority. In his judgment, Hamilton had erred because "the two powers to declare war and make treaties . . . can never fall within a proper definition of executive powers." Instead, the Constitution clearly invested powers in the legislature, especially regarding the authority to declare war. What Hamilton was looking to claim was an executive authority on a par with the "royal prerogatives in the British government."[6]

The Helvidius essays also dripped with contempt for Hamilton, who was generally known among politicians to be the author of the Pacificus series. At multiple points Madison approvingly cited Hamilton's old *Federalist* essays to suggest a contradiction between his current and previous views, and Madison concluded his final essay with dark suggestions about Hamilton's true motives. Madison noted that the "personal interest of an hereditary monarch . . . is the *only* security against the temptation" of an unfettered executive to undermine the "interests of the nation" regarding "its intercourse with the rest of the world." Thus, by arguing for an expansive scope of executive power, Hamilton was paving the way for a "hereditary magistrate." Madison also warned that investing the president with broad discretion on matters of peace implicitly gave him broad discretion on matters of war. "Every danger of error or corruption, incident to such a prerogative in one case, is incident to it in the other."[7]

The Helvidius-Pacificus exchange is interesting because it is the only time Madison and Hamilton came close to openly debating each other, yet the essays revealed little new about their philosophies or policy ideas. Where they stood depended greatly on where that had been sitting. Hamilton had long been an advocate of a strong executive and a firm admirer of the British system; moreover, he had been appalled by the atrocities of the French Revolution. Madison, on the other hand, had usually emphasized the centrality of the legislature in public affairs; he had detested the British sovereign from a young age and had been less bothered by the violence that occurred during the French Revolution.

The arguments were mostly academic, anyway. Washington did not have in mind the kind of hypervigorous executive that Hamilton advocated, and there was no way Congress was going to second-guess the president by declaring war on Great Britain. Hamilton and Madison tried to turn the proclamation into a battle over first principles of government, but in truth it was a pragmatic declaration of the plain facts of the case. The United States could not and would not involve itself in a European war. Somebody had to issue a statement to that effect, the sooner the better, and the president was the obvious choice. Even Jefferson admitted as much.[8]

The real question was the price the nation would have to pay for staying out of the war, and Great Britain would not make it easy on its former colonies. The Royal Navy was the most powerful the world had ever seen, and Britain quickly used it to punish the United States for failing to take its side. British ships began seizing American vessels bound from or to France or its possessions in the West Indies, and they captured American seamen, impressing them into service for His Britannic Majesty. On December 5,

1793, Washington reported to Congress on "the vexations and spoliation . . . on our vessels, by the cruisers and officers of some of the belligerent powers." As he put it, "The British government, [has] undertaken, by orders to the commanders of their armed vessels, to restrain generally our commerce in corn and other provisions to their own ports and those of their friends."[9]

Madison and Jefferson saw in Britain's hubris a political opportunity to push once again for an idea they had long advocated: commercial discrimination. During the debate over the Tariff of 1789, Madison had suggested offering better tariff rates for nations that had commercial treaties with the United States. Though he was typically counted among the free traders, he thought trade policy could induce other nations to change their conduct without resorting to warfare. Jefferson was of a like mind, and on December 16, 1793, he finally submitted his *Report on Commerce,* which he had begun working on in 1791. In it he called for a system of reciprocity in trade relations, punishing nations that refused to sign a trade treaty with the United States. On January 3, 1794, Madison introduced in the House seven resolutions that would implement Jefferson's recommendations.[10]

Their effort received a political boost from continued British aggressiveness. The French West Indies, as colonies under the French mercantile system, had previously been restricted to trading directly only with France. But after the war began, France had opened its colonies up to direct trade with the United States. Great Britain responded by reinstating the Rule of the War of 1756, prohibiting all trade that had not been allowed in peacetime. In other words, though France now permitted US trade with its West Indian colonies, the British Royal Navy would prohibit it. Orders in Council issued on November 6, 1793, instructed British commanders to "stop and detain all ships laden with goods . . . belonging to France, or carrying provisions . . . for the use of any such colony."[11]

Statesmen of all ideological stripes were outraged—including Hamilton. Hammond, the British minister to the United States, had developed a convivial relationship with Hamilton over the years and thought that he could explain Britain's position to him.

He was "surprised at perceiving that [Hamilton] did not receive those explanations with the cordiality I expected, but entered into a pretty copious recital of the injuries which the commerce of this country had suffered from British cruisers." Hamilton's lecture was more than just bluster. At around the same time he was reading the riot act to Hammond, he was suggesting to the president that the government fortify ports and raise an army of twenty thousand men. "War may come upon us, whether we choose it or not," he claimed, so the country "ought to be in a respectable military posture."[12]

The Orders in Council of November 6 had added to a large list of lingering problems between the two nations. After the Revolution, Britain had closed off trade between the United States and the British West Indies and had resisted multiple entreaties to reconsider. Moreover, outstanding issues remained from the Treaty of 1783, above all that Great Britain had refused to abandon its fortifications in the American northwest. Though the British had claimed that their recalcitrance was retribution for unpaid American debts, this was merely a pretext. The fur trade was simply too lucrative, and the British would have risked their place in it by abandoning the region. In fact, they had even entertained the fanciful notion of creating an independent, Native American nation to serve as a buffer between American settlements and British outposts, in the interests of securing this trade.[13]

Though Hamilton and his Federalist allies were angered by Britain's actions, they were deeply opposed to Madison and Jefferson's idea of trade discrimination. They recognized that *something* had to be done about British aggression, and they knew they had to counter the Republican proposals. So they prevailed upon Washington to nominate a special minister to Britain, who would hammer out a commercial treaty. Hamilton was the first choice of the Federalist leadership, but knowing that he was too controversial to be acceptable, they pushed for the nomination of John Jay, chief justice of the Supreme Court and a long-standing Hamilton ally. The estimable Jay was dispatched to Great Britain in the spring of 1794, and the rest of the government began to wait. Transatlantic communications were painfully slow in the eighteenth century, so there was nothing else to do.

Finally, in March 1795, news reached Philadelphia of the deal that Jay had brokered. It was, to say the least, controversial. The only firm concessions from the British were a commitment to abandon the northwest frontier—which it was obliged to do, anyway, by the Treaty of 1783—and to allow American boats of limited size access to the British West Indies. The British refused to deal on the issues of impressment and reinstatement of neutral shipping rights. In exchange for this, the United States basically acceded to the Rule of the War of 1756, which ran contrary to the agreements the young nation had reached with other countries. It also agreed to preferential duties for British goods, effectively granting Britain most-favored-nation status and foreclosing the possibility of commercial discrimination.[14]

The Republican press derided the Jay Treaty in vitriolic terms. For instance, in a lugubrious editorial, the *Independent Gazette* mourned the death of liberty itself, writing, "Our independence is not even nominal, and it is easy to presage our return to our former station in the scale of political depression. . . . Farewell thou radiant goddess that once inspired our souls! May we weep on thy tomb till our abject forms are changed to marble." Madison wrote to Robert Livingston that the "ruinous bargain" Jay had agreed to included "terms which would have been scorned by this country in the moment of its greatest embarrassment." The ever-cautious Washington had grave doubts about the treaty, though he submitted it to the Senate, which approved it by the minimum two-thirds majority necessary.[15]

The big political winner was Hamilton, for in a bold stroke he had accomplished his two great purposes in foreign policy. First, he drew the United States closer to Great Britain, which he judged essential to the nation's long-term prosperity. Second, he foreclosed the possibility that Madison and his Republican friends in Congress could enact a system of commercial discrimination. Unsurprisingly, he rushed to proclaim the virtues of the Jay Treaty. Under the pseudonym "Camillus," he produced a mind-boggling twenty-four essays in support of the agreement, plus another four essays as "Philo Camillus" that he wrote at the same time to comment on his other essays. Federalist senator King added another ten essays under the name Camillus, so that from the summer of 1795 to the winter of 1796, there was a constant stream of essays in support of the agreement. Hamilton argued that the treaty in general was good for the nation and consistent with its honor, and he then proceeded to break down each provision, often in excruciating detail. Amid this seemingly endless barrage, Jefferson complained to Madison that Hamilton "is really a colossus to the antirepublican party. Without numbers, he is an host within himself."[16]

Jefferson again exhorted Madison to issue a public response, but this time to no avail. Nevertheless, Madison was not prepared to give in. He led his Republican allies in the House in an effort to sink the Jay Treaty by refusing to appropriate the necessary funds to carry it into effect. His logic was that "the congressional power may be viewed as cooperative with the treaty power, on the legislative subjects submitted to Congress by the Constitution." When his opponents pointed out that this was contrary to the intent of the Framers at the Constitutional Convention, Madison waved the objection aside, arguing that "as the instrument came from them, it was nothing more than the draft of a plan, nothing but a dead letter." It only took on "life and validity . . . by the voice of the people, speaking through the several state conventions." The House did not accept this argument, and the Jay Treaty, having already been ratified by the Senate, was put into full effect.[17]

Madison's attempt to derail the Jay Treaty was not one of the finer moments of his political career. His adherence to the wisdom of the state ratifying conventions was, as noted earlier, inconsistent. And in his zeal to scuttle the treaty, he seemed to employ motivated reasoning, searching for an argument to justify his policy views. Hamilton did not exactly bring glory on himself, either. Throughout his Pacificus and Camillus essays, he demonstrated a willingness to overemphasize some facts, underemphasize others, strain logic, and level ad hominem attacks in pursuit of his policy goals.

Whatever the faults of reasoning or rhetoric, there was an important question at the root of this particular debate, a question that only foreign-policy issues could bring to the fore. Madison and Hamilton differed not only on whether Britain was a model that the new nation should follow but also on where the United States stood in the world in that moment. Madison, following the same economic and social views that informed his political philosophy, thought the young nation was dealing from a position of strength. Hamilton, on the other hand, believed the United States was operating from a point of weakness relative to Great Britain, which is why his financial system emphasized building the nation's economic foundations. This difference was crucial in shaping the two men's views on the diplomatic crisis of the mid-1790s.[18]

MADISON'S BELIEFS ABOUT the relative position of Great Britain and the United States were founded on his pessimistic take on *political economy,* a term of art used to describe the relationship between the government and commerce, agriculture, and manufacturing. In 1798, Thomas Malthus published *An Essay on the Principle of Population,* in which he argued that there was an inevitable tendency for population growth to outstrip the available resources, which subjects "the lower classes of the society to distress and . . . prevent[s] any great permanent amelioration of their condition." Although Malthus was the most notable proponent of this theory, it was not unique to him. In fact, such ideas had been circulating for some time, including in the United States. Madison was among those drawn to them.[19]

In a letter to Jefferson in 1786, Madison wrote that "a certain degree of misery seems inseparable from a high degree of populousness." Even if land and property were ideally distributed, a "great proportion" of the people would remain "unrelieved," for there was simply not enough to go around. It was fear of this development that reinforced his view of a Senate that protected property rights. At the Constitutional Convention, he warned that population growth would "of necessity increase the proportion of those who will labor under all the hardships of life, and secretly sigh for a more equal distribution of its blessings." Under the rule of equal suffrage, the leveling tendency of the masses would eventually win out—a danger that had to be "guarded against." Otherwise, "the rights of property and the public liberty" would be jeopardized.[20]

What was to be done with "this surplus" of humanity, he wondered, when there was no more land to go around? "Hitherto we have seen them distributed into manufacturers of superfluities, idle proprietors of productive funds, domestics, soldiers, merchants, mariners, and a few other less numerous classes." But even these occupations were "insufficient to absorb the redundant members" of society. The United States had not yet reached a point of crisis, although Madison believed the day was coming. During the Virginia ratifying convention in 1788, he calculated that it would take about twenty-five years until the unsettled parts of the nation would have "as great a population as there is now in the settled parts," where "manufactures are beginning to be established."[21]

It would be difficult to sustain republican government under these circumstances, Madison feared. Following the English philosopher James Harrington, Madison believed that landownership was the foundation of a stable, virtuous republic. The ideal citizen was the independent farmer, for his station in life inclined him to health, virtue, intelligence, and competency. "They are the best basis of public liberty," he believed, "and the strongest bulwark of public safety." Other occupations, such as manufacturing, were less favorable "to vigor of body, to the faculties of mind, or to the virtues or the utilities of life." The farmer cultivated the necessities of life, but the manufacturer produced luxuries, whose desirability is dependent upon the "mutability of fashion, and . . . the public taste." Madison's view of the future thus had a whiff of pessimism to it, at least over a long-enough timeline. A wise government might be able to delay the inevitable trajectory of humankind into moral, social, and civic decay, but could not put it off forever.[22]

The good news for the United States was that the country was still young, in the best sense of the word. It was stronger and more vigorous than its rivals in Europe, where people were increasingly being funneled into manufacturing jobs that left them vulnerable. Madison liked to tell the story of buckle manufacturers in Birmingham, England, who were virtually ruined because the Prince of Wales had begun using shoestrings—a fashion choice that had threatened nearly twenty thousand people who made their livelihoods off the buckle industry. He marveled at the contrast between the pitiable status of these manufacturers and "the independent situation and manly sentiments of American citizens."[23]

In the realm of foreign relations, this gave the United States the advantage over Great Britain. America exported necessities to Britain, which exported manufactured luxuries back to the United States. America was a land of virtuous, hardy republicans, whereas Britain was increasingly clogged with miserable people who owed their livelihood to the prince's taste in footwear. As Madison argued in a House debate over tariffs in 1789, Britain's "interests can be wounded almost mortally, while ours are invulnerable." He pressed the point again when advocating for commercial discrimination in the winter of 1794. "Our exports," he told the House, "are chiefly necessaries of life, or raw materials. . . . On the contrary, chief of what we receive from other countries, we can do without, or produce substitutes."[24]

Madison believed that the United States needed to drive a hard bargain. Eventually, the old mother country would yield. It would have to, because "where one nation consumed the necessaries of life produced by another, the consuming nation was dependent on the producing one." Madison scoffed at the Federalist rejoinder that this would lead to war. "What could Britain gain by a contest?" he asked the House on January 23, 1794. "Would war employ her starving manufacturers? Would war furnish provisions to her West India Islands which in that case, must also starve? Would war give employment to the vessels that had formerly imported luxuries to America?" No, Madison reasoned. Great Britain "will push her aggressions just so far and no farther, than she imagines we will tolerate." The United States could bring it to heel through strictly "just and pacific means."[25]

So Madison naturally detested the Jay Treaty. Likewise, he had no sympathy for Hamilton's solicitation of English good will. In his opinion, Great Britain was not a model to which the young nation should aspire. It was, instead, a civilization suffering from inexorable decline. There was no need to fear it. In Madison's view, Hamilton had lashed America to the mast of a sinking ship—a deeply regrettable decision that Madison believed could only be explained by his former ally's partiality to Great Britain and its corrupt system of mixed government.

HAMILTON DID NOT comprehend Madison's motives in dealing with Great Britain. In an October 1789 conversation, Hamilton and British agent George Beckwith agreed that Madison's support of commercial discrimination was peculiar. Beckwith said he was "surprised to find" Madison among its advocates, given that "his character for good sense, and other qualifications" should have led him to "a very different conduct." Hamilton concurred. "The truth is," he said, "that although this gentleman is a clever man, he is very little acquainted with the world. . . . He has the same end in view that I have, and so have those gentlemen who act with him, but their mode of attaining it is very different." As the events of the next six years would clearly demonstrate, Madison and Hamilton did not have "the same end in view"; rather, they imagined very different futures for the United States.[26]

Likewise, Madison did not understand the views of Hamilton on foreign affairs. The secretary's attitude was illustrated by a conversation he had in the spring of 1794 with Hammond, who succeeded Beckwith as Britain's representative in the United States. Jay was just about to be dispatched to Great Britain, and Hammond wanted some insight on what he would seek from his superiors. Hamilton responded that the United States would be looking for compensation for seized vessels and goods but said the request would "be couched in the most conciliatory language, and will evince the most sincere desire . . . to settle all the grounds of dispute . . . on an amicable and permanent principle." Madison knew that Hamilton was desperate to remain in the good graces of Great Britain, but he did not appreciate the rationale behind it. Hamilton was animated not by a bias toward kingly forms of government but, rather, by the belief that the success of the United States depended upon cultivating a favorable disposition from Britain.[27]

There were three specific reasons Hamilton held this view. First, his intricate financial system was built on the premise that the government would honor its full debt obligations, which meant that the Treasury coffers had to remain filled. Given that import duties were the government's primary source of revenue and that Great Britain was the nation's primary supplier of foreign goods, it was crucial to keep trade flowing. As Hamilton wrote to Washington in the spring of 1794, "The cutting off of intercourse with Great Britain . . . will give so great an interruption to commerce" that it might "interfere with the payment of the duties" owed by the government, "which would cut up credit by the roots." On the other hand, maintaining good trade relations would keep the Hamiltonian machine humming along and would continue to provide "astonishing progress in strength, wealth and improvement."[28]

Second, Hamilton believed that Great Britain was substantially more powerful than the United States at the time. His ideal of "one great American system," which he expounded in *Federalist* 11, was a long way off. In his judgment, achieving it would require a reliable system of public credit, a national bank, and the encouragement of a diversified economy—all of which Great Britain had implemented over the course of the eighteenth century. The United States, meanwhile, had only begun this project. Though Hamilton admitted that "being at war with us would be very far from a matter of indifference either to her commerce or to her credit," he doubted that it would "arrest her career or overrule those paramount considerations" that had created the crisis in the first place. "It is impossible," he wrote, "to imagine a more unequal contest, than that in which we should be involved in the case supposed; a contest from which, we are dissuaded by the most cogent motives of self preservation, as well as of interest."[29]

Third, Hamilton was convinced that Great Britain and the United States were natural allies. There was the simple fact of shared language, customs, and history. "We think in English," he told Beckwith, "and have a similarity of prejudices, and of predilections." There were good economic reasons for closer relations too. Before the Revolution, the thirteen colonies had directly serviced the British West Indies. That privilege had been granted to them as constituents of the British Empire, but the United States, as an independent nation, no longer possessed it. But Hamilton believed that open trade between the United States and the British West Indies was a good arrangement for both nations. As he told Beckwith in October 1789, it would be better to allow American cruisers "to carry our produce there, and to bring from thence the productions of those islands to our own ports" than to maintain a "rigid adherence" to Britain's mercantile restrictions.[30]

From Hamilton's perspective, the commercial-discrimination plan favored by Madison and Jefferson was nonsense. There was virtually no hope that it would induce a change of heart in Great Britain. It would hurt the United States more and would needlessly anger the nation that possessed the most powerful navy in the history of the world.

Little wonder that the political momentum favoring trade reciprocity in the winter of 1794 alarmed Hamilton. The idea to appoint a plenipotentiary minister to broker an agreement was a political stroke of genius, for it took the wind out of Madison's and Jefferson's sails. Moreover, by securing the appointment of Jay— whose views were in line with Hamilton's—the Federalists managed to hem Washington in. The choice the president faced in the spring of 1795 was either to sign a decidedly Hamiltonian agreement or to prepare for a lengthy commercial, and perhaps even military, struggle.

Unsurprisingly, Hamilton was a key player in formulating the terms that Jay would seek once he arrived in London, both influencing the formal instructions drafted by Secretary of State Edmund Randolph and offering informal advice to Washington and Jay. Hamilton even took the extraordinary step of opening a back channel with the British government, a channel through which he provided information that ran contrary to Jay's official instructions. Sweden, Denmark, and Russia had joined together in a league of armed neutrality to protect their rights on the high seas, and

Randolph told Jay that "if . . . the situation of things with respect to Great Britain should dictate," he should visit their ministers in Britain to sound them out "upon the probability of an alliance with their nations to support those principles." This was exactly what Hamilton did not want, and he took the liberty of assuring Hammond, and through him the British government, that "it was the settled policy of this government . . . to avoid entangling itself with European connections."[31]

In fact, the final agreement that Jay brokered with Foreign Secretary William Grenville looked strikingly similar to what Hamilton had advocated before Jay set sail: flexibility on the part of the United States regarding the Rule of the War of 1756 in exchange for a crack in Great Britain's mercantile wall protecting the West Indies, a final resolution to outstanding issues from the Treaty of 1783, and a firming up of the commercial alliance between Great Britain and the United States. Maybe Jay could have extracted more from Grenville, but he basically got everything Hamilton had really been hoping for.[32]

THE JAY TREATY has received mixed reviews over the years. Apart from limited access to the West Indies, it did not secure to America anything that it could not rightfully claim by the Treaty of 1783. And for this, it made a number of significant concessions to Great Britain. Nevertheless, the Jay Treaty—in conciliating America's main trading partner and the ruler of the high seas—facilitated another decade of commercial prosperity.

Neither Madison nor Hamilton was particularly acute in his analysis of the situation, though Madison made the larger mistakes. He fundamentally misunderstood the trajectory upon which western civilization was proceeding and its implications for republican government. Commerce, industry, diversification—these would become the keys to greater material prosperity, as Hamilton had argued in the *Report on Manufactures*. Hamilton's jibe to Beckwith that Madison was "very little acquainted with the world" may have been too harsh, but it was not altogether unfair, at least on the matter of Anglo-American relations. As secretary of state, and later as president, Madison would learn through hard experience just how dangerous a commercially powerful nation such as Great Britain could truly be.

If Madison erred on the economics, Hamilton misjudged the politics. He predicted that Great Britain would eventually come to realize that it was better off with the United States as a free and equal economic partner. But he was too optimistic, as Great Britain did not conceive its self-interests in the way Hamilton thought it should. Thus, the Jay Treaty simply bought the United States time; it did not produce a permanent reinvention of the relationship between the two countries. During the Napoleonic Wars, Great Britain began harassing American commerce once again, creating another diplomatic crisis and eventually leading to the War of 1812.

Hamilton and his Federalist allies won the political battle over the Jay Treaty, but the victory in the larger war between the two parties would eventually go to the Republicans. Jefferson's narrow victory in the presidential election of 1800 exiled the Federalists into the political wilderness and eventually led to their extinction. The Republicans would thus be free to reshape America's economic and foreign policy as they saw fit. But with that privilege came enormous responsibility. When Great Britain began acting in a condescending manner toward the United States during Jefferson's second term, he and Madison would finally have a chance to see if commercial discrimination would work. But it failed miserably and eventually forced them to reckon with American weakness, which Hamilton had appreciated all too well.

6

METAPHYSICAL WAR

By the time John Adams took the oath of office in 1797 to become the second president of the United States, Alexander Hamilton and James Madison were out of the government. Madison returned with his wife, Dolley, to his Orange County plantation after his final House term ended. Hamilton, who had resigned from the Treasury Department in 1795, was never far from the action—much to Adams's chagrin. The second president had Federalist inclinations, but he was not among the High Federalists who were devoted to Hamilton. Adams was often skeptical of the former secretary's economic plans, and he was a fiercely independent thinker, resistant to and resentful of Hamilton's behind-the-scenes machinations.[1]

Adams's presidency was dominated by foreign turmoil. When he sent a diplomatic commission to France, Foreign Minister Talleyrand refused to receive it. The diplomats were then approached by French agents demanding a bribe from Adams, causing a scandal known as the XYZ Affair. War fever gripped the United States, and the Federalist-dominated Congress voted to raise a provisional army, create the Navy Department, and authorize the arming of merchant vessels. Fearing civil insurrection at home, the Federalists also implemented the Alien and Sedition Acts to control immigration and criminalize some forms of political speech.[2]

Realizing that he had misjudged the American mood, Talleyrand extended an offer to make peace. Adams was also willing to make a deal, and the resulting Convention of 1800 resolved the tensions. The High Federalists were angered by it, believing that Adams should not have compromised with the French regime so eagerly, and schemed to replace him in the upcoming presidential election. Hamilton even went so far as to write a highly critical pamphlet about Adams. Federalist divisions, popular dissatisfaction with wartime taxes, and superior Republican organization gave Jefferson a narrow victory in the electoral college.[3]

Writing in retirement years later, Jefferson claimed that the election of 1800 was "as real a revolution in the principles of our government as that of '76." This was not really fair to Adams, who after all was a member of the committee assigned by the Continental Congress to draft the Declaration of Independence. He and Jefferson had been friends and would become friends once again. Nevertheless, Jefferson's victory did deliver a fatal blow to Hamilton and the High Federalists, who, in calling for a standing army and restrictions on the Republican press, had become unmoored from the liberal and republican foundations of the Revolution. Hamilton was always at his best when his ambitions were anchored by a strong, commanding presence, such as Washington. Without such guidance, his passions increasingly got the better of him, and he led his party to "suicide," as Adams put it. Hamilton himself would be killed in a duel with Vice President Aaron Burr in 1804—a tragic and senseless end to one of the great geniuses of the Founding.[4]

But Hamilton's ideas would endure. For more than a decade, Jefferson and Madison endeavored to govern according to Republican Party principles they had established over the 1790s. But that was easier said than done. One key assumption was their shared belief that an agrarian republic such as the United States was stronger and heartier than a commercial nation such as Great Britain, and that therefore the United States could rely on economic retaliation to force its former colonial master to behave reasonably. Over the course of Jefferson's second term and Madison's first term, this view would prove gravely wrong. Worse, the War of 1812—which began when Madison finally abandoned hope for a peaceable resolution of problems with Great Britain—demonstrated that simple Republican government, which emphasized deficit reduction, low taxes, and a spare military, was not dynamic enough to foster national development. After the war, Madison and his Republican congressional allies, recognizing the need for a more vigorous approach, returned to the economic ideas of Hamilton. It took Madison twenty years and an unsuccessful war against the world's strongest naval power to acknowledge the limits of his old views, but he eventually recognized the wisdom of Hamilton's economic ideas.

IN 1801, UPON assuming the office of the president, Jefferson brought Madison out of retirement to helm the State Department and installed Albert Gallatin—who had replaced Madison as head of the Republican Party in the House in 1797—at the Treasury Department. Along with James Monroe, they would govern the United States for the next twenty-four years. By the time they left office, the Republican Party had driven their Federalist opponents to the brink of extinction.[5]

At the top of the Jeffersonian agenda was the repeal of most internal taxes, which left import duties as the main source of federal revenue. Republicans were also intent upon paying down the national debt, which in their view had been the source of great political mischief during the 1790s. To do this while cutting taxes required aggressive spending cuts, and the administration targeted the military in particular. The Republicans also pursued territorial expansion. They feared that as populations exceeded the supply of land, yeoman farmers—in Republican thinking, the best citizens—would be forced into manufacturing work or other jobs that did not cultivate the independent spirit necessary for good citizenship. Fortunately, the vast territory to the west could sustain republicanism for generations, so the administration gladly purchased the Louisiana territory from France and tried to acquire Florida from Spain.[6]

To advance his vast and ambitious program, President Jefferson occasionally had to sacrifice some principles on the altar of practicality. Initially convinced that the federal government did not have the constitutional authority to purchase Louisiana from France, he penned several drafts of a constitutional amendment. Ultimately he went ahead with the purchase without an amendment, fearing that the unpredictable Napoleon would change his mind if he sensed any hesitation from the United States.[7]

Jefferson also abandoned his quest to do away with the Bank of the United States, at the insistence of Gallatin. Though an ardent Republican, Gallatin understood the utility of the bank. In his *Sketch of the Finances of the United States,* published in 1796, he praised the bank for the "accommodations which government receives" from it and for its "great commercial utility," particularly the way it brought "into circulation moneys which otherwise would remain inactive" and thus increased "the rapidity of the circulation." This was especially important in the United States, which, because of its "extensive trade to the East Indies," was vulnerable to "sudden drains of specie."[8]

When Gallatin came into the Treasury Department, he encouraged the expansion of the bank's branch network, which Hamilton had been leery of. In this way, the new secretary was the first party leader to appreciate that Hamilton's bank could be repurposed for Republican ends. In the fall of 1803 Jefferson learned of a proposal to establish a branch of the bank in New Orleans. He wrote to Gallatin, "This institution is one of the most deadly hostility existing, against the principles and form of our Constitution." Gallatin would have none of this. Though respectful in his response, he thoroughly dismissed Jefferson's warnings. He reiterated the old arguments that Hamilton had once made in the bank's favor, but he went beyond these old notions, linking the bank to the project of westward expansion. He told the president that the New Orleans branch would promote "our own security," for if the government was to collect impost and land revenue from the new territory, it needed an institution like a bank branch in operation nearby. Gallatin's strenuous case for the branch induced the president to yield.[9]

Excepting the elimination of the bank, Jefferson's first term accomplished just about everything the Republicans had originally hoped, including ending any serious challenge from the Federalist Party. Jefferson earnestly believed that most of his opponents were at bottom good republicans, so he was careful in his rhetoric and retained many Federalists who had been appointed to government posts by Washington and Adams. This helped bring a measure of civic calm to the nation and contributed to Jefferson's easy reelection in 1804 over the Federalist candidate, Charles Cotesworth Pinckney of South Carolina.[10]

Though Jefferson's first term was full of domestic successes, his second term was dominated by international frustrations. Like Washington and Adams before them, Jefferson and Madison generally sought a neutral course in foreign affairs, avoiding what Washington had called alliances that "entangle our peace and prosperity in the toils of European ambition, rivalship, interest, humor or caprice." In his first inaugural address, Jefferson gave thanks for "a wide ocean" that separated the nation "from the exterminating havoc of one quarter of the globe." Though he had originally supported the French Revolution, even at one point excusing its murderous excesses, he had no affection for the "cold-blooded, calculating, unprincipled" Napoleon. Republican fiscal policy reinforced the disposition toward neutrality. Eliminating most internal taxes meant that the government had to rely on import duties, which required open commerce. And cutting the military to a rump force meant that the nation was unprepared to honor any commitments that might come with such alliances.[11]

Washington and Adams had labored mightily to keep the United States out of the conflict between Britain and France, though it was the Republicans who at least for a while reaped the political benefit. The controversial Jay Treaty offered the United States few concrete benefits, but it did inaugurate a period of British forbearance toward American commerce. The seemingly interminable war with France had sapped the strength of Britain's merchant marine, a loss that its West Indian colonies felt most severely, as there were fewer commercial vessels available to convey goods back and forth. Accordingly, the walls of the old mercantile system began to come down as West Indian governors opened their ports to American ships. Even better, Britain all but suspended the Rule of the War of 1756, which had effectively outlawed American trade with the French West Indies. In the *Polly* decision, handed down in 1800, the British Admiralty Court ruled that American merchants who docked in an American port and paid a duty on their cargo were free to continue on their way, even if the goods originated from the French West Indies. The Rule of the War of 1756 was still technically in effect, but this "broken voyage" loophole facilitated an enormously profitable reexport trade for the United States, which peaked at roughly $60 million in 1806, compared to just $2 million in 1792.[12]

In due course, soaring American profits came to grate on the British public, who believed that their tiny island nation was protecting the whole world from Napoleonic tyranny and that the Americans were reaping a morally dubious reward. In 1805 the British Admiralty Court reversed course with the *Essex* decision, ruling that a broken voyage was no longer a legitimate loophole. At around this time Britain also stepped up its impressment of American sailors. Life in the Royal Navy was very hard, and desertions to the United States were common. Britain aimed to capture deserters from its navy, but the practice became so aggressive that many citizens of the United States were snatched up in the process. This disregard for US sovereignty wounded American pride at least as much as the end of the reexport trade drained the American wallet.[13]

By the end of 1805, the United States faced a grave dilemma. Horatio Nelson's victory at Trafalgar in October over the combined French and Spanish fleets made Great Britain the undisputed master of the high seas, but Napoleon gained dominion over Europe with his decisive victory at Austerlitz in December. As Jefferson put it, the world was faced with "one man bestriding the continent of Europe like a colossus, and another roaming unbridled on the ocean." Napoleonic decrees in 1806 and 1807 basically prohibited neutral countries from trading with Britain, and the British Orders in Council of 1807 prohibited neutrals from trading with France.

Having tried so long to avoid taking sides in the war, the United States found itself caught between the two dominant powers in Europe.[14]

American anger was primarily directed toward the British, even though after 1807 the French raided as many American vessels. Britain's longer history of abuses, combined with the humiliation of impressment, made it seem to Americans that Britain still did not respect their sovereignty. One particular event inflamed the situation and forced Jefferson to act. In 1807, the HMS *Leopard* boarded the USS *Chesapeake* in the belief that the latter was carrying British citizens. Yet the *Chesapeake* was no commercial vessel; it was a US Navy frigate, and national honor was deeply offended by Britain's supercilious act. In response, Jefferson called for an embargo, initially as a prelude to the armed conflict he expected. The Embargo Act of 1807 prohibited all American merchants from trading in foreign ports, its first motivation being to keep American ships off the high seas should a formal declaration of war be made.

By the spring of 1808 war fever had eased, yet the embargo remained in place. The policy evolved, in fits and starts, into a form of commercial retaliation of the sort that Madison had advocated back in the 1790s. The secretary of state was still enthusiastic about the usefulness of such measures as an alternative to war. In a series of essays for the *National Intelligencer,* a Republican newspaper, in December 1807, Madison praised the embargo as both a defensive and an offensive measure. Though the embargo "guards our essential resources," he wrote, it also had "the collateral effect of making it the interest of all nations to change the system which has driven our commerce from the ocean." This logic followed from his long-held conviction that the European powers were more dependent on American staples than America was dependent on European luxuries. At last, the long-awaited Republican experiment in peaceful, commercial resistance had arrived.[15]

Gallatin, for his part, was skeptical. Shortly after the embargo was enacted, he told Jefferson that he preferred "war to a permanent embargo" because of the "privations, sufferings, revenue, effect on the enemy, politics at home, etc." in the wake of embargo. As was so often the case, the treasury secretary turned out to be prescient, for the embargo was better in theory than in practice. A robust black market developed to export American staples across the ocean and into Canada, and Great Britain managed to find alternative ways to supply the West Indies. Importantly, the embargo did not prohibit British imports, an unexploited point of British vulnerability. And all the while, it was deeply harmful to America's economy, as merchant vessels sat idle in ports and farmers had no place to send their spare produce.[16]

An effective embargo required aggressive enforcement too, but there was no political will in Congress to maintain such a regime. At the end of Jefferson's term, Congress abruptly shifted course, replacing the embargo with the Non-Intercourse Act. This law excluded British and French ships from American harbors and technically lifted the embargo against all countries except Britain and France, although it was impossible to stop merchants from going where they pleased after they left American ports. An impracticable measure, its main purpose was to ease the burdens of the embargo without forcing Congress to cave in to British demands altogether.

MADISON SUCCEEDED JEFFERSON as president in March 1809. He was deeply disappointed with recent developments in Congress. For decades, he had argued that commercial retaliation was the rational alternative to violence and that eventually Great Britain would see the errors of its ways. But Congress, by replacing the embargo with the Non-Intercourse Act, effectively foreclosed this option just days before he took the oath of office. Years later, in retirement, he still maintained that a "faithfully executed" embargo would have eventually induced a crisis in the West Indies and "extorted justice without a resort to war." The problem was that the government "did not sufficiently distrust" the merchant community, "whose successful violations of the law led to the general discontent which called for its repeal."[17]

The new president also faced political problems, as the once-unified Republicans were now split in multiple ways. Some wanted a firmer posture toward Great Britain; others demanded peace at virtually any cost. Some were jealous of Virginia's monopoly on the presidency; others had personal vendettas, especially against Gallatin. This briar patch of ideological, regional, and personal rivalries would have been difficult for any president to navigate, but Madison was not well suited to such a task. Jefferson had skillfully managed the congressional Republicans, but Madison's stance toward his legislative caucus was more aloof. Like Washington, he preferred not to intervene directly in legislative affairs. Unlike Washington, Madison did not have a de facto prime minister such as Hamilton (or himself). The only person who could have occupied that role was Gallatin, but internal disputes in the Republican Party had weakened his political standing.[18]

Absent firm presidential leadership, a divided Congress passed what came to be known as Macon's Bill Number 2. This halfhearted measure reopened trade with Britain and France for three months, then promised thereafter to end trade with one of the nations, provided that the other ended its own restrictions. Though dissatisfied with the act, Madison nevertheless tried to make it work, concluding that Congress had presented Napoleon with an opportunity. British control of the oceans meant that blanket American decrees effectively hurt France more; Britain could enforce restrictions against American trade with France, but the French could not do likewise to American trade with Britain. So at least in theory, Napoleon had an incentive to liberalize trade as a way to punish the British. The problem was that Napoleon was completely unpredictable. In July 1810 the emperor seemingly rescinded his former decrees, provided that Britain revoked its Orders in Council and the United States reestablished prohibitions on British commerce. Yet the emperor's declaration was ambiguous, and incoming reports indicated that France was still harassing American merchants. Still, Madison gambled he could use this as leverage over Great Britain, so he declared France to be in compliance with Macon's Bill Number 2.[19]

It did not work. Great Britain protested that Napoleon had not actually revoked his prior decrees and accordingly refused to withdraw the Orders in Council. By the end of 1811, it was evident that war was looming, and Congress began making preparations—of a sort. Gallatin submitted a payment plan for the conflict that included internal taxes, a longtime Republican bugaboo that elicited howls of protest from members of Congress. Congress also played politics with military enlistment targets and balked at expanding the navy. On top of all this, Congress had already refused to recharter the bank, despite the fact that it had been run remarkably well during its tenure. Gallatin naturally supported the recharter bill and even prevailed upon Madison to privately endorse it. But the ever-stubborn Madison refused to do so publicly, as that would have required an admission of his previous error. Without explicit support from the president, the recharter bill was narrowly defeated by a coalition of conservative Republicans, state-bank cronies, and Gallatin's antagonists.[20]

While Congress "prepared" for war, Madison waited for some sign that the British were willing to come to terms. But no correspondence to that effect arrived from overseas. The British government, he had complained to Jefferson in April 1811, was "inflexible in its folly and depravity." Enough was enough. Madison sent a war message to Congress on June 1, 1812, which outlined British "acts, hostile to the United States, as an independent and neutral nation." Congress declared war on June 17, although the vote was not overwhelming. The war measure passed 79 to 49 in the House and only 19 to 13 in the Senate, reflecting staunch Federalist opposition and internal divisions among the Republicans.[21]

The War of 1812 remains a peculiar episode in American martial history. John Taylor of Caroline, an opponent of the conflict, called it a "metaphysical war—a war, not for conquest, not for defense—not for soil . . . this war for honor, like that of the Greeks against Troy." Even Madison sounded a similar note after the fact, when in his special postwar message to Congress in 1815 he called "the late war . . . a necessary resort to assert the rights and independence of the nation." The war was intended to show the European powers that America was finally owed some respect. The United States would assert its rights on the high seas and would push the British out of Canada for good measure.[22]

That is not the way it turned out. A decade of cuts to the military budget combined with a lack of public investment in industry and infrastructure had rendered the nation incapable of realizing its grand ambitions. Even the basic task of raising money to fund the war was a major struggle. The war virtually halted American trade, which, combined with congressional aversion to internal taxes, placed enormous strain on the federal budget. Without the Bank of the United States, Gallatin struggled to find the needed funds. New England financiers opposed the war and balked at lending to perpetuate it, ultimately forcing Gallatin to secure loans at very high interest rates.[23]

Most of the victories in the war were defensive, for both sides. Great Britain easily rebuffed the US invasion of Canada. The United States stood firm on the Great Lakes and won victories in the Battles of Plattsburgh, Baltimore, and New Orleans. By 1814, Great Britain—which had been at war for the better part of twenty years—had grown weary of conflict and agreed to open peace negotiations. Madison dispatched Gallatin, House Speaker Henry Clay, Minister to Russia John Quincy Adams, and former Federalist senator James Bayard to Belgium to broker a deal. Signed in December 1814, the Treaty of Ghent secured no material concessions for either side; instead, it returned the parties to the status quo ante. Six months later, Napoleon would suffer his final defeat at Waterloo, leaving no reason for Great Britain and the United States to quarrel on the high seas any longer. The two nations have been at peace ever since.[24]

OVER THE YEARS, Madison has come in for a good bit of criticism for his presidential tenure, much of it warranted. Considering that he had successfully led the congressional Republicans in the 1790s, he was surprisingly maladroit at the same task during his time in the White House. Still, there are important points in his favor. He faced the same dilemma that had plagued the United States since it declared its independence: the Old World refused to leave the New World alone. Like Washington, Adams, and Jefferson, Madison pursued a peaceful solution for as long as it was reasonably possible to do so, and perhaps even longer than that. And though the War of 1812 did not yield any significant concessions from Britain, it inaugurated a lasting peace between the two nations. And unlike later wartime presidents—Abraham Lincoln, Woodrow Wilson, Franklin Roosevelt—Madison's administration managed the conflict without abridging civil liberties, seizing power from Congress, or trampling on the principles of republicanism. For all this, Madison deserves to be praised.[25]

Even so, his presidential tenure did much to discredit the ideology by which he and Jefferson had governed. They had hoped to build a pacifistic, agricultural republic, populated by able-bodied, independent farmers whose hardy virtue would stand in stark contrast to the docile servility of European workers and the dandified barons who ruled over them. But the failures of diplomacy and the disappointments of the War of 1812 demonstrated that this vision of the republic was misguided, impractical, and even utopian.

The foundational idea of Madison's diplomacy was that the United States was stronger than Great Britain and could bring it to heel through commercial retaliation. This assumption was not true, as Hamilton had understood. The United States tried all manner of commercial reprisals between 1805 and 1812, but nothing seemed to induce Britain to relent. Madison maintained throughout his retirement that economic retaliation could have worked eventually if only it had been enforced strongly enough, but this was a dubious claim. Even if it could have had an effect on Great Britain, there was still a decided lack of political will in the United States to pursue his preferred course. America was more dependent upon British trade than he had realized.

Moreover, after more than a decade of Republican rule, the country was in no shape to carry on a war with a world power. Cutting military spending helped reduce the national debt, but when Madison summoned the armed forces in 1812, they were woefully unprepared to heed the call. Additionally, the Republicans had shown little interest in federal patronage of highways and canals and little regard for crucial industries, and as a result the economy was simply not ready to assume a wartime footing. And though cutting internal taxes had been politically popular during peace-time, the resulting reliance on import duties meant that when war came and international trade all but disappeared, the government faced a huge budgetary crunch. Worst of all, the Republicans had inherited a superb financial system but had allowed the bank char-ter to lapse.

By the end of the war, Madison's agrarian republicanism had become increasingly outdated anyway. The war had reduced the steady flow of imports into the United States to a trickle, which in-advertently created a huge stimulus to American manufactures. Still in its infancy when Hamilton issued the *Report on Manufactures,* manufacturing was developing into a major sector of the economy and would soon become a real political force. Though Madison al-ways praised household manufactures, his governing philosophy accorded no real place to industry, and the new generation of Re-publicans who took charge of the nation after the war would need to find room.

In sum, though it remained in power, the Republican Party was an ideologically adrift coalition at the end of the war, desperately in need of a new direction. In his final two years in office, Mad-ison would help chart such a course by drawing on the ideas of his old nemesis, Hamilton. The president embraced a program of vigorous national development that relied on the strategy of media-tion: individual factions within society would receive direct benefits from the government in the expectation that over time they would strengthen the nation as a whole.

Madison outlined several Hamiltonian policies in his seventh annual address to Congress, delivered in December 1815. The first was the Second Bank of the United States. The war had drained the nation of hard currency, at least outside New England—which had opposed the war and had been disinclined to share its precious metals—leading to a suspension of specie payments throughout most of the country. About $68 million in paper money—mostly state-bank notes that could not be redeemed for hard cash—was circulating, which was no basis for a sound currency. Wealthy merchants, including John Jacob Astor, David Parish, and Stephen Girard, were desperate for another national bank. Aligned with them were Treasury Secretary Alexander Dallas and Representative John C. Calhoun, the principal designers of the new institution. They saw the Second Bank as more than a bank. In the Hamiltonian rhetoric of Dallas, it could be used as a tool "of national policy, as an auxiliary in the exercise of some of the highest powers of the government." This time Madison explicitly advocated for the new bank, swallowing his pride and telling Congress that "the probable operation of a national bank will merit consideration." Chartered in 1816, the Second Bank was virtually a replica of the First Bank of the United States, with an initial capital of $35 million, 20 percent of which was subscribed by the government, which would also select five of the twenty directors.[26]

The second major policy Madison announced involved a further softening of his opposition to industrial protection. He had never been an absolute free trader, having long admitted the need to balance the economic efficiencies that come with open trade against the practical considerations of statecraft. Still, he could never abide Hamilton's program of bounties, or direct subsidies to specific industries, which he deemed an unconstitutional payoff to the wealthy and well connected. But by 1816, he was ready to advocate indirect subsidies in the form of protective tariffs. He still averred that it was "wise" for government to generally leave to individuals "the application of their industry and resources," but now he acknowledged that there had to be more exceptions than he had previously admitted. "So many circumstances must concur," he wrote to Congress in his seventh annual address, "in introducing and maturing manufacturing establishments" without public intervention, that a more expansive effort by government was necessary. He called for trade reciprocity, which he had long advocated, and he now favored protection for industries that would "relieve the United States from a dependence on foreign supplies, for articles necessary for public defence, or connected with the primary wants of individuals," and for materials that could be supplied by American agriculture. The goal, he said, was to provide safety "against occasional competitions from abroad" and to offer a "source of domestic wealth, and even of external commerce." The resulting Tariff of 1816 was the first truly protective tax law, placing duties of 25 percent on wool and cotton products and 30 percent on iron products.[27]

Third, Madison advocated for federal spending on infrastructure, arguing that "no objects within the circle of political economy, so richly repay the expense bestowed upon them" as internal improvements. Though the policy idea had not been taken up in the 1790s, Hamilton's *Report on Manufactures* had argued that there was "no doubt of the power of the national government to lend its direct aid" to a plan "facilitating of the transportation of commodities."[28] Once again, the strategy of mediation was at play: the United States would favor certain geographical locales with new roads and canals, but in so doing it would promote commerce throughout the whole nation. The benefits were not just economic either. Madison praised "the political effect of these facilities for intercommunication, in bringing and binding more closely together the various parts of our extended confederacy," a point reminiscent of his argument in the 1790s that a better intercourse of sentiments was good for republican government. Calhoun agreed. "The more enlarged the sphere of commercial circulation," he said, "the more extended that of social intercourse; the more strongly we are bound together, the more inseparable are our destinies.[29]

Republicans had been drawn to internal improvements for some time, as their vision of a successful republic depended upon farmers in the interior of the country being able to get their crops to foreign markets. Jefferson saw such improvements as a useful undertaking once the debt had been paid back. In his second inaugural address, he argued that "redemption once effected the revenue thereby liberated may . . . be applied in time of peace to rivers, canals, roads, arts, manufactures, education, and other great objects within each state." When Congress admitted Ohio as a state in 1803, it authorized funds from the sales of public lands to be used for building roads. That, in turn, led to the building of the Cumberland Road, which connected Cumberland, Maryland, to the Ohio River. Ever the visionary, Gallatin advocated a major commitment to infrastructure in his 1808 *Report on the Subject of Public Roads and Canals,* arguing that it would facilitate a "clear addition to the national wealth."[30]

Nevertheless, such national endeavors were sporadic until the nation struggled to transport men and matériel during the War of 1812. In the war's aftermath, it became clear to many leaders that the national infrastructure was desperately in need of improvement. In 1817, Congress passed the Bonus Bill, which would have applied the bonus the government received from the Second Bank of the United States to a fund for internal improvements. Madison, however, vetoed it for lack of precedent. Diverging from the bulk of his congressional allies, he argued that a constitutional amendment was necessary to initiate the project. Monroe, his successor, vacillated on the constitutionality of internal improvements. However, President John Quincy Adams—the last of the Madisonian Republicans to serve as president—had no such worries, and so federal spending on internal improvements increased quickly in the 1820s.[31]

Madison's postwar domestic agenda represented a notable change of heart from his prior opposition to Hamilton. Many of his fellow Republicans, who had also come up through the political ranks as opponents of Hamiltonian economics, changed their minds too. Of course, like any politicians in any era, they had a more charitable interpretation of their about-face. Monroe, once an ardent opponent of Federalism, offered a telling explanation of the Republicans' sudden fondness for government-directed national development. "By the war we have acquired a character and a rank among other nations," he argued. It was now the duty of the government "to support this rank and character" by adopting policies consistent with the country's new position in the world. "We cannot go back," he insisted. "The spirit of the nation forbids it." Along the same lines, Clay praised the nation for "nobly, manfully vindicat[ing] the national character" in the war, and he called on Congress to "do something to ameliorate the internal condition of the country," to "fulfill the just expectations of the public" by pursuing a "liberal and enlightened policy" of national development. This sort of sentiment informed the thinking of many postwar

Republicans. They saw the signing of the Treaty of Ghent as an epochal moment. It was now their duty to bind the nation together for its prosperity, security, and perpetuation. This was not a capitulation to Hamilton, in their view; it was a culmination of their long-term project.[32]

Republican rhetoric, though no doubt earnest, masked the underlying reality that with only a few exceptions (such as Gallatin), they had changed course, and quite dramatically. Given his once-vehement opposition, Madison was the most startling convert to Hamiltonianism. Though his earlier views cannot be reconciled to his later ones, his change of heart can at least be explained by recalling his commitments to both nationalism *and* republicanism. These principles were inextricably linked by his belief that only a firm union could secure republican government. Madison never renounced either of these positions. His opposition to Federalism in the 1790s was a defense of his republicanism, a reaction to his perception that the Hamiltonians were seeking to reward the moneyed elite at the expense of the general welfare. He changed course in his later years because the diplomatic and military conflict with Britain had forced the shift upon him. By 1815, the United States had tried and failed to peaceably dictate the terms of foreign affairs. Now a more vigorous approach had to be taken to secure the union.

To accomplish this task, Madison not only adopted old Hamiltonian policies but also accepted his approach to governance. Hamilton's program was built on the idea that the government could use select factions in society as mediators of the general welfare. In Hamilton's day, this primarily meant that debt holders, commercial merchants, and manufacturers would receive direct benefits from the state, all for the purpose of developing what he called "one great American System." These groups would gain in the short term, but eventually the whole country would prosper. This idea informed the three main planks of the postwar Republican economic agenda. The Second Bank of the United States would yoke the interests of its stockholders to the goal of economic stability and thus to the welfare of the whole nation. Protective tariffs would benefit manufacturers who provided goods that were vital to the national defense. And internal improvements would benefit key locales directly but would facilitate commercial intercourse and a unity of sentiment among all Americans.

Even the name eventually given by Clay to the new Republican program—the American System—hearkened back to Hamilton's *Federalist* 11. And Clay's first known invocation of the term involved precisely the same aim Hamilton had had when he first coined it: protecting the nation from foreign interference. As Clay argued in 1820,

> Was it possible we could be content to remain, as we now were, looking anxiously to Europe? . . . Our institutions now make us free; but how long shall we continue so, if we mold our opinions on those of Europe? Let us break these commercial and political fetters; let us no longer watch the nod of any European politician; let us become real and true Americans, and place ourselves at the head of the American system.

Hamilton's goal was for America to resist "transatlantic force and influence," dictating the "terms of the connection between the old and the new world." His economic package of 1790–1791 was to be the first step in developing American hegemony. As this passage illustrates, Clay had a similar goal in mind. And as the sharp-witted critic John Randolph of Roanoke put it, Clay's plan "*out-Hamiltons* Alexander Hamilton."[33]

But though the economics of postwar policy were Hamiltonian, the politics remained distinctively Madisonian. One of Madison's main concerns with Hamilton's system was that its benefits were too narrowly distributed. A very small slice of the country would win in the short run, but the vast majority would have to wait in the hope that benefits would come their way down the line. Madison consistently lodged this objection against Federalism: Hamilton's repayment proposal for the federal debt favored speculators over veterans; his assumption of the state debts favored the profligate states over the responsible ones; his bank charter favored those who lived closer to the seat of government; and his plan for patronizing manufactures aided a select few at the expense of the agricultural majority. Indeed, the name that Madison and Jefferson chose for their party—*Republican*—was meant to convey that they saw their coalition as representing a broad consensus, against the selectivity of the Federalists.

In adopting Hamilton's policies, the postwar Republicans rejected the Hamiltonian focus on a few constituencies. The two main Hamiltonian ideas they appropriated—a national bank and industrial protection—were substantially modified to draw in a larger network of factions. Hamilton had opposed opening branches of the bank, and when Jefferson took office there were only six in operation. But the Second Bank opened with eighteen and expanded over time. Hamilton's protective policy emphasized bounties for a relatively small number of manufacturing concerns. By contrast, the Republicans advocated protective tariffs on broad classes of goods, bringing many more manufacturers under the patronage of the government. And under a system of internal improvements, a wide array of regional and economic factions could benefit directly from federal munificence.[34]

Moreover, the whole of Republican policies was intended to be greater than the sum of the individual parts. The Second Bank would facilitate a uniform currency and would responsibly extend credit so the entire economy might grow. Protective tariffs would aid nascent American industries. And a network of roads and canals would enable farmers to get their products to market faster and cheaper. Combined, all the major economic groups and every region would benefit from some aspect of the plan, binding the country ever more tightly together.[35]

In sum, the Republican postwar program was no mere capitulation to Hamilton's way of thinking. It was, rather, a synthesis of Hamiltonian vigor and Madisonian balance. Politically speaking, it was a more durable approach to statecraft. Hamilton had sought to distribute benefits to such a narrow clique of society that it led to the discord in the 1790s, as many groups found themselves on the outside looking in. The Republican postwar system, on the other hand, roped in the vast majority of factions in the United States.

Thus the Republicans managed to do what Hamilton could not: inaugurate an ambitious program of national development without sowing political dissension.

Indeed, the fusion of Hamilton's and Madison's philosophies contributed to a lengthy era of political comity. By smartly placing itself between the elitism of the Federalists and the simplicity of the old Jeffersonian orthodoxy, the postwar Republicans became, for a time, the only party in the nation. In the election of 1816, the Federalists did not formally nominate a candidate, and Monroe easily won the contest as Madison's chosen successor. In 1820, Monroe faced no opposition whatsoever.

7

INTRIGUE AND CORRUPTION

AFTER HE WAS inaugurated the nation's fifth president in 1817, James Monroe embarked on a national goodwill tour. His visit to the Federalist bastion of Boston was so well received that it prompted the *Columbian Centinel* to declare that the country had entered an "era of good feelings." This was an apt description. By 1817 the United States was in the middle of a postwar export-driven economic boom. At least by its own reckoning, it had proven its mettle to the European powers in the War of 1812. The dark clouds of the sectional conflict over slavery were not yet on the horizon. And moreover, by fusing Alexander Hamilton's economic program with James Madison's republican politics, the Republicans had united a broad swath of the country behind a program of national development.[1]

But as the Era of Good Feelings began to give way to the Age of Jackson, the political consensus was fractured by a new array of challenges: divisive issues, economic hardships, and polarizing personalities. The nation's westward expansion triggered a fight over slavery, the first time under the Constitution that it became a national issue. The Panic of 1819 was the nation's first major experience with the severe recessions that inevitably strike modern economies. Rivalries among leading politicians were also intense. The end of Monroe's tenure in 1825 brought a conclusion to the Virginia dynasty that had occupied the White House for nearly a quarter century. A number of politicians scrambled to fill that vacuum—John Quincy Adams, Henry Clay, Andrew Jackson, and others—and each had his own personal and regional power bases.

And yet for all these new challenges, politics in Jacksonian America still had much to do with old disagreements over public policy, particularly the Second Bank of the United States. Basically a carbon copy of Hamilton's original bank, the Second Bank sparked an ideological conflagration that mimicked the fight from the 1790s.

The Second Bank has mostly been remembered for the way it was destroyed at the merciless hands of President Jackson. In 1832 he vetoed a bill to recharter it, and he justified his actions as a blow to the oligarchs in defense of the common man. "There are no necessary evils in government," Jackson thundered with righteous indignation in his veto message. "If it would confine itself to equal protection, and, as Heaven does its rains, shower its favors alike on the high and the low . . . it would be an unqualified blessing." However, he continued, "The act before me . . . seems to be a wide and unnecessary departure from these just principles." Jackson's veto message has reverberated through the ages. Ted Kennedy even quoted it approvingly in his speech to the 1980 Democratic National Convention.[2]

Rhetorical flourishes aside, Jackson's argument was deeply flawed. The constitutional issues had been settled for over a decade when he rehashed the old claim that the Second Bank lacked legal sanction. His economic argument against the Second Bank was premised on an agrarian vision of the nation that had little resemblance to the interconnected, diversified economy that was beginning to take shape. Even his reference to Madisonian balance rang false, for during the 1820s the Second Bank had followed through on the egalitarianism of the postwar American System. Granted, the bank was run by a financial elite in Philadelphia, but with branches throughout the country, it was a boon for the South and the West, which did not otherwise have well-developed financial institutions. Jackson harbored a personal distaste for banks, and as was his wont, he saw himself as engaged in a pitched battle against the forces of darkness. Economic historians have generally condemned his veto of the Second Bank, and rightly so.[3]

Still, the Second Bank was not without problems. It was a troubled institution, but not for the reasons Jackson outlined and not at the time he chose to strike it down. Putting aside Jackson's fit of pique and examining the Second Bank over its whole history—from 1816 until 1836—one sees an institution that justified both the genius of Hamilton's economic system and the sharp critiques that Madison had once made against such corporations. From the time that Nicholas Biddle became the bank's president in 1822 until Jackson's veto in 1832, the Second Bank was everything that Hamilton hoped it could be, and more. It regulated the currency, extended credit responsibly throughout the nation, and helped expand the economy while protecting it from overheating. Yet there were two distinct periods when the Second Bank behaved in ways that vindicated Madison's old warnings about corruption: under its first director, William Jones, between 1817 and 1819, and under Biddle after Jackson removed federal deposits from the Second Bank in 1833. During those periods, the leaders of the Second Bank used the public authority they had been granted not for the sake of the general welfare but, rather, for their own interests. In the early days of the institution, managers abused their power to line their own pockets. And in its final days, Biddle turned it into a political machine, intent upon exacting vengeance on Jackson by contracting credit and forcing an economic recession.

The Second Bank, then, was yet another reminder of both the utility and the danger of Hamilton's approach to public policy. Without the Second Bank's steady guidance, the economy would not have grown so steadily from 1822 to 1832. But its managers were nevertheless susceptible to bouts of avarice, arrogance, and ambition and were able to use the institution of the bank for their own agendas.

ONE CAN ONLY wonder what Hamilton would have said had he lived to see Madison sign the law establishing the Second Bank. After all, Madison had opposed the Bank of the United States in 1791 on the grounds that the Constitution did not explicitly grant Congress the power to issue charters, but a quarter century later he himself chartered its successor. In a letter to Charles Ingersoll in 1831, Madison defended his change of heart by analogizing the legislative process to the judicial process. What is the "wisest and most conscientious judge" to do, Madison asked, when his opinion "has been overruled by the matured opinions of the majority of his colleagues?" He answered, "He will find it impossible to adhere to . . . his solitary opinions . . . in opposition to a construction reduced to practice, during a reasonable period of time; more especially where no prospect existed of a change of construction by the public or its agents." Accordingly, Madison was obliged to approve the Second Bank, which had been validated by "deliberate and reiterated precedents," having "undergone ample discussions in its passage through the several branches of the government; . . . carried into execution throughout a period of 20 years with annual legislative recognitions; . . . and with the entire acquiescence of all the local authorities."[4]

Of course, Madison still had to account for the potential problem of corruption. The danger with such an institution, Madison had originally argued, was that by granting the bank unique privileges (such as the right to hold federal tax deposits), the government transferred public resources to a private faction, namely, its stockholders. Moreover, these monetary subsidies were tantamount to political authority, for as the bank wielded economic influence, it could exert corresponding political leverage, corrupting the republican quality of the government. This is what Madison meant when he warned in 1791 that the bank risked becoming a "political machine." Jefferson added some color to this assertion in a letter to Albert Gallatin in 1803 in which he suggested that the bank could be overcome by the "avarice of the directors . . . for personal emolument" and that, "penetrating by its branches every part of the Union, acting by command and in phalanx, [it] may, in a critical moment, upset the government."[5]

The intensity of Jefferson's and Madison's anxiety over the bank gradually waned after the Federalists were removed from office: Jefferson had acquiesced to Gallatin on the New Orleans branch in 1803; Madison had quietly agreed to a recharter in 1811 and had made his endorsement public in 1815. There remained a handful of die-hard conservative Jeffersonians who opposed the Second Bank, but most of the party made peace with the idea of such an institution after the War of 1812. Why the new level of comfort?

Madison never addressed this question head-on, but he seems to have concluded in retrospect that the real danger was the Federalist ambitions for the bank, not, as he originally claimed, the institution itself. During the 1790s, Madison came to believe that there was a top-down plot in the works, with Hamilton as the leader and with his High Federalist partisans marching behind in lockstep. The alleged plan was to use the public debt and the bank as a form of patronage in order to bribe members of Congress into undermining the republican character of the government and thus to bring an American monarchy into being. Now that the perpetrators of the scheme were no longer on the scene, there was less reason to worry about the late secretary's program.

Writing in 1821, Madison noted, "There have been epochs when the general government was evidently drawing a disproportion of power into its vortex." One such instance, he believed, was the Federalism of the 1790s, whose leaders were trying to transform the government "into something very different from its legitimate character as the offspring of the national will." But by 1821, the Federalists were long gone and the danger they had posed had passed. "In the present condition and temper of the community," Madison argued, "the general government cannot long succeed in encroachments contravening . . . the people." Gallatin had made a similar point to Jefferson in 1803, assuring the president that there was no need to fear the directors of the bank. "They may vote as they please and take their own papers," he admitted, "but they are formidable only as individuals and as merchants, and not as bankers. Whenever they shall appear to be really dangerous, they are completely in our power and may be crushed." With Republicans firmly in control of the government, the institutions of Federalism were no longer to be feared.[6]

The history of the Republican era certainly seemed to justify this newfound confidence. During its twenty-year charter, the bank lived up to Hamilton's billing, and Madison's worry that it could become a political machine turned out to be unwarranted. Moreover, the country felt the bank's absence quite keenly during the War of 1812. Without a central institution to regulate the financial sector, a plethora of state banks filled the vacuum, lending recklessly and eventually draining most of the country of hard currency. After the war, an institution like the bank was at least as necessary as it had been in 1791.

But the Republicans had been wrong about Hamilton. The threat of the 1790s was not an incipient monarchy but an oligarchy. Though the wealthy had benefited from Hamilton's system and were flexing their political muscle to maximize their gains, the secretary himself was not at the helm of this clique. Far from it. As demonstrated by his desperate pleas to Jefferson about cutting a deal on the state debts in the summer of 1790 and by his effort to tamp down the speculative excesses of 1791–1792, he was often chasing frantically after men like William Duer. Accordingly, pushing Hamilton and his allies out of the government would do little to ease the threat of corruption, for he was not the proximate cause of the problem. Rather, his policies—in particular the way they pulled private factions into the government as mediators of the general welfare—were the actual danger. Insofar as the Republicans appropriated this governing strategy, they were running the same risks once again. That the bank had been well run did not alter the fact that such an institution could potentially become a political machine, corrupting the careful balance of power the Constitution tried to distribute among the people.

If anything, the dangers were more pronounced the second time around. After all, the Republicans had grander designs for the Second Bank than Hamilton had considered for the First Bank. Though the late secretary had wanted to keep the number of branches to a minimum so that the institution could be centrally controlled more effectively, the Republicans were eager to expand its operation as part of their political ambition to settle the western frontier. More than a dozen Second Bank branches had been opened by the end of 1817. This broadened the economic influence of the Second Bank—for good and possibly for ill, as its errors or misdeeds would reverberate throughout the whole economy.

The Republicans compounded the danger by failing to insist on solid leadership for the Second Bank—a mistake that Hamilton never made. Thomas Willing, who had previously served as the president of the Bank of North America, helmed the First Bank for most of its existence. A wealthy merchant with a lengthy résumé of government service, he was well attuned to the unique problems of national finance and was a solid choice for the bank's presidency. As for the Second Bank, its first president was William Jones, a thoroughly unspectacular functionary who consistently expressed reluctance when offered government posts, complained about his duties when he accepted them, and indicated a desire to be relieved from the burdens of public service. His main qualification seems to have been his early and energetic participation in Republican politics, going back to 1793 when he was still a merchant in Philadelphia. This earned him a stint as secretary of the navy, then as acting secretary of the treasury when Gallatin went as a diplomat to Europe during the War of 1812, and finally as president of the Second Bank.

Though the Republicans were right to recognize that the nation could use an institution like the Second Bank, they were wrong to set aside their old worries about corruption. Where they diverged from Hamilton—creating a broader branch network and employing second-rate managers—the Republican scheme tended to exacerbate rather than mitigate the threat. Little wonder, then, that the Second Bank was a problem from the very start.

JONES WAS LARGELY ignorant of the intricacies of public finance. He was hardly better with personal finance, either, having been forced into bankruptcy some years earlier. As president of the

Second Bank, he indulged corrupt officials and speculators as they misused the institution to enrich themselves. His eagerness to condone unmitigated greed may have actually helped secure him the presidency of the Second Bank in the first place. Stephen Girard—a wealthy merchant who purchased most of the First Bank's stock after its charter expired and who was an important advocate for chartering the Second Bank—complained that "intrigue and corruption had formed a ticket for twenty directors of the Bank of the United States who I am sorry to say appear to have been selected for the purpose of securing the presidency for Mr. Jones."[7]

The government had chartered the Second Bank to be a stabilizing force on the national economy, but because of the indulgence of Jones and the directors toward the investors, it began operations short on hard currency. They allowed subscribers to pay their second installment of specie on a pledge from the stock itself, permitted them to discount their stock at an advance of 25 percent, and waived the specie payment if subscribers gave up their first dividend. As a consequence, the Second Bank only raised $2 million in hard currency, well short of its $7 million goal, and allowed a handful of speculators to snatch up large quantities of stock for very little cash down. The machinations of the directors frustrated Hamilton's old ally Rufus King, once again serving in the Senate, who thought the "dispensation" would "prove . . . seriously mischievous in the early resumption of cash payments." Worse, speculators evaded the rule that a stockholder could hold no more than thirty votes by spreading nominal ownership among dummy holders. For instance, George Williams, director of the Second Bank branch in Baltimore, held 1,172 shares of stock, for which he received 1,172 votes because he registered them under 1,172 names.[8]

With control over so many shares and with a permissive administrator in Philadelphia, speculators all across the country used Second Bank branches to line their pockets. Fraud was common during Jones's tenure, but the Baltimore branch stood out, not only because the speculative scheme was so ambitious in scope (roughly $1.5 million was embezzled, a staggering sum for the 1820s) but also because the fraud went undetected for years. The central players in the drama were Williams, James Buchanan (not the future president of the United States, but the branch president and a partner at the financial house of Smith and Buchanan), and James McCulloch, the clerk at the branch, who is primarily remembered as a party to the famous *McCulloch v. Maryland* case. Buchanan and McCulloch purchased nearly thirty thousand shares of Second Bank stock for $4.5 million, financed partly from Second Bank loans on a pledge of stock and partly on advances from the Second Bank to themselves. This fraud continued for years, yet Jones did not notice. In fact he accepted an $18,000 "gift" from the managers, which they paid from the profits they made speculating in Baltimore. Eventually Congress detected some hints of misbehavior, and former speaker of the house Langdon Cheves of South Carolina, Jones's successor to the presidency of the Second Bank, uncovered the fraud. By that point McCulloch had taken about $425,000 in unsecured loans and Smith and Buchanan had taken another $350,000. John Quincy Adams recounted the sordid affair in his diary after it became public. "The house of Smith and Buchanan," he recollected, "were Tyrian merchants" who "used the funds of the bank as if they were their own." Worse, Adams wrote, "This explosion has brought on others: the failures are numerous and for heavy sums," for Smith and Buchanan were not the only ones making mischief. "The presidents and cashiers of other banks have been playing the same game."[9]

In theory, the Second Bank could have been an asset to the economy. By collecting tax revenue mostly in the form of state-bank paper, the Second Bank was a creditor to the state banks and thus had the power to induce them to behave properly. But under Jones it was too often a tool for speculators, and it facilitated an egregious overexpansion of credit. Upon taking charge of the bank, he had told Treasury Secretary William Crawford that he intended to pursue a more expansionary policy than the First Bank, whose approach to lending had been "less enlarged, liberal, and useful than its powers and resources would have justified." But crucially, he failed to set the capital levels for the various branches. This meant, in effect, that he let the inmates run the asylum. Of the $33 million in total bank loans made by October 1817, more than $8 million had originated from Baltimore alone. Another $13 million were sourced from Philadelphia, where fraud was also rampant. And though these two offices were extremely irresponsible, they were still part of a general pattern. In region after region, local branches were captured by parochial interests and made loans with gross irresponsibility, without regard to the financial well-being of the Second Bank or of the economy at large.[10]

By July 1818 the Second Bank had liabilities of $22.4 million and a specie reserve of just $2.4 million, a ratio that was double the legal limit. This was not just irresponsible; it was disastrous. The country had been enjoying a postwar export boom, but cotton hit a peak value of thirty-two and a half cents a pound on the Liverpool exchange that year and then quickly tumbled through 1819. Land values fell accordingly, and the Panic of 1819 was on. Even a responsible institution would probably not have been able to stop the onset of the depression, though it could have checked the irrational exuberance of the postwar years and kept itself in a position to provide relief when the contraction came. But the Second Bank had fueled the fire and was now forced to contract its own credit, worsening the crisis.

Enough was enough. A frustrated Girard organized a faction of stockholders to replace Jones with Cheves, who was tasked with the unenviable job of bringing order to the chaos. That meant extending the contraction that Jones had started and cleaning out the speculators who had taken control of the local branches. As Cheves later recalled, this would be no mean feat. "I was satisfied that there was a great want of financial talent in the management of [the Second Bank]," he wrote, "but I had not the faintest idea that its power had been so completely prostrated, or that it had been thus unfortunately managed or grossly defrauded." On taking the reins of the institution in 1819, he complained to Crawford that "with the present organization of the Second Bank it can never be managed well. We have too many branches, and the directors are frequently governed by individual and local interests and feelings." Eventually Cheves restored financial solvency to the Second Bank, whose specie reserve reached $8 million and whose total note issuance declined from $68 million to $45 million.[11]

The aggressive contraction amid the economic crisis drew a heated public rebuke. William Gouge spoke for many when he wryly commented that under the Jones-Cheves contraction, "the Bank was saved, and the people were ruined." When Chief Justice John Marshall declared in the 1819 *McCulloch* decision that the Second Bank was constitutional, using the same arguments that Hamilton had made long ago, he was salvaging an institution that, had it been up for recharter at the time, might have been cast aside.[12]

On initial inspection, the early years of the Second Bank do not seem consistent with the dire warnings issued by Madison at the height of the partisan melodrama of the 1790s. After all, he feared that the First Bank was facilitating a hierarchical clique, a brigade of speculators led by the monarchist Hamilton. The misbehavior by the Second Bank from 1817–1819 was hardly orchestrated by Jones, who was a man entirely out of his depth. Moreover, the real antagonists did not wish to establish a royal order in the United States. Buchanan and McCulloch were motivated by simple greed.

Even so, the Second Bank had been captured—not by a band of Hamiltonian monarchists but by a faction of greedy stockholders and managers. The sordid ambitions of this particular "praetorian band" did not change the fact that it owed its position to a government sanction, and it wielded its powers to dominate American monetary policy for its own interests. As Madison himself argued in an unpublished essay from around 1820 entitled "Banks":

> The greatest, certainly the most offensive abuses of Banks proceed from the opportunity and interests of the Directors. They can obtain discounts for themselves, even it is said to privileged amounts: They *can* suspend limit and resume the discounts to others as they please: Their stations inform them of the wants and business of all who deal with and depend on the Bank under their management. With these advantages alone they may by first lending money to themselves, and then immediately

shutting the Bank to others, with a knowledge of the effect on others, carry on speculations as gainful as reproachful.

This is a near-perfect description of the oligarchic cabal of Williams, Buchanan, and McCulloch. Though the rhetoric coming from the Republican Party in the 1790s connected the First Bank to Hamilton's supposed royalist machinations, simple private gain could also be a motive for corruption.[13]

IT IS A credit to Cheves that the corrupt managers of the Second Bank branches were removed from power in fairly short order. By 1822, with the Second Bank back in sound fiscal health, the stockholders were ready for the resumption of dividend payments and an expansion of credit. They also, at least by Cheves's telling, wanted a Philadelphian running the institution. So the South Carolinian was pushed aside for Biddle, then just thirty-six years old.

Biddle's performance as president of the Second Bank in the 1820s was nothing short of spectacular. He advanced the concepts of central banking further than anyone else had by that point, outdoing even the heads of the Bank of England. Under Biddle, the Second Bank served as a fiscal steward of the government, just as the First Bank had done under Hamilton and Gallatin. Biddle also regulated the supply of credit throughout the country, and unlike Jones, he retained tight control over the branches, so he could expand or contract credit as necessary in any given region. His adroit use of the Second Bank can be appreciated by comparing the Panic of 1819 to the Panic of 1825. The first overwhelmed the Second Bank, which was awash in incompetence and graft, but in 1825 Biddle had the foresight to see trouble in England before it hit American shores, and the Second Bank was in a good position to provide relief as needed. Additionally, the Second Bank promoted interregional and international trade by popularizing bills of exchange, which enabled merchants to buy and sell goods across vast distances with only modest transaction costs.

It is a common misconception that President Jackson acted as the tribune of the people when he vetoed the bill to recharter the

Second Bank in 1832. Jackson was the hero of the Battle of New
Orleans, the lionhearted defender of the national honor during
the War of 1812. In a head-to-head political battle, he was bound
to crush Biddle. Even so, by 1832 people liked the Second Bank,
which is truly remarkable. When Biddle became its president in
1822, people were so angry about the Second Bank's role in the
Panic of 1819 that it seemed as if Congress might revoke its charter.
A decade later, when Biddle applied for recharter, testimonials in
its favor flooded in from all across the country, especially from the
South and the West, which otherwise lacked strong financial institutions and—despite having voted overwhelmingly for Jackson—
appreciated the service Biddle had rendered. Naturally, these public
statements came primarily from the financial class, but when combined with the broad support from the regions' members of Congress, it is fairly clear that Biddle had greatly improved the Second
Bank's reputation in the decade he had been in charge.[14]

Legislative support in favor of the recharter was strong, but it
was not enough to overcome Jackson's veto pen. Old Hickory detested banks and had long professed a preference for hard currency
as the circulating medium. Voting to sustain his veto in Congress
were the conservative Jeffersonians who had always opposed the
Second Bank on principle. Jackson also drew support from a faction motivated not by republican propriety but by concrete matters of dollars and cents—namely, rival banking interests and their
patrons in Congress. The Second Bank was a welcome facilitator
of the regional economies in the South and the West, but the Mid-
Atlantic and New England had more sophisticated banking sys-
tems, and financiers in those regions chafed under Biddle's rule.
It did not help matters that though the Second Bank served many
functions that a modern central bank does, it was still a for-profit
institution mostly held in private hands. Many state banks were
thus inclined to see Biddle's institution not as a public servant but
as a competitor favored by the government.

The hostility to the Second Bank in the state of New York was
especially acute. Secretary of the Treasury Richard Rush informed
Biddle in December 1828, "You have probably as much or more to
fear for the Second Bank, from New York, as from Virginia, and

with even less excuse. In Virginia, there are still constitutional scruples. In New York, none." With the Erie Canal driving commerce between the East Coast and the Great Lakes region, New York City was now the commercial center of the nation. Yet the tax revenue from the port of New York was held not in native New York banks but, rather, in the New York branch of the Second Bank, whose main office was located in Philadelphia, whose stock was largely owned by Philadelphians, and whose president, Biddle, was a native of the city. As such, as Rush warned Biddle, "the ox of Wall Street" was increasingly jealous of the Second Bank's power, "and will not have you abuse him."[15]

The main antagonist from New York was Thomas Olcott, cashier of the Mechanics and Farmers Bank of Albany. His institution already held state tax revenue in its vaults, making it the preeminent bank in upstate New York's system. Olcott was aligned with Edwin Croswell of the *Albany Argus,* the main newspaper of the Albany Regency (the state's political machine) and holder of the state printing contracts, and with Benjamin Knower, principal stockholder of the Mechanics and Farmers Bank. This group had also acquired stakes in several New York City banks. If Jackson shattered Biddle's institution, "this cabalistic political combination," as John Quincy Adams called it, would be well positioned to pick up the pieces, and the largest share of economic power would finally transfer from Philadelphia to New York.[16]

Taken together, the antibank prejudices of Jackson, the old Jeffersonians of the South, and the Albany Regency of New York were sufficient to block the recharter. It is highly unlikely that Biddle could ever have overcome this alliance, even if he had been a political maestro. Alas, Biddle was a poor politician, which made the Second Bank's situation all the more difficult.

Throughout the 1820s, Biddle had employed Second Bank patronage cleverly, offering salaries, generous loans, or advances on paychecks to newspapermen and politicians. But he made several significant mistakes in his effort to shield the Second Bank from Jackson's wrath. He joined forces with Clay, who was running against Jackson in the 1832 election, thereby turning the Second

Bank into a campaign issue and undercutting a decade of effort to establish a nonpartisan reputation. Biddle's supercilious attitude also played right into Jackson's people-versus-the-powerful message. When asked by Congress whether the Second Bank oppressed the state banks, Biddle offered a very impolitic line that illustrated his tin ear. "Never," he answered. "There are very few banks which might not have been destroyed by an exertion of the power of the Bank." Moreover, he blundered his way into New York politics, whose byzantine ways were totally foreign to this Philadelphia patrician. He essentially bribed the antibank *Courier and Enquirer* to change its position on the Second Bank—and though the ethical standards of his day were often blurrier than those of our own, he endeavored to hide the gift from the Second Bank board, which was certainly inappropriate. As it turned out, his malfeasance was a waste of time anyway. Biddle's main political contact in New York was a con man who did not have the foggiest idea about how Empire State politics actually worked. Yet Biddle naïvely followed the bad advice he received, and he got nowhere because of it.[17]

Jackson believed that Biddle was not only trying to protect the Second Bank but also endeavoring to take down his presidency. Late one summer night in 1832, as the election neared, Jackson told Martin Van Buren, "The bank . . . is trying to kill me *but I will kill it*." His veto message was written with this idea in mind, that he would transform the Second Bank into a referendum on whether the people or the elites should rule. Once safely reelected to a second term, Jackson instructed William Duane, the secretary of the treasury, to remove the federal deposits from the Second Bank. When Duane refused, arguing that he could legally remove them only if they were deemed unsafe, Jackson replaced Duane with Roger Taney, who followed the president's orders. The Senate censured Jackson for his actions, the only time in American history the Senate has censured a US president, but Old Hickory was unbowed. His cronies distributed the federal funds to state banks, mostly pets whose managers had proven themselves loyal Jacksonians (or who had at least not backed Clay during the campaign).[18]

Jackson's removal of the deposits was bound to provoke a contraction from the Second Bank. After all, Biddle was a responsible lender, and he was not going to allow the reserve ratio of his institution to get out of hand, especially because he was uncertain of how far Jackson was prepared to go. However, still oblivious to the political realities, Biddle thought he could yet snatch victory from the jaws of defeat. He used the removal of the deposits as an excuse to initiate a contraction that was longer and deeper than the security of the Second Bank required, decreasing earning assets by 25 percent and demand liabilities by 22 percent and increasing specie reserves by 34 percent. This produced a mild recession—not very painful, but considering its origins in Biddle's political concerns, completely egregious.[19]

Biddle's Second Bank was similar to what scholars today call *government-sponsored enterprises,* like Fannie Mae and Freddie Mac. Empowered by a federal charter, the Second Bank had advantages that competitors lacked, and though it was obliged to carry out certain responsibilities on behalf of the government, it was still mostly free from interference. Biddle had been long aware of his unique position. In a May 1824 letter, he informed President Monroe that the board would "respectfully consider" any proposals from the government regarding payments related to a treaty with the Spanish and would "cheerfully agree" to any proposal, provided that it was "not inconsistent with [his] duty to the institution." At the same time, he still felt a keen obligation to support the public interest. The Second Bank's independence had been a national blessing in the 1820s, as it had allowed him to develop new techniques in central banking.[20]

But Biddle felt that Jackson's removal of the deposits had "relieved" him of his "responsibility for the currency" and forced him to "look primarily to the interest of the stockholders committed to our charge." And to do that, Biddle intended to hold the nation's economy hostage. As he told William Appleton in January 1834, "The ties of party allegiance can only be broken by the actual conviction of existing distress in the community. Nothing but the evidence of suffering abroad will produce any effect in Congress." Biddle had to stay the course and not "be frightened or coaxed into any relaxation of [the bank's] present measures," for that would be proof that "the measures of the government are not injurious or oppressive." It was only through a "steady course of firm restriction" that Biddle could acquire "the recharter of the Bank." The next month, Biddle swore to John Watmough that "all the other Banks and all the merchants may break, but the Bank of the United States shall not break."[21]

As it turned out, however, Biddle did indeed break. The clamor of the merchant and financial classes for relief, amplified by an infusion of capital from England, induced him to ease his assault by the end of 1834. When the Second Bank's charter expired in 1836, Biddle secured a state charter from Pennsylvania, but the institution was badly equipped for the Panic of 1837. It suspended specie payments in 1839 and was liquidated in 1841.

Though Biddle's inventive leadership of the Second Bank in the 1820s demonstrated his brilliance as a financier, the political games he played with the nation's economy in the early 1830s illustrated that he was no statesman. His outrageous politicking seemed to realize Madison's warnings about Hamilton's bank in the 1790s:

> The power of granting Charters, he observed, is a great and important power, and ought not to be exercised, without we find ourselves expressly authorized to grant them: Here he dilated on the great and extensive influence that incorporated societies had on public affairs in Europe: They are a powerful machine, which have always been found competent to effect objects on principles, in a great measure independent of the people.

Hamilton's bank was not much of a threat, and for most of his tenure as president of the Second Bank Biddle was an earnest and effective agent of the national interest. But when Jackson removed the deposits, Biddle turned the full force of the Second Bank against the people in the hope they would demand the government restore its status.[22]

And where did Biddle get such power? From the government itself, of course. Because the Second Bank had been the depository for federal tax moneys, Biddle was in a position to build an immensely powerful financial institution. The Second Bank's stockholders were, in other words, a faction that had been blessed by government benefits—including the Republican desire to expand the branch network as part of its egalitarian project. Biddle used these state-sponsored resources not only to help the economy but also to expand the scope and importance of his institution—and, when the time came, to wield them against the Jackson administration.

THOUGH THE SECOND Bank was a national blessing during the 1820s, its earlier and later years illustrated how such institutions could foment oligarchy. The misbehavior of the Second Bank during these two periods was substantially worse than anything that had happened in the 1790s. The efforts of the speculators to maximize their gains from Hamilton's system, though no doubt egregious, did not do nearly as much harm to the nation as the Second Bank did in 1817–1819 and 1833–1834.

Madison reflected on this theme around 1820, in an essay on monopolies. He warned that the "growing wealth" of all corporations, religious or secular, can be a "source of abuses." Europe offered a harrowing example. In his estimation, the established churches had acquired too much wealth and power, creating a "disordered state of things" that contributed to the Reformation. But thanks to their public sanctions, the churches had acquired their vast holdings—"half *perhaps* the property of some European nations"—in entirely legal ways. Ultimately, the only way to correct their "gross . . . corruptions" was to "disregard the sanctions of the law, and the sacredness of property," ideals that were at the very foundation of western civilization. Likewise, by 1833 the Second Bank had become so integral to the American economy that correcting its abuses could not be done without great exertion and at enormous expense.[23]

Just as he got the better of most men during his life, Jackson ultimately defeated Biddle, who shrank from the national scene and passed away in 1844. The Second Bank building, a brilliant example of the Greek revival style, stands to this day on Chestnut Street in Philadelphia, just a short walk from Independence Hall. It is open to the public as an art gallery, housing many famous paintings from the Founding era by Charles Willson Peale. The only testament inside to Biddle's brilliant economic management is a small bust in a corner room. Towering over the Biddle sculpture is a large, imposing portrait of Old Hickory himself—triumphant in life, and triumphant in memory, too.

8

THE VILEST OF CHEATS

THE SECOND BANK was not the only nationalist initiative from the end of James Madison's term that created problems after he retired. The protective tariff became a source of political conflict too. But whereas the Second Bank was a partisan issue—between the Democrats of Andrew Jackson and the National Republicans, later the Whigs, of Henry Clay—the protective tariff divided the country along sectional lines. The measure was a winner for the industries of the North and the farmers of the West, but the South—which drew much of its income from exports—was a loser in the scheme.

In theory, this need not necessarily have been a problem. The protective tariff, along with the Second Bank and a program of internal improvements, were part of a Madisonian package that Clay had called the American System. What really mattered was that, on balance across these policies, the South was treated equitably. But that just was not the case. In practice, the protective tariff became a way for economic groups in the North and the West to enrich themselves at the expense of the South.

So once again, the Madisonian-Hamiltonian hybrid facilitated a corruption of the republican form of government. But whereas the Second Bank had shades of oligarchy, the protective tariff facilitated an ochlocracy, or mob rule, what Madison in *Federalist* 10 called a "majority faction." He had argued that the extended republic would make it difficult to form majority factions, as a diversity of interests would check one another. However, the Hamiltonian-Madisonian synthesis, by employing a vast array of mediators, generated a work-around: diverse groups with little or nothing in common could use the tariff to bargain with each other, creating a legislative logroll in which they enriched themselves, harmed the South, and did nothing for the national interest.

For a republic in which the majority rules, such corruption can be very difficult to root out; because the offending policies benefit a majority of the people, there is little hope for remediation at the ballot box. Vice President John C. Calhoun of South Carolina, who had been one of the great nationalists during Madison's tenure, was so troubled by this development that he renounced his commitment to the American System and tried to establish the right of the states to nullify federal laws. His effort prompted the first bona fide constitutional crisis of the young nation and was a harbinger of the Civil War.

HAMILTON'S 1791 *REPORT on Manufactures* notwithstanding, there was little political pressure for industrial protection in the early years of the republic. Prior to the Orders in Council of 1807, the Atlantic trade was enormously profitable for New England, and the South's prosperity depended upon exporting agricultural products to Europe. However, the Jeffersonian embargo and then the War of 1812 served as massive stimuli for domestic industry. Imports collapsed from an average of $130 million per year in 1805–1807 to $64 million per year in 1808–1811 and to just $38 million per year in 1812–1815. The sudden want of cotton and woolen goods was particularly significant, as it induced the country to quickly develop its nascent textile industry. After the Treaty of Ghent, trade was reopened with Great Britain, which began dumping its surplus products on the American market, posing a dire threat to domestic manufacturers.[1]

The Madison administration considered this situation dangerous to the national interest. Having experienced two wars with England in his lifetime, the president had no way of knowing that
the Treaty of Ghent would inaugurate a durable peace. He and his
Republican allies expected more trouble and resolved to prepare the
nation for the next conflict. Then representative Calhoun argued
in the House that Great Britain would not "permit us to go on
in an uninterrupted march to the height of national greatness and
prosperity." Instead, he expected "future wars, long and bloody,"
between the two nations. Thus the United States had to prepare immediately by expanding the navy and militia, sponsoring internal
improvements to facilitate military transport, fortifying the coasts,
and protecting domestic industries that would offer "the necessary
materials for clothing and defense." In calling for protection, Calhoun explicitly placed "the claims of the manufacturers entirely out
of view"; instead, he defended it "on general principles, without regard to [the manufacturers'] interest."[2]

Judged by subsequent tax legislation, the Tariff of 1816 was not
very protective; the rates turned out to be too low to have much im-
pact. Still, its manifest purpose was to offer protection, albeit tem-
porarily. It raised duties on cotton and woolen goods to 25 percent
until 1819 and then dropped them to 20 percent thereafter, thus
stimulating domestic industry without burdening consumers for
too long. The measure's mildness and brief lifespan helped create a
broad, transregional coalition in its favor. House members from the
Mid-Atlantic and the West voted overwhelmingly for it, and New
England gave it a small majority. Though the South voted against
it, 14 to 31, the bill enjoyed a respectable share of the vote, and
South Carolina's representatives broke 4 to 3 in its favor.[3]

The passage of the Tariff of 1816 was just the beginning of agitation for protection. The Society for the Encouragement of Manufactures was founded in 1816 as a host of regional interests began
to push for more assistance, and during the Panic of 1819 they
claimed that protection of their industries would amount to a mass
employment policy. Their efforts resulted in the Baldwin Tariff of
1820, a measure that went down to a narrow defeat at the hands of

New England and the South. After the congressional reapportionment following the census of 1820, political power shifted toward the Mid-Atlantic and the West, which allied to pass the Tariff of 1824. This law increased duties on all manner of goods, including iron, lead, raw wool, hemp, cotton bagging, and textiles; on average the rate increased to 50 percent on dutiable imports.

The Tariff of 1824 marked the end of the national consensus regarding protection, as henceforth the tariff would pit region against region. The James Monroe administration refused to endorse the measure, but the president signed it into law because he did not think it was unconstitutional (the typical practice prior to Jackson's administration). Opposition was intense in the South, whose main exports had not fully recovered from the Panic of 1819. Overexpansion of cotton acreage left planters in the South Carolina up-country particularly vulnerable. Given their precarious economic situation, they were unwilling to abide a government-mandated increase in the price of imported goods, and in addition they feared potential retaliatory tariffs from foreign governments against their cotton, tobacco, and other exports. Nevertheless, the measure passed on the strength of support from the Mid-Atlantic and the West, with New England in opposition and just one southern House member supporting it.

Taken by itself, there is little doubt that the Tariff of 1824 was partial in the sense that Madison would have found objectionable in the 1790s. It had little to offer the South except a higher cost of living, and it imposed its burdens when cotton, the region's most profitable product, was struggling to earn half of what it had a decade earlier. Arguing against the legislation from the Senate floor, John Taylor of Caroline warned:

> For in truth, this is not a tariff bill to encourage manufacturers. It is a bill of bargains, to enrich a pecuniary aristocracy. This aristocracy is a polygamist, and is, by this bill, courting a number of local interests, with a design to marry them for the sake of their fortunes. . . . It proposes to bribe them with small portions of their own estates, to get the rest for itself.

Taylor was describing a legislative logroll. Such coalitions were not unprecedented in American history up to that point. Madison sought to form one during the impost fight of the 1780s, and the Compromise of 1790—whose supporters included eastern speculators, Hamiltonian loyalists, indebted states, and the Potomac River districts—had a similar quality, in that the final measure provided disparate benefits for several factions. But the impost and the assumption compromises were ultimately about paying the nation's bills, whereas the Tariff of 1824, according to Taylor, was nothing more than a way for certain factions to reward themselves at the expense of others.[4]

Taylor's views on the matter became commonplace in the South during the 1820s. For instance, petitioners from Richland County, South Carolina, complained to Congress in 1828 about the tariff:

> Your memorialists, deeply suffering under this system of protecting duties . . . desire to express their deliberate conviction that Congress possesses no power under the Constitution . . . to favor, in any manner, one class of citizens at the expense of the rest; that such a system has been long felt in this State as equally unjust in its principle and in its operation; that it arrays the pursuits and the interests of one section of the Union against those of another, conferring advantages and privileges arbitrarily, unequally, and in no degree sanctioned by the Constitution or by justice; and that it is liable to great abuse, as a political engine, by bribing one section of the Union with the plunder of another.

Like Taylor's lament, this argument harkens back to Madison's commitment to impartiality. The government should not play favorites among factions; instead, it should be committed strictly to the general welfare.[5]

How could this kind of "polygamist" aristocracy form in a republic like the United States? In *Federalist* 10, Madison had argued that the diversity and extent of the nation would make it difficult for such a coalition to form. At the time, his primary worry was to prevent a singular interest with some "common motive" from invading "the rights of other citizens." Madison believed that in a diverse republic, factions would rarely amount to a majority and could therefore be dispensed via "the republican principle, which enables the majority to defeat its sinister views by regular vote." However, as Taylor saw it, the principle of protection had enabled minority interests to create a majority by bargaining with one another for their mutual gain. Previously, such disparate factions would have little reason to join together, but now they could support each other's preferred tariff rate in exchange for support on their own. Meanwhile, the South, whose economy relied heavily on exports, could not, for all intents and purposes, join the logroll.[6]

Taylor's argument against the Tariff of 1824 was disputed in its day. Clay, who had by that point become the leading advocate of Madisonian nationalism, thought the measure was consistent with the American System. Clay still maintained that it was part of a package that, on the whole, balanced the interests of each region in a fair and judicious manner. The same, however, cannot be said about the Tariff of 1828, commonly known as the Tariff of Abominations. Reviled in its day and condemned by subsequent generations of scholars, it was, as historian George Dangerfield put it, "an undisguised hunt for special advantages," demonstrating that "the central government was expected to give assistance, but never to plan the assistance that it gave." The Tariff of Abominations legitimized Taylor's critique, perverting Clay's grand ambition for a coherent system of national development into a mad scramble for plunder.[7]

THE TARIFF OF 1824 hardly provided the protection for which the wool manufacturers had hoped. In that same year, Parliament abolished the duty on raw wool, which enabled English manufacturers to lower their prices in the United States. It was not long until the woolen interests in the United States were calling upon Congress for more assistance, but the narrow scope of their request made it a losing proposition. A protective measure for their benefit failed in the Senate in 1827 by the vote of Vice President Calhoun, who was forced to take this step (harmful to his presidential ambitions) because Senator Martin Van Buren (an ally of Calhoun's old rival, Treasury Secretary William Crawford, and soon to be his nemesis in the Jackson administration) withdrew, causing a tie in the roll-call vote.

The woolen manufacturers responded by broadening the scope of their coalition. If their congressional allies were to offer a bill that granted assistance to a wider range of industries, they could cobble together a majority coalition. That summer in Harrisburg, the Pennsylvania Society for the Promotion of Manufacturers and the Mechanic Arts held a convention that included such luminaries as Representative Rollin Mallary, an ally of President John Quincy Adams and chairman of the House Committee on Manufactures, and Hezekiah Niles, editor of the influential *Niles Weekly Register* of Baltimore. The convention's report called for increased protection for manufactured and raw wool, as well as iron, hemp, distilled spirits, and printed cotton.[8]

Coming as it did at the start of an election campaign, the society's report created a political problem for presidential hopeful Jackson. As a senator he had voted for the Tariff of 1824 (as did his political confidant and co-senator from Tennessee, John Eaton), but Old Hickory had otherwise remained ambiguous on the subject, merely telling the public during the 1824 presidential campaign that he favored a "judicious examination and revision" of the tariff. Heading into the 1828 election, Jackson could count on support from the South, which was staunchly opposed to protection, but the election would be decided in the Mid-Atlantic and the West, which supported it. The Adams administration, in which Clay served as secretary of state, was squarely on the side of protection. The National Republicans (as this political coalition was called at the time) threw its weight behind an upward adjustment of the tariff, in keeping with the society's recommendations. The Jackson partisans could not suffer an alliance in the presidential election between New England—whose burgeoning manufacturing sector was making the region more comfortable with protection—and the Mid-Atlantic and the West, especially when Jackson did not offer a clear position on the issue. Such an alliance had already begun to form in Congress—hence the passage of the Tariff of 1824—and the Jacksonians had to stop the pro-tariff vote from cohering around Adams's reelection bid without alienating the South.[9]

So the Jackson men (or, as they came to be known, the Democrats) in Congress cleverly schemed to write a bill that could not pass. Though Mallary was chair of the Manufactures Committee, it was full of Democrats, including Silas Wright, a close ally of Van Buren, who was well on his way to becoming indispensable to Jackson. The bill the committee produced was stuffed with all sorts of goodies for the Mid-Atlantic and the West—including protections the society never requested—but it did not protect the woolen manufacturers of New England, who had been prime movers in the initiative. Moreover, the Democrats went out of their way to burden New England by hiking tariffs on raw materials critical to their industries. They proposed taxing not only the higher grades of wool that were grown in the United States but also the lower grades that were not, a maneuver whose only purpose was to harass the woolen industry. Likewise, they made no distinction between the quality of hemp in their duties, meaning that the higher grades imported by the New England cordage industry were heavily taxed. They played similar games with flax and molasses, all in order to burden northeastern manufacturers. On the House floor, southern Democrats refused any amendments, believing that the bill as written would be opposed by a critical mass of New Englanders. Responsibility for its defeat—and with it the calumny of the Mid-Atlantic and the West—would thus fall on Adams, not on Jackson, whose northern partisans would vote for passage.[10]

That the law was wholly disingenuous is not merely an interpretation of subsequent generations of scholars; it was evident to many at the time. Representative Thomas Mitchell of South Carolina, for instance, justified his opposition to an amendment that would lower the molasses impost because "keeping it in the bill would get votes against the final passage." John Randolph of Roanoke declared that the only manufacturing the bill supported was "the manufacture of a president of the United States." An anonymous letter published in the *Franklin Repository* quoted future president James Buchanan, a Democrat from Pennsylvania, as saying he would "bring before Congress a tariff bill so larded with other than protection to wool growers and manufacturers of wool, and involving principles which we know the East will not agree to, [that] we will . . . throw the odium of its rejection off the South on . . . the East." In private, Clay denounced the bill as "the vilest of cheats" because it "demolishe[d]" the woolen manufactures "with the professed purpose of protecting them." After he returned to the Senate in 1831, he blamed Van Buren for the mess, stating that the tariff "was framed on principles directly adverse to the declared wishes of the friends of the policy of protection . . . upon the advice of a prominent citizen, now abroad [Van Buren], with the view of ultimately defeating the bill, and with assurances that, being altogether unacceptable to the friends of the American system, the bill would be lost." In 1837, Calhoun made a similar claim on the Senate floor, arguing that Van Buren had offered "assurances" to place "the representatives of the South at ease" that the bill would fail.[11]

Nevertheless, the same regional coalition that drove the Tariff of 1824 pushed the 1828 measure over the finish line. In the House, the Mid-Atlantic and the West gave it a combined 86 votes in favor and 20 opposed; New England broke narrowly against, 16 to 23; and the South was staunchly opposed, 3 to 51. In the Senate, Van Buren held firm with the South, except on the all-critical woolen provisions. When amendments were offered to provide more protection for this important industry, Van Buren broke with his Jacksonian allies from the South and approved the adjustment. Eaton did, too. This was sufficient to secure its passage in the upper chamber, and President Adams—having no constitutional objections to the principle of protection—signed it into law, even though he recognized that it burdened the South unfairly.[12]

By stopping efforts to improve the bill, southern legislators had badly miscalculated, and they ended up with a tariff that was more burdensome than it otherwise would have been. Nevertheless, the South, which gave Jackson 80 percent of its vote in 1828, was optimistic that Old Hickory would provide remediation. However, in his first message to Congress, Jackson offered only disappointment. He wrote, "No very considerable change has occurred during the recess of Congress in the condition of either our agriculture, commerce, or manufactures. The operation of the tariff has not proved so injurious to the two former or as beneficial to the latter as was anticipated." Moreover, he suggested that when the national debt was extinguished, the revenue from the tariff should be "apportion[ed] among the several States according to their ratio of representation."[13]

To many planters in the South, Jackson's plan was a betrayal of the principles of republicanism. Government was supposed to be administered impartially and strictly for the benefit of the whole nation, but the tariff had come to pit region against region and had placed the South on the losing end. Southerners would pay higher prices on imports, their products would receive no benefit, and Jackson's plan to redistribute the spare revenue to the states based on population effectively meant the South would subsidize the rest of the nation. The National Republicans, meanwhile, had little to offer the South either. They too wanted protective tariffs, but they sought to use the surplus revenue to fund internal improvements. A decade earlier, Calhoun had supported the Bonus Bill, which would have created a fund for such expenditures, but ten years of spending on such projects showed that the money was bound to travel northward and westward. Though the West had just 13 percent of the population, it had received nearly a third of federal disbursements for internal improvements in the 1820s; meanwhile, the South had received less than 20 percent of those dollars. So, either way, under the Democrats or the Whigs, the South seemed bound to lose.[14]

THAT PROSPECT HAD a profound effect on Calhoun. Elected to the House in 1810, he was one of the War Hawks who demanded a tough posture toward Great Britain, and after the War of 1812 he had became one of the premier southern nationalists in Congress. A strong advocate of Madison's domestic agenda, he served as secretary of war under Monroe and was elected vice president in 1824 under Adams. He was elected vice president once again in 1828 under Jackson, making him the last person to serve in that office under two different presidents. Yet Calhoun's political fortunes took a turn for the worse over the course of the decade. Like most southern politicians, he had opposed the Tariff of 1824, which had alienated him from many of his old northern allies. Moreover, his rivalry with Van Buren undermined his relationship with President Jackson. By the end of Jackson's first term, Calhoun was a man without a party.

It was during this period that Calhoun started to execute one of the most amazing backflips in the history of American politics as his old nationalism gave way to a sectionalist orientation over the tariff and, by the 1840s, to a bitter isolationism in defense of slavery. His unequivocal support of the institution of slavery was highly controversial in his day and is thoroughly offensive in our own. But it is worthwhile to consider the critique of the tariff he developed during the 1820s and 1830s, for he was a man acute of intelligence, philosophical depth, and uncompromising stubbornness. Not content merely to oppose the tariff itself, he instead developed a full-blown theoretical critique of the principle of majority rule, drawing on classical republicanism and on debates from the American Founding.

Like Taylor before him, Calhoun saw a polygamous majority at work in the tariff coalition. "The woolen manufactures," he claimed, "found they were too feeble" to pass a law on their own. So they began to collect "other interests, till a majority be formed" that favored increasing duties "on more than a dozen other of the leading articles of consumption." Writing privately to Senator Littleton Tazewell in 1827, Calhoun bemoaned the formation of "combinations" with "separate and opposing interests" and worried that their potential political power was "the weak part of our system." He warned his cousin James Edward Calhoun that though the tariff had divided the "wisest men of the country . . . on principle," the power was "highly dangerous" because through it "one section of the country may really be made tributary to the other."[15]

Calhoun saw the tariff as a threat to the stability and justice of the government, issues that had vexed not only the Founders but also political theorists for millennia. Aristotle had observed that each general form of government—rule by one, by the few, and by the many—has a "right constitution" as well as a "perversion," depending on the purpose to which the government is directed. Each right constitution, regardless of the form, governs "with a view to the common interest," and the perverted ones govern for the sake of the rulers. While preparing for the Constitutional Convention in 1787, Madison enumerated a list of abuses by the state governments that, in sum, suggested that they had become a corruption of democracy. This is why the "enlarged republic" was so central to his political philosophy, for it would inhibit self-interested majority factions from forming, thereby curing the disease of popular government via solely democratic means.[16]

Through his analysis of the tariff, Calhoun came to reject Madison's argument that the extended republic was a sufficient safeguard. Calhoun argued that though "various interests" would struggle "to obtain a majority" in the republic, eventually "a combination will be formed between those whose interests are most alike;—each conceding something to the others." In fact, he told Monroe that the "vast extent and diversity" of the country made it more, not less, likely that "some portions of the country may be enriched by legislation at the expense of others." A diversity of factions only meant more opportunities for bargains. The system of checks and balances was no safeguard, either. "No government," he claimed, "based on the naked principle that the majority ought to govern, however true the maxim in its proper sense, and under proper restrictions, can preserve its liberty even for a single generation." Eventually, a hodgepodge majority would overrun these protections.[17]

Calhoun concluded that the maintenance of republican government required much stronger protections for minority rights. This was the basis for his theory of the *concurrent majority,* more commonly known as the *principle of nullification.* The general government should continue to possess supreme authority to rule in all cases where "a community of interests" exists across the nation. But in disputes where "the states have distinct and separate interests, over which no supervision can be excised by the general power without injustice and oppression," individual states should hold a veto over the federal authority, with the only remedy being a constitutional amendment adopted by a supermajority of the other states to override the minority.[18]

The theory of the concurrent majority had a lot in common with the old notion of mixed estates as a hedge against the excesses of popular majorities. The British model in particular was celebrated during the eighteenth century, by Hamilton and others, because it balanced popular majorities against self-constituted authorities, such as the monarch, who was entitled to rule regardless of public opinion. Calhoun sought to establish the state governments as an independent sovereign for a similar purpose. Just as the king could veto unjust or unwise laws enacted by Parliament, the states could nullify acts of Congress that violate the terms of the Constitution. So, ironically, in endeavoring to mitigate the excesses of Hamiltonian economics, Calhoun promoted a somewhat Hamiltonian view of the government.

Calhoun refused to acknowledge that his system was an innovation. Instead, he and his allies wrongly claimed that the concurrent majority was a constitutional principle, and in so doing they drew an aged Madison back into the political fray. The nullifiers pointed out that in 1798 he had anonymously authored the Virginia Resolutions for the Virginia legislature, which—so they claimed— nullified the Alien and Sedition Acts. However, Madison, still as staunch a nationalist as ever, rejected this interpretation. The Virginia Resolutions, he reminded the nullifiers, were an example of "interposition," not nullification. The goal was to rally the other states, to mobilize public opinion against Federalist abuses, similar to what he had done in his essays for the *National Gazette*. In fact, Madisonian interposition was not far from Hamilton's argument in *Federalist* 26 that the state legislatures could "sound the alarm" when the federal government overstepped its boundaries. And anyway, Madison noted, protective tariffs had always been considered constitutional. His objections to Hamilton's *Report on Manufactures* had to do with the secretary's program of bounties, or direct subsidies to specific firms.[19]

The deviations from Madisonian republicanism ran deeper still. In the essay "British Governments," written for the *National Gazette* in 1792, Madison argued that the "boasted equilibrium" of the British system "is maintained less by the distribution of its powers, than by the force of public opinion." If the people wanted a truly republican form of government, the king would have no choice but to yield to their demand. The United States, Madison argued in "Spirit of Government," was different, for its energy was derived "from the will of society, and operating by the reason of its measures, on the understanding and interest of the society." In time, Madison knew that any state, "operating by corrupt influence," could enervate the republican spirit of the nation, but he trusted there was time to call upon the love of liberty that still lived within the people. Calhoun, on the other hand, was not calling upon public opinion to vindicate the principles of the Revolution. Rather, he was trying to limit the sovereignty of the public. Nullification would allow the few to outvote the many, which stood in direct contrast to the principles upon which Madison argued the government had been founded.[20]

Considering Calhoun's promising start as a nationalist, it is hard not to be disappointed by his descent into sectionalism in the latter half of his career. One wonders what kind of statesman he might have been if he had endeavored to keep the South within the main current of American politics. Instead, outraged by the protective tariff, he employed his efforts in the 1820s and 1830s to argue against the popular sovereignty enshrined in the Constitution. And in the 1840s, he redeployed his theory of nullification as a bulwark for slavery, the vilest institution in the nation's history.

It is especially frustrating because Calhoun's critique of the protective tariff was extremely incisive, illustrating a formidable problem posed by the Hamiltonian-Madisonian synthesis. In its original Hamiltonian version, mediation lent itself to oligarchy: government benefits were distributed to a select few who, thanks to their close relationships with politicians or formal grants of power, were able to acquire political power they would not otherwise have possessed in a republic. The postwar tariff, on the other hand, was a more egalitarian use of mediation, as it distributed benefits broadly across society. This did not eliminate the danger of corruption; rather, it altered its nature. The tariff was abused not by a select few but by what Madison in *Federalist* 10 called a "majoritarian faction," a group united by its desire to enrich itself at the expense of the minority and the general welfare. Such factions were supposed to be too difficult to form in a diverse republic, but the strategy of mediation, employed on a grand enough scale, gave otherwise disparate parties an opportunity to bargain with one another. For all of Calhoun's many mistakes, he rightly understood that this is indeed corruption of republican government, albeit not in the manner we usually think of it today. In contemporary parlance, "corruption" usually implies the sacrifice of the public interest for the sake of wealth or prestige—in other words, oligarchy. But a republic is corrupted when the public interest is sacrificed for *any* other interest. What Calhoun saw in the 1820s was the makings of not an oligarchy but, rather, an ochlocracy.

Such majority factions, as Madison knew, are extremely dangerous to popular government. Whereas an oligarchy can be rooted out by popular elections, ochlocracy is actually fueled by the principle of majority rule. In the original Hamiltonian approach to public policy, this was not a large concern; the scope of mediation was so narrow that a majority of the public could not benefit from special government considerations. But after Madison and the Republicans enlarged the number of groups to be brought under the umbrella of government patronage, mob rule became a distinct possibility. Calhoun was so distraught over this development that he swung from being a nationalist to being a sectionalist. For all his many other failings, he was right to be worried.

If an extended sphere could no longer protect majority factions from abusing the principle of mediation, what could? According to Madison, there was one final safeguard: public opinion, the "only true sovereign" in a free government. The people could abuse the powers of the state to advance their parochial interests at the expense of the common good, but, alternatively, they could heed the sort of call to unity that Madison had made in the *National Gazette*. They could extract from their neighbors everything they could get, or they could remember that virtuous citizens must refrain from such abuses. Unfortunately, Calhoun chose to promote parochialism, sectionalism, and divisiveness—thereby inflaming the very sorts of passions he was so anxious about. This us-versus-them attitude would dominate politics after the Civil War and facilitate grave abuses of the Hamiltonian-Madisonian synthesis.

THE SITUATION FOR the South was not as hopeless as Calhoun believed, for the region still had some political chips left to play. In 1829, Senator Robert Hayne of South Carolina tried to peel the West away from the North by throwing the South's weight behind a liberal land policy. This was a priority of the West, but the North feared its population would be drained away as a consequence. In December, Senator Samuel Foote of Connecticut proposed limiting the sale of public lands, which drew the ire of Thomas Hart Benton of Missouri, who tied the issue to the tariff; the implication was that northern industrialists were harming both the South (by forcing artificially high prices for its wares) *and* the West (by preventing migration to keep the labor supply cheap). Hayne, who had been working with Benton to develop an alternative coalition, jumped into the debate to support a speedy and cheap dispersal of the lands.

This incipient coalition was thwarted by Daniel Webster, who artfully blocked the alliance by invoking the specter of disunion. His famous second reply to Hayne, written with the newspaper-reading public in mind, turned the political question of regional alliances into a constitutional debate over whether South Carolina's nullification plan was an affront to the nation. Webster extolled the virtues of the Union with the full force of his rhetorical power. "While the Union lasts," he said, "we have high, exciting, gratifying prospects spread out before us and our children. Beyond that

I seek not to penetrate the veil. God grant that in my day, at least, that curtain may not rise!"[21]

Eloquence notwithstanding, Webster's maneuver was only a temporary expedient. In 1832, South Carolina, following Calhoun's arguments, declared the Tariff of Abominations null and void. This brinksmanship infuriated President Jackson, but it also served as the catalyst for a durable compromise. Clay and Calhoun came together to negotiate the Tariff of 1833, which slowly scaled rates down over the next decade. By then, Hayne and Benton's South-West political coalition had ripened, and the Democratic party came to stand for low tariffs and aggressive expansionist policies. As a consequence, tariff rates would remain reasonable until the Civil War.

That conflict saw the North and the West once again join together in a political coalition. And the abuses of the protective tariff would return, worse than ever. The architects of the new tariff would stitch together a massive coalition in its favor, one that—despite the South's protestations against the injustice of the system—would endure to the Great Depression. Calhoun was right that the South could "be made tributary" to the other regions, but it happened after the Civil War, not before it.

CONCLUSION

DURING THE EARLY years of the new nation, the task of securing the principles of liberalism, republicanism, and nationalism faced two distinct challenges. The first was to design an instrument of government that enshrined these ideals. This project was advanced by the ratification of the Constitution, a document that united the thirteen states into a single union premised on the rule of the people, and a Bill of Rights to guarantee civil and religious liberty. Though the debate about the particular meaning of this or that clause of the Constitution continued during this period (and persists into our own), there was a widespread consensus at the time that it provided a secure framework for the American project.

But filling in that framework with public policy—the second task—was a different challenge altogether. The Founders quickly divided over how to accomplish it in a way that was consistent with their political principles, and the dispute lasted for more than a generation. The primary difficulty was in reconciling their republican scruples to their nationalist ambitions.

Alexander Hamilton wanted to develop the national economic marketplace by transforming the moneyed class into mediators of the national interest. His system called for favoring this select group in order to fortify the currency, build a financial infrastructure, spur economic diversification, and eventually generate prosperity for all. His plan was ingeniously nationalistic and largely successful on its own terms, but it had negative effects on the republican project. With its relentless favoritism toward the wealthy few, it created a policy imbalance that offended James Madison's political philosophy. Madison held that though many of the principles of Hamilton's program were more or less sound, its benefits should have been more broadly distributed across society.

Moreover, Madison detected a dynamic relationship between economic benefits and political power. The clique of speculators that Hamilton favored did not sit idly by as the treasury secretary developed his program. Taking advantage of inside information, they plunged further into their ventures and extorted immediate assumption of the state debts from their opponents. They were able to do this because many legislators were themselves invested in public certificates; when Hamilton proposed to favor the speculators, he created for the legislators a conflict between the interests of their constituents and the interests of their pocketbooks. Ultimately, Madison and the opponents of assumption had no choice but to relent. But that was not the end of the story. Hamilton's program was premised on maintaining a stable price for government securities, which meant that the government was, in a sense, bound to those who owned the public debt. Within a year after Hamilton's program was passed, not one but two manias began, and in both cases the secretary felt obliged to stabilize the market by bailing out the bulls with money from the sinking fund.

Madison considered this to be corruption of republican government, substituting the sovereignty of the people for the rule of the rich. In private correspondence to Thomas Jefferson, he called the speculators "the praetorian band of the government—at once its tool and its tyrant; bribed by its largesses, and overawing it, by clamors and combinations." This description was not far from the mark. Hamilton had hoped his financial program would rope the interests of the moneyed class to the government, and it did, but the opposite also happened. The wealthy transformed their bounties into real power over public policy, guiding it toward their own ends rather than toward the demands of the general welfare.[1]

Hamilton's system, favorable as it was to the commercial class, was not well suited to a still mostly agrarian America. In due course, the Republican Party—the political vehicle Madison and Jefferson used to mobilize the people against Hamilton—took control of the national government and initiated a second effort at balancing the competing ideals in the founding creed. They cut taxes, reduced military expenditures, and promoted territorial expansion. Jefferson and Madison saw the future of the country as largely agricultural, pushing farther and farther into the western frontier. For a while this endeavor seemed to work, but its success was illusory, dependent mostly upon British toleration of American shipping. When Britain returned to war with the French, it clamped down on American merchants, prompting a diplomatic crisis that led ultimately to the War of 1812, a conflict for which the United States was wholly unprepared. The military was understaffed and poorly equipped, the country lacked good roads to move men and matériel, and the government—having foregone Hamiltonian finance—had no ability to borrow money reliably and at low interest rates. A combination of luck and American panache kept the nation from embarrassing itself, but Republican leaders realized that they had to adopt a more aggressive course of national development.

For this, President Madison returned to Hamilton's old program—and not just to his policy specifics. He embraced the strategy of mediation, which he had once decried, but he and the Republicans made substantial political modifications to Hamilton's economic prescriptions. They broadened the scope of mediation so that each policy was designed to benefit more people directly and the total benefits would accrue to all major economic and regional groups in society.

When Madison left office in 1817, there seemed to be a sensible middle ground between the extremes of Republican simplicity and Federalist elitism. In his final years as president, he had enacted a modestly protective tariff whose purpose was to develop domestic industries for the sake of national security, chartered the Second Bank of the United States, and advocated federal involvement in internal improvements. James Monroe's overwhelming victories in 1816 and 1820 testified to the broad popularity of this hybrid program.

Yet over the course of the 1820s and 1830s, the problems of this fusion were made evident. The features of oligarchy, which had begun to emerge in the 1790s, returned once more. Though Hamilton's First Bank of the United States had performed ably during its twenty-year tenure, the Second Bank was a cesspool during its early years, and in its final years Nicholas Biddle—an able financier but a terrible politician—used the power of the institution to create a recession that, he hoped, would induce President Andrew Jackson to sanction its recharter. In both these instances, the Second Bank embodied the worries Madison had expressed thirty years prior when he opposed it: that it would become an institution unto itself, using its federal authority to advance its own interests rather than the nation's.

Moreover, the Federalist-Republican synthesis facilitated a different kind of corruption by encouraging a sort of mob rule, or governance by a majority faction for its own ends rather than for the good of the nation. In the 1790s, Madison's problem was that Hamilton was dispensing benefits to the few at the expense of the many, so he and the postwar Republicans sought to broaden the scope of potential mediators. But this had the effect of creating opportunities for what John Taylor of Caroline aptly called "polygamist" coalitions, disparate interests united only by their common desire for self-enrichment. This problem manifested itself primarily with the protective tariff. Though a transregional coalition had approved the Tariff of 1816, the Tariff of 1824 was highly sectional by nature, as was the Tariff of 1828. This last measure—the so-called Tariff of Abominations—was a parochial push for self-enrichment, spurred on by partisan angling for the presidency. It was a "popular" bill, in the sense that a majority of representatives believed their constituents would gain something from it, but it failed to advance the national welfare and did material damage to the South. John C. Calhoun—himself one of the architects of the Federalist-Republican synthesis—was so appalled by the nature of the postwar tariff that he abandoned much of his old nationalism. Ultimately, he decided that the only way to protect the nation from the factional designs of a numerical majority was a near-absolute veto for states over federal legislation.

Thus, by the time of Madison's death in 1836, the country had succeeded in framing an instrument of government that was broadly consistent with the principles of liberalism, republicanism, and nationalism, but it had not yet developed a political economy that did the same.

DESPITE ITS FAULTS, the Federalist-Republican fusion turned out to be very durable. Between the Civil War and the Great Depression, policy makers, particularly in the Republican Party of Abraham Lincoln, proposed protective tariffs and internal improvements as the way to promote national development in a fair, republican manner. They frequently won electoral majorities on these pledges, but the reality rarely matched the rhetoric. Instead, the civic problems of the 1790s and the 1820s–1830s grew substantially worse than anybody from those earlier eras could have imagined.

By the end of the nineteenth century, the tariff had become a massive logroll. Its main beneficiaries were the industries that had to compete with foreign manufacturers, but the scope of the coalition was broadened substantially to build a political majority. Certain agricultural products were brought onboard to secure the support of key midwestern voters. On top of that, the revenue from the tariff was used to fund a pension program for Union veterans, who were well represented by the Grand Army of the Republic, a powerful lobbying organization that sprang up after the Civil War. In this way, the tariff was an effective political instrument used by the Republican Party, but it failed to serve any nationwide economic purpose.[2]

Worse, the tariff harmed the farmers of the Great Plains and the planters of the South, who were burdened with a higher cost of living. Under Jackson, the Democratic Party had once been ambivalent regarding the tariff, but by the 1840s it had become the home of those who counted themselves as losers in this great scheme. The party's 1892 platform rejected the tariff system in uncompromising terms:

> We denounce Republican protection as a fraud, a robbery of the great majority of the American people for the benefit of the few. We declare it to be a fundamental principle of the Democratic Party that the Federal Government has no constitutional power to impose and collect tariff duties, except for the purpose of revenue only, and we demand that the collection of such taxes shall be limited to the necessities of the Government when honestly and economically administered.[3]

This reads like a verse from the ancient Republican hymnal. Under the Constitution, the government is authorized only to lay and collect taxes for "the general welfare." The protective system was not consistent with this purpose, by the party's logic; instead, it rewarded Republican voters at the expense of Democratic voters. Unfortunately for those on the outside looking in, the tariff coalition was a majority faction, meaning that reform efforts usually ended in failure. It was only the Great Depression that destroyed public support for the tariff regime, because the Smoot-Hawley Tariff of 1930—the most onerous since the Tariff of Abominations—was widely believed to have worsened the economic crisis.[4]

The tariff was propped up by a majority faction, but it had oligarchic qualities as well. Its gains were primarily concentrated among wealthy industrialists, who plied legislators with all sorts of kickbacks to protect the regime. Consider the case of Nelson Aldrich, Republican senator from Rhode Island from 1881 until 1911. He is rightly celebrated for his role in drafting the Federal Reserve Act, which finally filled the vacuum created by Jackson's reckless destruction of the Second Bank. But Aldrich was also "the commercial ideal of a political character," as muckraker Lincoln Steffens argued, and the faithful defender of the protective tariff for thirty years. There was nobody in the Senate who understood its arcane rate schedules better, and time and again he could be counted on to thwart House-driven efforts to reform the regime. As progressive journalist David Graham Phillips put it, Aldrich was "the head of it all."[5]

By the 1890s, a senator's life had lost its appeal to Aldrich, who dreamed of owning a fine estate on Warwick Neck, Rhode Island. His retirement would have been calamitous for the great concatenation of business interests that profited from the tariff. No interest depended on the tariff more than the American Sugar Refining Company. It needed the rates on raw sugar kept low, which the cane growers in Louisiana hated, and rates on refined sugar kept high, which burdened consumers and contributed to the embarrassingly high surplus in the federal coffers. It was essential to have a fixer like Aldrich in the Senate, so John Searles, the company's chief lobbyist, made Aldrich an offer he could not refuse. Searles would stake roughly $6 million to form the United Traction and Electric Company, which would modernize street railways in Rhode Island. Aldrich would become president of the company, despite investing none of his own money. All he had to do was supply the votes in the Rhode Island legislature to grant the company a new franchise. It was thus a certain winner, and $100 par value shares sold for $40 in 1896 and $110 in 1901. Aldrich became a millionaire many times over, just as he had always dreamed of, and he remained in the Senate, protecting the interests of the trusts for another decade.[6]

Aldrich was hardly alone. The list of politicians who were bought off by the great industrial trusts during this period was seemingly endless: Simon and Donald Cameron, Matthew Quay, Philander Knox, and Boies Penrose of Pennsylvania; Thomas Platt and Chauncey Depew of New York; Richard Allison of Missouri; John Spooner of Wisconsin; William Foraker, Marcus Hanna, and John Sherman of Ohio; and more. In 1912 William Randolph Hearst published the "Standard Oil Letters," which showed how a representative for John D. Rockefeller's massive concern traded campaign contributions and personal kickbacks for governmental favors. The tariff was at the foundation of the relationship—it provided the money that businesses and politicians needed—but as

Hearst's scoop demonstrated, the conflicts of interest stretched far beyond trade policy, reaching even into the smallest matters of state politics. US senators whom Standard Oil purchased were expected to use their influence to pressure state and local politicians on any issue of concern to Rockefeller.[7]

And the corruption extended beyond just the tariff and the trusts. Federal sponsorship of internal improvements eventually helped create a spectacular network of railroads that crisscrossed the continent, but it also corrupted the legislative process for the sake of the rich. Railroad tycoons who built their companies on government loans used just a small slice of their fortunes to purchase the support of politicians to ensure that the government would continue to bless them. James G. Blaine, the Republican nominee for president in 1884 and one of the most charismatic politicians of the Gilded Age, was a key ally of the railroads. In 1877, when several railroads had failed to repay overdue government loans worth $65 million, Senator Allen Thurman of Ohio introduced legislation to impose a schedule of repayment. But Jay Gould of the Union Pacific and Collis Huntington of the Central Pacific called on Blaine to defeat it, which is precisely what he did. This prompted Senator George Edmunds of Vermont to complain bitterly:

> It is my opinion that Mr. Blaine acts as the attorney of Jay Gould. Whenever Mr. Thurman and I have settled upon legislation to bring the Pacific railroads to terms of equity with the government, up has jumped James G. Blaine, musket in hand, from behind the breastworks of Gould's lobby, to fire at our backs.[8]

Blaine was always well compensated for his troubles. In 1869, for instance, he secured a land grant for a southern railroad, and as a gratuity he received $150,000 in land and bonds to sell to his friends. When the venture went belly up, Thomas Scott, president of the mighty Pennsylvania Railroad, bought the stock from Blaine at a price far greater than the market value. The kickback became public knowledge prior to the 1876 presidential campaign and damaged Blaine's efforts to win the Republican nomination that year.[9]

Blaine was hardly the sole politician in the pocket of the railroads. The Crédit Mobilier scandal, which the *New York Sun* crowned "the King of Frauds," ensnared dozens of government officials, including Vice President Schuyler Colfax, future vice president Henry Wilson, and future president James Garfield. The managers of the Union Pacific Railroad created a dummy corporation named Crédit Mobilier to do construction work, at a handsome profit for its owners. As a way to hide this fraud from the government (the Union Pacific, after all, had been incorporated by the federal government in 1862), its managers contracted Representative Oakes Ames of Massachusetts to sell stock in Crédit Mobilier to members of Congress. There was little initial interest in the shares, but when Ames allowed members to buy stock with no money down, so long as they forfeited the first dividend payment, he set off a scramble. The newspapers blew the lid off the scheme, but Congress quickly put it back on. The ensuing investigation found Ames guilty of buying congressional influence, but no member of Congress was found guilty of selling it.[10]

All of this was similar to what Madison had feared about Hamiltonian mediation, but on a much grander scale. Directing some benefit to a particular faction of society has the potential to corrupt the power relations of republican government, as that faction has an incentive to mobilize to maximize its gains from the state, even if the bounties are not in the interest of the public. And because legislators are so often governed by personal ambition and greed, they are easy marks for such factions. Men like Aldrich and Blaine were charged with exercising their authority on behalf of the public, but they misused that power to satisfy their personal greed.

This corruption inspired reform movements throughout the late nineteenth and early twentieth centuries. The most prominent group was the Progressive Party, led by former president Theodore Roosevelt, whose 1912 platform had a decidedly Madisonian flavor. It declared, "Behind the ostensible government sits enthroned an invisible government owing no allegiance and acknowledging no responsibility to the people." The Progressives offered an ambitious series of proposals "to destroy this invisible government" and "dissolve the unholy alliance between corrupt business and corrupt politics"—including by reforming the tariff code along "scientific" principles, regulating business, and installing protections for workers. In *The Promise of American Life,* Herbert Croly, one of the premier intellectuals of the progressive movement, characterized this approach as employing Hamiltonian means for Jeffersonian ends.[11]

But Croly overlooked a crucial point. The second generation of Republicans, led by Madison, thought they were doing *precisely that* after the War of 1812 when they implemented these now-inequitable policies in the first place. They thought they could repurpose the Hamiltonian machine for Republican ends, but they were wrong. Instead, a century later it had become clear that their fusion had in fact laid the groundwork for the corruption that the Progressives were struggling against.

FOR ALL ITS high drama, the battle between Madison and Hamilton can be understood through a more modern framework too, that of *public-choice economics,* which applies economic theories to the problems of politics and governance. Public-choice economists are particularly interested in how public goods are produced. Because everybody can enjoy public goods, and because one person's enjoyment of them does not interfere with another's, no single individual has an incentive to actually produce them. Instead, it is in everybody's interest to sit back, let others do the hard work, and just enjoy the results; however, if everybody does that, then the goods will not be produced. This is where the government comes into play. There are many ways it can facilitate the production of public goods; one strategy is to offer private subsidies to factions or groups capable of creating them, thus getting around the problem of free riding. This was, in effect, what Hamiltonian mediation was intended to do: incentivize the wealthy to create a sound currency and a diversified economy, which would be good for everybody.

Again, borrowing from the language of public-choice economics, this strategy produces *negative externalities,* or bad side effects significant enough to compromise the original policy. Mediation is really a form of outsourcing national projects to groups that themselves do not necessarily share the same nationalistic viewpoint, and side benefits are provided to make it worthwhile for the factions to provide the service. But as we have seen, government benefits can often become interchangeable with political power, enabling those groups to wield authority that they would not otherwise have possessed. So one negative externality of mediation is corruption of republican government, as the state behaves according to the interests of the faction rather than of the people at large. The corruption can happen through the law itself—for instance, when a public charter or other government license disrupts the balance of power in the republic. It can also happen informally, via conflicts of interests that legislators feel between the public good and their own personal loyalties. When the faction that gains control is a majority of the nation, the sort of corruption that occurs is what the classical republicans called mob rule or ochlocracy, what Madison called majority factionalism. When it is a minority, the corruption is oligarchy, rule by the wealthy. Historically, mediation has been more likely to facilitate oligarchy, but in some cases—for instance, in the case of the Tariff of Abominations—it has created majority factions that barter among themselves for their own benefit. Either way, this is a corruption of the republican form of government.[12]

That the fight between Madison and Hamilton can be restated in the rather dry language of economics demonstrates that it was more than just a momentary clash of personalities. Instead, it illustrates a paradox at the heart of the American constitutional order. Our Constitution simultaneously promotes the notions of liberalism, republicanism, and nationalism. "We the people" are to form a "more perfect union," yet the sorts of policies that strengthen our national fiber can also diminish the republican character of our government, most often in ways that redound to the benefit of the wealthy.

This dynamic is more evident today than ever before. We have a government that over the last hundred years has taken on a large number of nationalistic endeavors, primarily by promoting economic growth, continuing to develop the national infrastructure, and building a military force superior to those of the nation's enemies. Moreover, the liberal project has evolved since the New Deal, as well. In the Founding era, rights were understood in a negative sense: the government would leave you alone to enjoy your property, speak your mind, and worship God as you please. But in the twentieth century, rights have taken on a positive cast: the government takes responsibility for providing a minimum standard of living for those who cannot maintain it themselves. For all of these tasks, mediation is the primary tool employed by the government. How is economic growth promoted? By creating incentives for business owners. How is our overawing military properly equipped? By contracting weapons manufactures. How is medical care for seniors provided? By reimbursing doctors and hospitals. How is housing promoted? By encouraging home builders and financial-service institutions. The government does not build MRI machines, fighter jets, or homes. It pays people to do that, employing them as mediators between the state and the people.

Yet for all of the ostensible public-spiritedness in today's government, we the people have a stark lack of confidence in the republican project. Average citizens do not feel as though the government really represents them. Instead, it seems to speak for the "special interests"—in the terms of this book, the mediators. Even though we are all entitled to vote for federal offices on the second Tuesday of November in even-numbered years, it seems as though the government does not much belong to us.

This is one reason why the story of Madison and Hamilton remains vital, more than 180 years after they perished. Our anxieties about our government, our fights over what it should do and how it should do it, our recriminations and suspicions about each other's motives—these resemble the battle between the two founders, so long ago. Madison and Hamilton debated how to keep our national ambitions and our republican principles properly ordered; today, we still feel as if we do not have a good balance between these values.

How can we rediscover that equilibrium? There is a raft of potential policy fixes that could help root out corruption from the government: reforming campaign finance, tightening restrictions on lobbyists, devolving more power to the states, encouraging greater civic participation, and so on. These are all fine ideas, but corruption is not a problem that simply needs a few policy tweaks. It requires consideration of the larger framework of what Montesquieu called "the spirit of the laws"—or how law relates to a nation, its people, and its form of government.

The classical republicans believed that corruption was an endemic feature of any unmixed commonwealth. According to Cicero, each type of good government (monarchy, aristocracy, and democracy) "has a path—a sheer and slippery one—to a kindred evil" (tyranny, oligarchy, or mob rule). Roman historian Polybius expanded on this idea to develop a cycle through which he believed all governments pass: from monarchy to tyranny, aristocracy, oligarchy, democracy, and finally mob rule, in a perpetual process of "growth, zenith, and decadence." As a consequence, Machiavelli advised "prudent legislators" to refrain "from adopting any one of those forms" and to instead create a system that included the rule of the one, the few, and the many; "such a government would be stronger and more stable," for the defects of each form would be countered by the virtues of the others. The republican revolution brought about by the Founders was to dispense with such mixed estates and found a government solely on the authority of the people at large.[13]

How can corruption be arrested or reversed, once it has begun to set in? According to Machiavelli, the solution is to make changes "for their conservation which lead them back to their origins." He analogized the corruption of a republic to the decay of a physical body due to age, and he suggested that the way to reverse civic degeneration was "to return to its original principles," thereby "restor[ing] the prestige that it had at the outset." In Madison's view, "no government is perhaps reducible to a sole principle of operation"; rather, "different and often heterogeneous principles mingle their influence in the administration," akin to what Montesquieu called the "spirit which predominates in each."[14]

In a suggested preamble to the Constitution, Madison offered a comprehensive view of the principles upon which the United States was founded:

> That all power is originally vested in, and consequently derived from the people.
>
> That government is instituted, and ought to be exercised for the benefit of the people; which consists in the enjoyment of life and liberty, with the right of acquiring and using property, and generally of pursuing and obtaining happiness and safety.
>
> That the people have an indubitable, unalienable, and indefeasible right to reform or change their government, whenever it be found adverse or inadequate to the purposes of its institution.

In this proposal, Madison made explicit the three principles that combine to form the spirit of the laws in the United States: nationalism, liberalism, and republicanism. The people of the United States—bound together in a single nation—are free because the government respects their rights and because they participate in the creation of the laws that govern them.[15]

Purging our government of corruption, therefore, requires us to return to these three principles—but not in some vague, anodyne sense of gratitude. Instead, we have to reengage with them and relearn critical lessons that seem to have been forgotten. To start, we must appreciate that the Constitution did not settle the relationship among liberalism, republicanism, and nationalism for all time. Public policy, in all forms, necessarily advances or hinders each principle. Though we typically do not think of contemporary political questions in these foundational terms, Madison understood this, and we should follow his example.

We must also remember that these values are often in tension with one another. Republicanism and liberalism come from different traditions of political thought. They overlap in some ways but conflict in others. And nationalism is different altogether; a strong nation need not be either republican or liberal. Thus, holding these three values in their proper balance has to be a constant struggle. Neither Madison or Hamilton "solved" the problem, for it is a paradox that admits of no final answer. But both are to be credited for trying to solve it, for in so doing they helped bring about a better understanding of how government functions in practice. We the people must endeavor to do likewise.

We should further appreciate that the republican quality of government has proven itself to be the most difficult to maintain over the generations. Our government vigorously pursues all sorts of national endeavors, and individual rights—both negative and positive—are more respected than ever before, but it feels as though our government has been hijacked from the people. It is easy to assume that our country is a republic because elections are free and open to all adult citizens, but this is a mistake. As Madison noted in the *National Gazette,* it is possible for a government to "support a real domination of the few, under an apparent liberty of the many. Such a government, wherever to be found, is an imposter." Madison appreciated that the policies that Hamilton was promoting were undermining the principle of popular sovereignty, even though they had no effect on the form of government. We must remain mindful of this and appreciate that policies that advance the national project or the liberal project must *also* remain consistent with the republican principles that are just as essential to the American creed.[16]

Above all, we should remember that sovereignty ultimately belongs to the people, and if we wish the government to become more republican, we ourselves must rediscover that lost tradition. As Madison put it, "the force of public opinion" is what maintains government in practice. "If the nation were in favor of absolute monarchy, the public liberty would soon be surrendered by their representatives. If a republican form of government were preferred, how could the monarch resist the national will?" We get the government we deserve, in other words. So when the American people demand a return to republican propriety, the government will acquiesce, for "public opinion sets bounds to every government, and is the real sovereign in every free one."[17]

ACKNOWLEDGMENTS

I WOULD LIKE to thank my wife, Lindsay, for her years of encouragement and feedback. Thanks to Nathan Tarcov, Mark Hansen, and James Wilson for their outstanding assistance on this project. Thanks to Dan Gerstle of Basic Books for his superb editorial guidance. Thanks to my parents, John and Lyn Cost, for their enduring commitment to my education. Thanks to Dan and Kaye McKenzie, for helping me in innumerable ways. Thanks to Jeffrey Anderson, Patrick Colby, Eric Cost, Eric Jantsch, Roger Kimball, Yuval Levin, Scott Lincicome, Matthew Mitchell, Mike Needham, Richard Samuelson, Bradford Wilson, Dan Wilson, Jean Yarbrough, and Andy Zwick, all of whom offered feedback, support, or both at critical junctures during the researching and writing of this book.

ABBREVIATIONS

Individuals

AG	Albert Gallatin
AH	Alexander Hamilton
EP	Edmund Pendleton
ER	Edmond Randolph
GW	George Washington
HC	Henry Clay
JCC	John C. Calhoun
JM	James Madison
JMe	James Monroe
JQA	John Quincy Adams
NB	Nicholas Biddle
TJ	Thomas Jefferson

Collections

AC *Annals of Congress.* Compiled by Joseph Gales. First Congress–Eighteenth Congress. Washington, DC: Gales and Seaton, 1834–1856. http://memory.loc.gov/ammem/amlaw/lwaclink.html.

AP *The Avalon Project: Documents in Law, History, and Diplomacy.* Yale University Law School. http://avalon.law.yale.edu.

APP *The American Presidency Project.* Edited by Gerhard Peters and

John T. Woolley. Accessed August 26, 2016. www.presidency .ucsb.edu.

ASP *American State Papers, Finance.* Edited by Walter Lowrie et al. 5 vols. Washington, DC: Gales and Seaton, 1832–1858.

CNB *The Correspondence of Nicholas Biddle Dealing with National Affairs, 1807–1844.* Edited by Reginald C. McGrane. Boston: Houghton Mifflin, 1919.

LSHC *The Life and Speeches of Henry Clay.* Compiled by Daniel Malloy. 2 vols. New York: Robert P. Bixby, 1844.

MJQA *Memoirs of John Quincy Adams.* Edited by Charles Francis Adams. 12 vols. Philadelphia: J. P. Lippincott, 1874–1877.

PAH *The Papers of Alexander Hamilton.* Edited by Harold C. Syrett et al. 26 vols. New York: Columbia University Press, 1961–1979. http://founders.archives.gov.

PGW *The Papers of George Washington.* Edited by Donald Jackson et al. Charlottesville: University Press of Virginia, 1976–. http:// founders.archives.gov.

PJM *The Papers of James Madison.* Edited by William T. Hutchinson et al. Chicago: University of Chicago Press; Charlottesville: University Press of Virginia, 1962–. http://founders.archives.gov.

PTJ *The Papers of Thomas Jefferson.* Edited by Julian P. Bond et al. Princeton: Princeton University Press, 1950–. http://founders .archives.gov.

RD *Register of Debates in Congress.* Compiled by Joseph Gales. Eighteenth Congress–Twenty-Fifth Congress. Washington, DC: Gales and Seaton, 1824–1837. http://memory.loc.gov/ammem /amlaw/lwrdlink.html.

WAG *The Writings of Albert Gallatin.* Edited by Henry Adams. 3 vols. Philadelphia: J. B. Lippincott. http://oll.libertyfund.org.

WTJ *The Works of Thomas Jefferson*, edited by Paul Leicester Ford. 12 vols. New York: G. P. Putnam's Sons, 1904. http://oll.liberty fund.org

NOTES

INTRODUCTION

1. Articles of Confederation, *AP*.

2. Stanley M. Elkins and Eric L. McKitrick, *The Age of Federalism* (New York: Oxford University Press, 1993), 234. For defenses of Madison, see, for instance, Adrienne Koch, *Madison's "Advice to My Country"* (Princeton: Princeton University Press, 1966), 116; Ralph Ketcham, *James Madison: A Biography* (Charlottesville: University Press of Virginia), 314–315; Marvin Meyers, ed., *The Mind of the Founder: Sources of the Political Thought of James Madison* (Hanover, MA: Brandeis University Press, 1973), xlii; and Garrett Ward Sheldon, *The Political Philosophy of James Madison* (Baltimore: Johns Hopkins University Press, 2001), xiv. Scholars in the Madisonian camp have also highlighted philosophical differences between Madison and Hamilton, endeavoring to distill the "Madisonian Madison," distinct from the Hamiltonian caricature. The most comprehensive such effort is Lance Banning, *The Sacred Fire of Liberty: James Madison and the Founding of the Federal Republic* (Ithaca, NY: Cornell University Press, 1998). See also Alan Gibson, "Madison's 'Great Desideratum': Impartial Administration and the Extended Republic," *American Political Thought* 1, no. 2 (Fall 2012): 181–207; Alan Gibson, "The Madisonian Madison and the Question of Consistency: The Significance and Challenge of Recent Research," *Review of Politics* 64, no. 2 (Spring 2002): 311–338; and Colleen A. Sheehan, "Madison v. Hamilton: The Battle Over Republicanism and the Role of Public Opinion," *American Political Science Review* 98, no. 3 (August 2004): 405–424.

3. Declaration of Independence, *AP;* and Virginia Declaration of Rights, *AP*.

4. Cicero, *"On the Commonwealth" and "On the Laws,"* ed. James E. G. Zetzel (Cambridge: Cambridge University Press, 2010), 18; and JM,

Federalist 14, *PJM* 10. See Aristotle, *Politics,* trans. Ernest Barker (Oxford: Oxford University Press, 1995), 156–160; Machiavelli, *The Discourses,* ed. Bernard Crick (New York: Penguin Books, 1998), 109; and Montesquieu, *The Spirit of the Laws,* ed. Anne M. Cohler, Basia C. Miller, and Harold S. Stone (Cambridge: Cambridge University Press, 1989), 70 and 156–166.

5. See Colleen Sheehan, *The Mind of James Madison: The Legacy of Classical Republicanism* (Cambridge: Cambridge University Press), 29–30.

6. "The founders wandered the unmarked borderlands between classical republicanism and liberalism, scavenging for building materials. The specific materials selected on each foray depended upon the nature of the problem and upon the mood of the scavenger." Carl Richard, *The Founders and the Classics: Greece, Rome, and the American Enlightenment* (Cambridge, MA: Harvard University Press, 1994), 6. See also Lance Banning, *Jefferson and Madison: Three Conversations from the Founding* (Lanham, MD: Rowman and Littlefield, 1995), 57–102.

7. AH, *Federalist* 11, *PAH* 4; and Andrew Burstein and Nancy Isenberg, "Mike Lee's Bad History," *Salon,* June 17, 2017, www.salon.com/2017/06/17 /mike-lees-bad-history-utah-senators-book-is-an-ignorant-hodgepodge -concocted-to-justify-the-modern-gop.

8. Constitution of the United States, *AP.*

Chapter One: The Great Desideratum

1. See Richard K. Matthews, *If Men Were Angels: James Madison and the Heartless Empire of Reason* (Lawrence: University Press of Kansas, 1995), 17–25.

2. As Adrienne Koch put it, what one makes of Madison's inconsistencies "depends upon the degree of historical imagination brought to the act of criticism—that of sledgehammer literalness? Or something like the tempered subtlety adequate to experience?" Koch, *Madison's "Advice to My Country"* (Princeton: Princeton University Press, 1966), xix–xx.

3. JM, "Vices of the Political System of the United States," *PJM* 9; JM to GW, April 16, 1787, *PJM* 9; and JM, speech of June 6, 1787, *PJM* 10. The best study of Madison's conception of justice as impartiality is Alan Gibson, "Madison's 'Great Desideratum': Impartial Administration and the Extended Republic," *American Political Thought* 1, no. 2 (Fall 2012): 181–207.

4. David Hume, *Political Essays,* ed. Knud Haakonssen (Cambridge: Cambridge University Press, 1994), 20; and JM, *Federalist* 10, *PJM* 10.

5. JM, speech of June 26, 1787, *PJM* 10.

6. JM, *Federalist* 51, *PJM* 10; and JM to William Bradford, January 24, 1774, *PJM* 1.

7. JM, *Federalist 39, PJM* 10; JM to ER, January 10, 1788, *PJM* 10; and JM, *Federalist* 10, *PJM* 10.

8. JM, "Notes for the *National Gazette* Essays," *PJM* 14; JM, *Federalist* 10, *PJM* 10; and JM, speech of June 6, 1787, *PJM* 10.

9. JM, speech of July 17, 1787, *PJM* 10; and JM, speech of June 8, 1787, *PJM* 10. Madison said "he had brought with him into the Convention a strong bias in favor of an enumeration and definition of the powers necessary to be exercised by the national Legislature; but had also brought doubts concerning its practicability." JM, speech of May 31, 1787, *PJM* 10.

10. JM, speech of June 12, 1787, *PJM* 10; and JM, "Observations on Jefferson's Draft of a Constitution for Virginia," *PJM* 11.

11. JM, *Federalist* 10, *PJM* 10; JM, *Federalist* 51, *PJM* 10; JM, "Public Opinion," *PJM* 14; and Greg Weiner, *Madison's Metronome: The Constitution, Majority Rule, and the Tempo of American Politics* (Lawrence: University Press of Kansas, 2012), 40. See also Colleen Sheehan, *James Madison and the Spirit of Republican Self-Government* (Cambridge: Cambridge University Press), 84–124.

12. JM, *Federalist* 10, *PJM* 10.

13. Irving Brant observed, "Though he had no thought of making a gift to posterity, Madison at that moment invented one of the most sacred, most effective and tenacious of American political institutions—the congressional system of logrolling." Irving Brant, *James Madison,* 6 vols. (Indianapolis, IN: Bobbs-Merrill, 1941–1961), 2: 233.

14. JM to ER, April 1, 1783, *PJM* 6. See also JM to TJ, April 22, 1783, *PJM* 6; and JM, "Notes on Debates, 4–5 March 1783," *PJM* 6.

15. JM, speech of April 17, 1789, *PJM* 13. See also JM, speech of April 9, 1789, *PJM* 13.

16. Constitution of the United States, *AP.*

17. JM, "Detached Memoranda," *PJM* Retirement Series 1.

18. JM to William Bradford, January 24, 1774, *PJM* 1; and JM to William Bradford, April 1, 1774, *PJM* 1. See also JM, "Memorial and Remonstrance Against Religious Assessments," *PJM* 8.

19. See, for instance, JM to TJ, January 9, 1785, *PJM* 9; and JM, "Bill for Granting James Rumsey a Patent for Ship Construction," *PJM* 8.

20. JM to EP, January 8, 1782, *PJM* 4.

21. JM, *Federalist* 10, *PJM* 10; and JM, "Vices of the Political System of the United States," *PJM* 9.

22. JM, *Federalist* 51, *PJM* 10.

23. JM, *Federalist* 55, *PJM* 10; and JM, *Federalist* 10, *PJM* 10.

24. JM, "Autobiography," December 1830, *PJM* Early Access Document. Madison has been misrepresented on this issue. Ron Chernow

wrongly stated, "Madison and Henry Lee speculated in land on the Potomac, hoping to earn a windfall profit if the area was chosen for the capital." Ron Chernow, *Alexander Hamilton* (New York: Penguin Books, 2004),
326. Forrest McDonald made a similar claim in his biography of Alexander
Hamilton—a generally fine study of Hamilton's life that is undercut by frequent, thinly sourced speculations about the motivations and character of
Madison and Jefferson. See McDonald, *Alexander Hamilton: A Biography*
(New York: Norton, 1979), 175. Bluntly stated, there is no documentary
evidence to support the claims of Chernow or McDonald, which regards
an investment in Great Falls, Virginia. McDonald, as he so often did with
Madison, chose to read dark designs between the lines of history. And in this
case, he and Chernow both overlook plenty of evidence to dispute the accusation. For starters, there is Madison's unequivocal denial of having engaged
in such a practice, which, considering the generally high esteem he was held
in among his contemporaries, should carry enormous force. Moreover, Lee
had an interest in purchasing this land *before* the Constitution was even
ratified, so the idea that Madison was trying to cash in on the future site of
a capital of a government whose existence was in doubt is dubious. Additionally, according to Ralph Ketcham, Madison ultimately did not make a
full investment. See Ketcham, *James Madison: A Biography* (Charlottesville:
University Press of Virginia), 148. Irving Brant noted that his resources were
tied up in an investment on the Mohawk River in upstate New York and
that "his sole apparent contribution" to the Great Falls investment "was a
panegyric on it, written at Lee's request, for publication in monthly maga-
zines." Brant, *James Madison*, 2: 374. And, most importantly, according to
Dorothy Twohig, the investment had nothing to do with speculating about
the future site of the capital. Rather, "Lee viewed the site as the gateway
to a network of rivers and canals which would bring western trade to the
Potomac region." Twohig, "Editorial Note," JM to GW, November 5, 1788,
PGW Presidential Series 1. Ketcham averred that the investment hinged on
the expectation that the Potomac Canal would be built through the acreage.
In sum, Chernow and McDonald are simply incorrect. Instead, according to
Brant, Madison's limited investment in this project was "unaffected by his
current political activities." Brant, *James Madison*, 2: 374.

25. See JM to ER, April 22, 1787, *PJM* 9; and JM to TJ, August 8,
1791, *PJM* 14.

26. See Brant, *James Madison*, 2: 89–92.

27. JM, "Motion Regarding the Western Lands," *PJM* 2.

28. JM to Joseph Jones, September 19, 1780, *PJM* 2; and JM to Joseph
Jones, November 21, 1780, *PJM* 2.

29. JM to EP, October 30, 1781, *PJM* 3. See also JM to EP, November
13, 1781, *PJM* 3.

Chapter Two: One Great American System

1. AH to James A. Bayard, April 16–21, 1802, *PAH* 25; David Hume, *A Treatise of Human Nature* (New York: Penguin Books, 1985), 22; JM, *Federalist* 10, *PJM* 10; AH, "The Defense of the Funding System," *PAH* 19; and JM, *Federalist* 10, *PJM* 10. See also Michael P. Federici, *The Political Philosophy of Alexander Hamilton* (Baltimore: Johns Hopkins University Press, 2012), 92.

2. AH, "JM's Version of AH's Plan of Government," *PAH* 4; and AH, "Notes on Plan of Government," *PAH* 4.

3. AH, "Robert Yates's Version of AH's Plan of Government," *PAH* 4.

4. Ibid.; and AH, "JM's Version of AH's Plan of Government," *PAH* 4.

5. AH, speech of June 22, 1787, *PAH* 4.

6. David Hume, *Political Essays,* ed. Knud Haakonssen (Cambridge: Cambridge University Press, 1994), 26.

7. AH, speech of June 22, 1787, *PAH* 4; and AH, "John Lansing's Version of AH's Plan of Government," *PAH* 4.

8. See AH, Publius Letters I–III, *PAH* 1.

9. See Lance Banning, *The Jeffersonian Persuasion: Evolution of a Party Ideology* (Ithaca, NY: Cornell University Press, 1978), 16–17.

10. AH, *Federalist* 6, *PAH* 6.

11. AH, *Federalist* 7, *PAH* 6.

12. AH, *Federalist* 8, *PAH* 6.

13. AH, *Federalist* 11, *PAH* 6.

14. AH, *Federalist* 12, *PAH* 6.

15. See Forrest McDonald, *Alexander Hamilton: A Biography* (New York: Norton, 1979), 84–85; and Greg Schofield, "Madison and the Founding of the Two-Party System," in *James Madison: The Theory and Practice of Republican Government,* ed. Samuel Kernell (Stanford: Stanford University Press, 2004), 310–315.

16. See Clinton Rossiter, *Alexander Hamilton and the Constitution* (New York: Harcourt, Brace and World, 1964), 138–141.

17. To be precise, Hamilton's repayment plan did include a very modest reduction in the rate of interest, in exchange for an option for creditors to purchase western lands. For all intents and purposes, this was a "full" repayment, and for the sake of narrative clarity that is the word I will use to describe Hamilton's proposal.

18. AH, "Report on Public Credit," *PAH* 6.

19. Ibid.

20. AH, "Report on a National Bank," *PAH* 7.

21. Ibid. See also AH, "Opinion on the Constitutionality of an Act to Establish a Bank," *PAH* 8.

22. AH to James Duane, September 3, 1780, *PAH* 2; and AH to ———, December 1779–March 1780, *PAH* 2.

23. AH to James Duane, September 3, 1780, *PAH* 2. See also Edward Channing, *A History of the United States,* 6 vols. (New York: Macmillan, 1905–1925), 4: 93; and John Thom Holdsworth and Davis R. Dewey, *The First and Second Banks of the United States* (Washington, DC: Government Printing Office, 1910), 22–23.

24. See AH, "Opinion on the Constitutionality of an Act to Establish a Bank," *PAH* 8.

25. See Douglas Irwin, "The Aftermath of Hamilton's 'Report on Manufactures,'" *Journal of Economic History* 64, no. 3 (September 2004): 800–821.

26. AH, "Report on Manufactures," *PAH* 10.

27. Ibid.

28. Ibid.

29. See AH, "Attendance at a Meeting of the Society for Promoting the Manumission of Slaves," February 4, 1785, *PAH* 3.

Chapter Three: Doing Full Justice

1. AH, speech of November 26, 1782, *PAH* 3; and JM, "Notes on Debate, 26 November 1782," *PJM* 5.

2. JM, speech of September 3, 1789, *PJM* 12.

3. TJ to JM, September 6, 1789, *PJM* 12; and JM to TJ, February 4, 1790, *PJM* 13.

4. JM to ER, March 14, 1790, *PJM* 13; JM, "Money," *PJM* 1; and JM, speech of March 11, 1790, *PJM* 13. Madison would later endorse a more Jeffersonian view in an essay for the *National Gazette,* where he disdained the instrument of "perpetual debts" and recommended "a subjection of each generation to the payment of its own debts." JM, "Universal Peace," *PJM* 14.

5. See James E. Ferguson, *The Power of the Purse* (Chapel Hill: University of North Carolina Press, 1961), 252–257.

6. JM, speech of February 11, 1790, *PJM* 13.

7. Ibid.

8. JM to TJ, February 14, 1790, *PJM* 13.

9. AH, "Report on Public Credit," January 9, 1790, *PAH* 6.

10. The Revolutionary War had a relatively high percentage of "battle deaths" among all soldiers "in theater." See "America's Wars," US Department of Veterans Affairs, May 2016, www.va.gov/opa/publications/fact sheets/fs_americas_wars.pdf.

11. JM, speech of February 24, 1790, *PJM* 13. See Ferguson, *The Power of the Purse*, 306–310.

12. AH, "Report on Public Credit," January 9, 1790, *PAH* 6; Thomas Fitzsimmons, speech of February 8, 1790, *AC* 1: 1177–1179; and JM to EP, March 4, 1790, *PJM* 13. See also Stanley M. Elkins and Eric L. McKitrick, *The Age of Federalism* (New York: Oxford University Press, 1993), 148.

13. JM, speech of February 24, 1790, *PJM* 13; and AG, "A Sketch of the Finances of the United States," *WAG* 3. See "Historical Debt Outstanding—Annual 1790–1849," TreasuryDirect, US Treasury Department, accessed June 30, 2017, www.treasurydirect.gov/govt/reports/pd/histdebt /histdebt_histo1.htm.

14. JM to TJ, July 10, 1791, *PJM* 14.

15. JM, speech of April 22, 1790, *PJM* 13. See also JM, speech of April 25, 1783, *PJM* 6; and JM to Henry Lee, April 13, 1790, *PJM* 13.

16. See Jacob E. Cooke, "The Compromise of 1790," *William and Mary Quarterly* 27, no. 4 (October 1970): 523–545. Cooke also doubts that placing the capital on the Potomac was even part of the compromise.

17. See Ralph Adams Brown, *The Presidency of John Adams* (Lawrence: The University Press of Kansas, 1975), 190.

18. AH to James Duane, September 3, 1780, *PAH* 2.

19. JM, speech of February 8, 1791, *PJM* 13; and JM, "Draft Veto of the Bank Bill," *PJM* 13.

20. JM, "Draft Veto of the Bank Bill," *PJM* 13. See also "The First Bank of the United States: A Chapter in the History of Central Banking," Federal Reserve Bank of Philadelphia, June 2009, www.philadelphiafed.org /publications/economic-education/first-bank.pdf.

21. JM, speech of February 8, 1791, *PJM* 13.

22. JM, *Federalist* 44, *PJM* 10; and AH, "Opinion on the Constitutionality of an Act to Establish a Bank," *PAH* 8. See JM, "Madison Debates," September 14, 1787, *AP*.

23. Nicholas P. Trist, "Memoranda from Montpellier [*sic*], 27 September 1834," in *The Records of the Federal Convention of 1787*, ed. Max Farrand, 3 vols. (New Haven: Yale University Press, 1911), http://oll.libertyfund.org /titles/1787#Farrand_0544–03_1664.

24. JM, speech of April 20, 1789, *PJM* 12; and JQA, *MJQA* 5: 364–365. Madison similarly could read broad powers into the Articles of Confederation. In 1781 Madison supported a congressional resolution that declared Congress had a "general and implied power" to enforce its decrees against recalcitrant states. See JM, "Proposed Amendment of Articles of Confederation," March 12, 1781, *PJM* 3.

25. JM, speech of February 8, 1790, *PJM* 13.

26. JM, speech of April 9, 1789, *PJM* 13. See also JM, speeches of April 21, April 28, and May 4, 1789, *PJM* 13.

27. JM, "Property," *PJM* 14; emphases in original.

28. JM to EP, January 21, 1792, *PJM* 14; emphases in original. Hamilton argued that the phrase "general welfare" was "as comprehensive as any that could have been used; because it was not fit that the constitutional authority of the Union, to appropriate its revenues should have been restricted within narrower limits than the 'General Welfare' and because this necessarily embraces a vast variety of particulars, which are susceptible neither of specification nor of definition." AH, "Final Version of the Report on the Subject of Manufactures," *PAH* 10.

29. See Greg Schofield, "Madison and the Founding of the Two-Party System," in *James Madison: The Theory and Practice of Republican Government,* ed. Samuel Kernell (Stanford: Stanford University Press, 2004), 310–315.

30. JM, speech of April 22, 1790, *PJM* 13.

Chapter Four: The Tool and the Tyrant

1. TJ to Philip Freneau, February 28, 1791, *PTJ* 19.

2. JM, "Public Opinion," *PJM* 14; and JM, *Federalist* 10, *PJM* 10.

3. See, for instance, William Howard Adams, *Gouverneur Morris: An Independent Life* (New Haven: Yale University Press), 226; Edward Channing, *A History of the United States,* 6 vols. (New York: Macmillan, 1905–1925), 4: 98–99; Robert F. Jones, *The King of the Alley: William Duer, Politician, Entrepreneur, and Speculator, 1768–1799* (Philadelphia: American Philosophical Society, 1992), 152–155; and Leonard D. White, *The Federalists: A Study in Administrative History* (New York: Free Press, 1948), 153–195.

4. William Maclay, *The Journal of William Maclay,* ed. Edgar S. Maclay (New York: D. Appleton, 1890), www.constitution.org/ac/maclay/journal .htm. See also Whitney K. Bates, "Northern Speculators and Southern State Debts: 1790," *William and Mary Quarterly* 19, no. 1 (January 1962): 46–47; Charles Beard, *An Economic Interpretation of the Constitution of the United States* (New York: Macmillan, 1921), 89–133, 179, and 195; and Edmund Berkeley and Dorothy Smith Berkeley, *John Beckley: Zealous Partisan in a Nation Divided* (Philadelphia: American Philosophical Society), 86.

5. See "Election for the Directors of the Bank of the United States," *General Advertiser,* 5 January 1792; Bates, "Northern Speculators and Southern State Debts," 38; Joseph Stancliffe Davis, *Essays in the Earlier History of American Corporations, Numbers I–III* (Cambridge, MA: Harvard University Press, 1917), 352–374; Bray Hammond, *Banks and Politics in America*

from the Revolution to the Civil War (Princeton: Princeton University Press, 1957), 127, 125; and Jones, *The King of the Alley,* 159.

6. Craigie quoted in Davis, *Essays in the Earlier History of American Corporations,* 88. See also Archer B. Hulbert, *Andrew Craigie and the Scioto Associates* (Worcester, MA: American Antiquarian Society, 1913); Archer B. Hulbert, "The Methods and Operations of the Scioto Group of Speculators," *Mississippi Valley Historical Review* 1, no. 4 (March 1915): 502–515; and Jones, *The King of the Alley,* 163.

7. Maclay, *The Journal of William Maclay.*

8. Craigie quoted in Anthony J. Connors, "Andrew Craigie: Brief Life of a Patriot and Scoundrel: 1754–1819," *Harvard Magazine,* November 2011, http://harvardmagazine.com/print/33313?page=all; Davis, *Essays in the Earlier History of American Corporations,* 111 and 133–146; and Jones, *The King of the Alley,* 118–121.

9. JM to TJ, December 8, 1788, *PJM* 11.

10. See Bates, "Northern Speculators and Southern State Debts," 39; Beard, *An Economic Interpretation of the Constitution of the United States,* 119; Irving Brant, *James Madison,* 6 vols. (Indianapolis: Bobbs-Merrill, 1941–1961), 3: 300–303; Connors, "Andrew Craigie"; Davis, *Essays in the Earlier History of American Corporations,* 159–168; and Charles Rappleye, *Robert Morris: Financier of the American Revolution* (New York: Simon and Schuster, 2010), 388–389.

11. Craigie quoted in Davis, *Essays in the Earlier History of American Corporations,* 177.

12. See John Catanzariti, "Editorial Note: Jefferson and the Giles Resolutions," *PTJ* 25.

13. See Jacob E. Cooke, "The Compromise of 1790," *William and Mary Quarterly* 27, no. 4 (October 1970): 523–545.

14. See Forrest McDonald, *Alexander Hamilton: A Biography* (New York: Norton, 1979), 171–188. A notable exception is Irving Brant, whose six-volume study of Madison—still the most comprehensive history on the subject—makes careful note of the speculative motives of Madison's opponents. See Brant, *James Madison,* 3: 306–318.

15. Foreigner [pseud.] to JM, February 17 1790, *PJM* 13.

16. Ibid. See also JM to James Madison Sr., February 27, 1790, *PJM* 13.

17. JM, speech of March 3, 1790, *PJM* 13.

18. JM to JMe, July 4, 1790, *PJM* 13.

19. Fitzsimons quoted in Jacob E. Cooke, "The Compromise of 1790," *William and Mary Quarterly* 27, no. 4 (October 1970): 540. See Thomas Fitzsimons, speech of February 8, 1790, *AC,* 1177–1179. Daniel Carroll of Maryland, another advocate of assumption, was likewise distraught over the

vehemence of its most ardent advocates. See James E. Ferguson, *The Power of the Purse* (Chapel Hill: University of North Carolina Press, 1961), 317–318.

20. JM to ER, May 19, 1790, *PJM* 13. See JM, "Vices of the Political System of the United States," *PJM* 9.

21. JM, speech of April 22, 1790, *PJM* 13.

22. JM to JMe, April 17, 1790, *PJM* 13; and JM to Henry Lee, April 13, 1790, *PJM* 13. See "First House Page," *VoteView,* comp. Keith Poole, accessed August 25, 2016, http://voteview.org/house01.htm.

23. Maclay, *The Journal of William Maclay.*

24. See JM to JMe, April 17, 1790, *PJM* 13; and Brant, *James Madison,* 3: 306–318.

25. See Cooke, "The Compromise of 1790," 541.

26. JM, speech of April 22, 1790, *PJM* 13.

27. Maclay, *The Journal of William Maclay;* and TJ, "Account of the Bargain on the Assumption and Residence Bills," *PTJ* 17.

28. JM to the Governor of Virginia, May 25, 1790, *PJM* 13; JM to Ambrose Madison, May 27, 1790, *PJM* 13; and JM to JMe, June 17, 1790, *PJM* 13.

29. TJ, "Account of the Bargain on the Assumption and Residence Bills," *PTJ* 17; and JM to James Madison Sr., July 31, 1790, *PJM* 13.

30. JM to JMe, July 25, 1790, *PJM* 13, emphasis in original.

31. AH, "Report on Public Credit," *PAH* 6.

32. See Channing, *A History of the United States,* 93; and John Thom Holdsworth and Davis R. Dewey, *The First and Second Banks of the United States* (Washington, DC: Government Printing Office, 1910), 22–23.

33. JM to TJ, July 10, 1791, *PJM* 14; and Henry Lee to JM, August 24, 1791, *PJM* 14.

34. AH to William Duer, April 4–7, 1790, *PAH* 6, emphasis in original. See also Jones, *The King of the Alley,* 169.

35. Rufus King to AH, August 15, 1791, *PAH* 9; and AH to Rufus King, August 17, 1791, *PAH* 9. See also Davis, *Essays in the Earlier History of American Corporations,* 202–203; Hammond, *Banks and Politics in America,* 123; and Jones, *The King of the Alley,* 169.

36. AH to William Duer, August 17, 1791, *PAH* 9.

37. AH to Henry Lee, December 1, 1789, *PAH* 6.

38. AH to William Seton, August 16, 1791, *PAH* 9, emphasis in original. See also AH to William Seton, August 15, 1791, *PAH* 9.

39. See David J. Cowen, Richard Sylla, and Robert E. Wright, "The U.S. Panic of 1792: Financial Crisis Management and the Lender of Last Resort," paper prepared for NBER DAE Summer Institute, July 2006,

www.helsinki.fi/iehc2006/papers1/Sylla.pdf; and "When Markets Are Too Big to Fail," editorial, *New York Times*, September 22, 2007.

40. See Forrest McDonald, *Alexander Hamilton: A Biography* (New York: Norton, 1979), 244–245. Jones argues that Hamilton's "aid" had "possibly allowed him to recover much faster." Jones, *The King of the Alley*, 172. See also Ron Chernow, *Alexander Hamilton* (New York: Penguin Books, 2004), 360; Channing, *A History of the United States*, 102; Davis, *Essays in the Earlier History of American Corporations*, 360; and Jones, *The King of the Alley*, 176.

41. AH to William Seton, January 18, 1792, *PAH* 10.

42. Hamilton biographer Ron Chernow argues that Hamilton instructed Wolcott to act against Duer, thereby communicating publicly that Duer's time was up. However, the Treasury Department had been pushing Duer to settle his accounts for some time, and Wolcott, as a semijudicial official, was empowered to act outside Hamilton's purview. In fact, it was the friendly relationship between Duer and the Treasury Department that created such a lengthy delay in settling Duer's account in the first place. Wolcott probably acted against Duer because he realized that the end for Duer was near and he wanted to secure the money Treasury was owed, rather than because Hamilton encouraged him to stop the expansion of the bubble. See McDonald, *Alexander Hamilton*, 246–247; Chernow, *Alexander Hamilton*, 381–382; Davis, *Essays on the Earlier History of American Corporations*, 292; and Jones, *The King of the Alley*, 177.

See AH to the president and directors of the Bank of New York, April 12, 1792, *PAH* 9; and AH to William Seton, April 12, 1792, *PAH* 9. Cowen, Sylla, and Wright credit Hamilton with having developed "Bagehot's rules" for financial-crisis management nearly a century before they were compiled by their namesake, Walter Bagehot. Cowen, Sylla, and Wright, "The U.S. Panic of 1792."

43. AH to William Duer, March 23, 1792, *PAH* 9; and AH to William Seton, May 25, 1792, *PAH* 9, emphasis in original. See also Davis, *Essays on the Earlier History of American Corporations*, 420–421.

44. AH, "Report on Public Credit," *PAH* 6. See also Cowen, Sylla, and Wright, "The U.S. Panic of 1792."

45. JM to TJ, May 1, 1791, *PJM* 14.

46. JM, "A Candid State of Parties," *PJM* 14; and JM, "Spirit of Governments," *PJM* 14.

47. TJ, "Explanations of the 3. Volumes Bound in Marbled Paper," *WTJ* 1; JM, "The Union. Who Are Its Real Friends?" *PJM* 14; and JM, "Government of the United States," *PJM* 14.

48. JM, "Parties," *PJM* 14. See also AH, "JM's Version of AH's Plan of Government," *PAH* 4.

49. See AH to Angelica Church, December 8, 1794, *PAH* 17. The most that can be said about Hamilton's royalist tendency is twofold. First, he admired aspects of the British system, namely, its separation of the few from the many, and the ability of the monarch to use patronage to induce members of Parliament to support the general welfare. Second, in contemplating the possible failure of the Constitution in 1787, Hamilton thought a "reunion with Great Britain . . . [was] not much to be feared." AH, "Conjectures About the New Constitution," *PAH* 4. He speculated that one of the sons of George III might be persuaded to rule in America, after a negotiation reminiscent of the one that brought William of Orange to the British throne during the Glorious Revolution. This is an awfully thin firmament upon which to build Madison's elaborate inferential structure regarding Hamilton's cryptomonarchism.

50. AH, *Federalist* 6, *PAH* 6.

Chapter Five: Vexations and Spoliation

1. GW, "Neutrality Proclamation," *PGW* Presidential Series 12.

2. JM to TJ, June 19, 1793, *PJM* 15; and TJ to JM, June 29, 1793, *PTJ* 26, emphasis in original.

3. AH, *Pacificus,* nos. I, II, III, IV, and VI, July 3–17, 1793, *PAH* 15, emphasis in original.

4. See TJ to JM, June 29, 1793, *PTJ* 26.

5. TJ to JM, July 7, 1793, *PTJ* 26; and JM to TJ, July 30, 1793, *PJM* 15. See Thomas A. Mason, Robert A. Rutland, and Jeanne K. Sisson, "Madison's 'Helvidius' Essays, 24 August–18 September 1793 (Editorial Note)," *PJM* 15.

6. JM, *Helvidius* 1, *PJM* 15.

7. JM, *Helvidius* 4, *PJM* 15, emphasis in original.

8. See AH, *Americanus* 1, *PAH* 15. In April 1793, after the execution of Louis XVI and the first waves of violence eventually known as the Terror, Madison still accepted the National Assembly's declaration that he be made an honorary citizen of France. He considered it an "honor" to be so named, and he offered his "anxious wishes for all the prosperity and glory to the French nation." He made no mention of the recent regicide, nor of the many innocents who had been slain by the blades of the guillotine. JM to the minister of the interior of the French Republic, April 1793, *PJM* 15.

9. GW to the US Senate and House of Representatives, December 5, 1793, *PGW* Presidential Series 14.

10. See JM, speech on tonnage duties, May 4, 1789; John Catanzariti, "Editorial Note: Report on Commerce," *PTJ* 27; and TJ, "Final State of the Report on Commerce," *PTJ* 27.

11. Order in Council quoted in Wilhem and Jan Willink, Nicholaas and Jacob Van Staphorst, and Nicholas Hubbard to AH, January 14, 1794, *PAH* 15. See also JM, *An Examination of the British Doctrine Which Subjects to Capture a Neutral Trade Not Open in Time of Peace* (London: Ellerton and Byworth, 1806), 305; Ron Chernow, *Alexander Hamilton* (New York: Penguin Books, 2004), 459; Stanley M. Elkins and Eric L. McKitrick, *The Age of Federalism* (New York: Oxford University Press, 1993), 390; and James Thomas Flexner, *George Washington,* 4 vols. (Boston: Little, Brown, 1963–1972), 4: 131.

12. AH, conversations with George Beckwith, April 15–16, 1794, *PAH* 16; and AH to GW, March 8, 1794, *PAH* 16.

13. See Samuel Flagg Bemis, *Jay's Treaty: A Study in Commerce and Diplomacy* (New Haven: Yale University Press, 1965), 1–31; and Bradford Perkins, *The First Rapprochement: England and the United States, 1795–1805* (Philadelphia: University of Pennsylvania Press, 1955), 1–2.

14. See "John Jay's Treaty, 1794–95," US State Department, accessed June 30, 2017, https://history.state.gov/milestones/1784-1800/jay-treaty; Forrest McDonald, *The Presidency of George Washington* (Lawrence: University Press of Kansas, 1974), 154; and Perkins, *The First Rapprochement,* 5.

15. Quoted in Donald Stewart, *The Opposition Press of the Federalist Period* (Albany: State University of New York Press, 1969), 199–200; and JM to Robert R. Livingston, August 10, 1795, *PJM* 16. See also GW to AH, July 29, 1795, *PAH* 18.

16. TJ to JM, September 21, 1795, *PTJ* 28. See Harold C. Syrett, "Introductory Note: *The Defence* No. 1, 22 July 1795," *PAH* 18.

17. JM, speech of March 10, 1796, *PJM* 16; and JM, speech of April 6, 1796, *PJM* 16.

18. Some of the disagreement was also regional. Hamilton was willing to include a payment of prewar debts owed to the British, mostly by Maryland and Virginia tobacco farmers, as part of an agreement. He also was not interested in having the slaves the British confiscated returned to the United States. See McDonald, *The Presidency of George Washington,* 142–143.

19. Thomas Malthus, *An Essay on the Principle of Population, and Other Writings,* ed. Robert J. Mayhew (New York: Penguin Classics, 2015), 22.

20. JM to TJ, June 19, 1786, *PJM* 9; JM, speech of June 26, 1787, *PJM* 10; and JM, speech of August 7, 1787, *PJM* 10. See also JM to Nicholas P. Trist, April 1, 1827, *PJM* Early Access; and JM to Edward Everett, November 26, 1783, *PJM* Early Access.

21. JM to TJ, June 19, 1786, *PJM* 9; and JM, speech of June 12, 1788, *PJM* 11.

22. JM, "Republican Distribution of Citizens," *PJM* 14; and JM, "Fashion," *PJM* 14.

23. JM, "Fashion," *PJM* 14. See Drew McCoy, *The Elusive Republic: Political Economy in Jeffersonian America* (Chapel Hill: University of North Carolina Press, 1980), 136–184.

24. JM, speech of May 4, 1789, *PJM* 12; and JM, speech of January 3, 1794, *PJM* 15. See also Forrest McDonald, *Novus Ordo Seclorum: The Intellectual Origins of the Constitution* (Lawrence: University Press of Kansas, 1985), 135.

25. JM, speech of January 14, 1794, *PJM* 15; JM, speech of January 23, 1794, *PJM* 15; JM to Horatio Gates, March 24, 1794, *PJM* 15; and JM, speech of January 31, 1794, *PJM* 15.

26. AH, conversation with George Beckwith, October 1789, *PAH* 5.

27. AH, conversation with George Hammond, April 15–16, 1794, *PAH* 16.

28. AH to GW, April 14, 1794, *PAH* 16; and AH, *Americanus* 2, *PAH* 16.

29. AH, *Federalist* 11, *PAH* 4; AH, *Americanus* 1, *PAH* 16; and AH, *Pacificus* 3, *PAH* 15. See also AH, *The Defence* 2, *PAH* 18; and AH to GW, April 14, 1794, *PAH* 16.

30. AH, conversation with George Beckwith, October 1789, *PAH* 5.

31. AH, "Points to Be Considered in the Instructions to Mr. Jay," *PAH* 16; and AH, conversation with George Hammond, July 1–10, 1794, *PAH* 16.

32. See AH, "Points to Be Considered in the Instructions to Mr. Jay," *PAH* 16; AH, "Suggestions for a Commercial Treaty," *PAH* 16; and Bemis, *Jay's Treaty*, 291.

Chapter Six: Metaphysical War

1. See Ralph Adams Brown, *The Presidency of John Adams* (Lawrence: The University Press of Kansas, 1975), 118.

2. John Adams, address to Congress, May 16, 1797, *APP*. See also Brown, *The Presidency of John Adams*, 34–49; and AH to Rufus King, January 5, 1800, *PAH* 24.

3. See AH, "Letter Concerning the Public Conduct and Character of John Adams, Esq. President of the United States," *PAH* 25.

4. TJ to Spencer Roane, September 6, 1819, *PTJ* Early Access; and John Adams to James Lloyd, February 6, 1815, in *The Adams Papers*, ed.

L. H. Butterfield et al. (Cambridge: Harvard University Press, 1961–), http://founders.archives.gov. See also Ron Chernow, *Alexander Hamilton* (New York: Penguin Books, 2004), 88.

5. Believing that the bulk of the Federalist Party could be peeled away from the High Federalists, Jefferson employed moderate rhetoric to discuss his opponents, and he also left many Federalist appointees in office. See Leonard D. White, *The Jeffersonians: A Study in Administrative History, 1801–1829* (New York: Free Press, 1951), 347–368.

6. See TJ, First Annual Message, November 27, 1801, *PTJ* 35; JM to Robert R. Livingston and JMe, March 2, 1803, *PJM* Secretary of State Series 4; Alexander Balinky, "Albert Gallatin, Naval Foe," *Pennsylvania Magazine of History and Biography* 82, no. 3 (July 1958): 293–304; Drew McCoy, *The Elusive Republic: Political Economy in Jeffersonian America* (Chapel Hill: University of North Carolina Press, 1980), 185–208; and Robert W. Tucker and David C. Hendrickson, *Empire of Liberty: The Statecraft of Thomas Jefferson* (New York: Oxford University Press), 87–174.

7. See TJ, "Revised Amendment," *PTJ* 4; TJ to AG, July 9, 1803, *PTJ* 40; TJ to JM, August 24, 1803, *PTJ* 41; and TJ, "Amendment for Annexation of Louisiana and Florida," *PTJ* 41.

8. AG, "A Sketch of the Finances of the United States," *WAG* 3. See Forrest McDonald, *The Presidency of Thomas Jefferson* (Lawrence: University Press of Kansas, 1976), 38–43; and Raymond Walters, *Albert Gallatin: Jeffersonian Financier and Diplomat* (Pittsburgh, PA: University of Pittsburgh Press, 1969), 145–147.

9. TJ to AG, December 13, 1803, *WTJ* 10; and AG to TJ, December 13, 1803, *WAG* 1. See also AH to William Seton, November 25, 1791, *PAH* 9; Bray Hammond, *Banks and Politics in America from the Revolution to the Civil War* (Princeton: Princeton University Press, 1957), 127; Robert Allen Rutland, *The Presidency of James Madison* (Lawrence: University Press of Kansas, 1990), 68–69; and Walters, *Albert Gallatin,* 171.

10. See White, *The Jeffersonians,* 347–368.

11. GW, Farewell Address, *PGW* Early Access; TJ, First Inaugural Address, March 4, 1801, *APP*; and TJ to John Adams, July 5, 1814, *PTJ* Retirement Series 7. See also Bradford Perkins, *Prologue to War: England and the United States, 1805–1812* (Berkeley: University of California Press, 1961), 50.

12. See JMe to JM, July 1, 1804, *PJM* Secretary of State Series 7; and Bradford Perkins, *The First Rapprochement: England and the United States, 1795–1805* (Philadelphia: University of Pennsylvania Press, 1955), 73–74.

13. See, for instance, JM to George Joy, May 22, 1807, *PJM* Early Access.

14. TJ to Thomas Lomax, January 11, 1806, *PTJ* Early Access.

15. JM, editorial in the *National Intelligencer,* December 23, 1807, *PJM* Early Access. See also JM to TJ, September 14, 1805, *PJM* Secretary of State Series 10; JM, editorial in the *National Intelligencer,* December 25, 1807, *PJM* Early Access; JM, editorial in the *National Intelligencer,* December 28, 1807, *PJM* Early Access; and JM to William Pinkney, April 30, 1808.

16. AG to TJ, December 18, 1807, *PTJ* Early Access.

17. JM to Henry Wheaton, July 11, 1824, *PJM* Early Access.

18. See William Branch Giles to JM, February 27, 1809, *PJM* Early Access.

19. See JM to TJ, April 23, 1810, *PJM* Presidential Series 2; JM to William Pinkney, May 23, 1810, *PJM* Presidential Series 2; and JM to TJ, May 25, 1810, *PJM* Presidential Series 2. The president was not blind to the potential for French duplicity. Madison was accused of being Napoleon's dupe during his own day and responded that the charge was "as foolish as it is false." JM to Henry Wheaton, February 26, 1827, *PJM* Early Access. See JM to William Pinkney, May 23, 1810, *PJM* Presidential Series 2; JM to TJ, May 25, 1812, *PJM* Presidential Series 4; and JM to John Armstrong, October 29, 1818, *PJM* Presidential Series 2.

20. See JM to Caesar A. Rodney, September 30, 1810, *PJM* Presidential Series 2; JM to TJ, May 25, 1812, *PJM* Presidential Series 4; AG to Ezekiel Bacon, January 10, 1812, *WAG* 1; AG to NB, August 14, 1830, *WAG* 3; and AG, "Memorial to the House of Representatives," *RD* 23: 4862–4864.

21. JM to TJ, April 19, 1811, *PJM* Presidential Series 3; JM to Congress, June 1, 1812, *PJM* Presidential Series 4. See also Roger H. Brown, *The Republic in Peril: 1812* (New York: Columbia University Press, 1964), 44–66.

22. John Taylor, "The Letters of John Taylor of Caroline (Concluded)," *Virginia Magazine of History and Biography* 52, no. 2 (April 1944): 128; and JM to US Congress, February 18, 1815, *APP.*

23. See Rutland, *The Presidency of James Madison,* 126–127. In the fall of 1812, Gallatin estimated to Madison that the government would need to borrow $21 million to fund the war. See AG to JM, ca. November 19, 1812, *PJM* Presidential Series 5.

24. See the Treaty of Ghent, 1814, *AP;* and JM to Richard Rush, May 10, 1819, *PJM* Retirement Series 1.

25. See "Presidential Historians Survey, 2017: James Madison," C-SPAN, accessed August 6, 2017, www.c-span.org/presidentsurvey2017/?personid =39787; and Drew McCoy, *The Last of the Fathers: James Madison and the Republican Legacy* (Cambridge: Cambridge University Press, 1989), 12–14.

26. Alexander J. Dallas to JCC, December 24, 1815, in *Legislative and Documentary History of the Bank of the United States,* comp. M. St. Clair and

D. A. Hall (Washington, DC: Gales and Seaton, 1832), 616; JM to US Congress, December 5, 1815, *PJM* Early Access.

27. JM to US Congress, December 5, 1815, *PJM* Early Access. Madison was not the first Republican to advocate industrial protection. Jefferson had hinted at this idea to Gallatin, arguing in 1808, for instance, that a certain type of lead might be "worthy of being placed within the pale of protection." TJ to AG, December 24, 1808, *PTJ* Early Access. Early in his career, Clay was also an advocate of protection, arguing for it as a means of defending American self-sufficiency against encroachments by the European powers. See HC, "On Domestic Manufactures," *LSHC*, 197.

28. AH, "Report on Manufactures," *PAH* 10.

29. JM to US Congress, December 5, 1815, *PJM* Early Access; and JCC, speech of February 4, 1817, *AC* 14: 854. See also JM, "Public Opinion," *PJM* 14.

30. TJ, Inaugural Address, March 4, 1805, *APP;* and AG, *Report on the Subject of Public Roads and Canals* (Washington, DC: R. C. Weightman, 1808), http://oll.libertyfund.org/titles/gallatin-report-of-the-secretary-of-the -treasury-on-the-subject-of-public-roads-and-canals.

31. See John Lauritz Larson, *Internal Improvements: National Public Works and the Promise of Popular Government in the Early United States* (Chapel Hill: University of North Carolina Press, 2008), 39–70; and John Joseph Wallis and Barry R. Weingast, "Equilibrium Impotence: Why the States and Not the American National Government Financed Economic Development in the Antebellum Era," National Bureau of Economic Research, working paper 11397, June 2005, www.nber.org/papers/w11397 .pdf.

32. JMe to the Military Committee of the Senate, February 22, 1815, in *The Writings of James Monroe,* ed. Stanislaus Murray Hamilton, 7 vols. (New York: G. P. Putnam's Sons, 1902–1903), 5: 322; and HC, "On the Direct Tax," *LSHC,* 285.

33. HC, "Mission to South America," *LSHC,* 486; and AH, *Federalist* 11, *PAH* 6. Randolph quoted in David S. Heidler and Jeanne T. Heidler, *Henry Clay: The Essential American* (New York: Random House, 2011), 124, emphasis in original. See also HC, speech of February 2–6, 1832, *RD* 22: 257–296.

34. See AH to William Seton, November 25, 1791, *PAH* 9; Hammond, *Banks and Politics in America,* 256; and Lawrence A. Peskin, "How the Republicans Learned to Love Manufacturing: The First Parties and the 'New Economy,'" *Journal of the Early Republic* 22, no. 2 (Summer 2002): 239–248.

35. See Heidler and Heidler, *Henry Clay,* 228.

Chapter Seven: Intrigue and Corruption

1. *Columbian Centinel* quoted in Harlow G. Unger, *The Last Founding Father: James Monroe and a Nation's Call to Greatness* (Cambridge, MA: Da Capo Press, 2010), 271.

2. Andrew Jackson, veto message of July 10, 1832, *APP*; and Ted Kennedy, "1980 Democratic National Convention Address," American Rhetoric, accessed October 11, 2017, http://www.americanrhetoric.com/speeches /tedkennedy1980dnc.htm.

3. Bray Hammond called his condemnation "an unctuous mixture of agrarianism and laissez faire." Hammond, *Banks and Politics in America from the Revolution to the Civil War* (Princeton: Princeton University Press, 1957), 405.

4. JM to Charles J. Ingersoll, June 25, 1831, *PJM* Early Access. Madison was prepared to follow this reasoning only so far. In his view, precedent validated the Second Bank but not federal sponsorship of roads and canals, so, surprisingly, he broke from Clay and the Republicans on the Bonus Bill of 1817, which would have used the bonus owed the federal government from the Second Bank as a fund for internal improvements. In one of his last acts as president, he vetoed the measure for "insufficient precedents," despite the fact that the federal government had already made investments, particularly in the Cumberland Road. In retrospect, this appears to have been an ad hoc, rearguard action to keep the constitutional grant of authority to Congress from morphing into a plenary power. See JM, veto message of March 3, 1817, *APP*.

5. TJ to AG, December 13, 1803, *WTJ* 10.

6. JM to John G. Jackson, December 28, 1821, *PJM* Retirement Series 2; and AG to TJ, December 13, 1803, *PAG* 1.

7. Girard quoted in Hammond, *Banks and Politics in America*, 252.

8. Rufus King to C. Gore, December 26, 1816, in *The Life and Correspondence of Rufus King*, ed. Charles R. King, 6 vols. (New York: G. P. Putnam's Sons, 1894–1900), 6: 38. See Ralph C. H. Catterall, *The Second Bank of the United States* (Chicago: University of Chicago Press, 1903), 40–41; Edward K. Eckert, "William Jones: Mr. Madison's Secretary of the Navy," *Pennsylvania Magazine of History and Biography* 96, no. 2 (April 1972): 177–178; Thomas P. Govan, *Nicholas Biddle, Nationalist and Public Banker, 1786–1844* (Chicago: University of Chicago Press, 1959), 51; and Hammond, *Banks and Politics in America*, 251–258.

9. JQA, *MJQA*, 4: 382–383.

10. Jones quoted in Hammond, *Banks and Politics in America*, 253.

11. Langdon Cheves, "Exposition of the President of the Bank to the Stockholders," in *Niles Weekly Register*, ed. Hezekiah Niles and William

Ogden Niles, 52 vols. (Baltimore: Franklin Press, 1814–1837), 23: 91; and Langdon Cheves to William Crawford, May 27, 1819, in *Report on the Condition of the Bank of the United States,* comp. Committee of Inspection and Investigation (Philadelphia: William Fry, 1822), 73.

12. Gouge quoted in Edward Kaplan, *The Bank of the United States and the American Economy* (Westport, CT: Greenwood Press, 1999), 64.

13. JM to TJ, August 8, 1791, *PJM* 14; and JM, "Banks," *PJM* Retirement Series 1.

14. See Catterall, *The Second Bank of the United States,* 96–108; Phil Davies, "The 'Monster' of Chestnut Street," Federal Reserve Bank of Minneapolis, September 1, 2008, www.minneapolisfed.org/publications/the-region/the-monster-of-chestnut-street; Hammond, *Banks and Politics in America,* 323–324: Govan, *Nicholas Biddle,* 85–87; and Jean Alexander Wilburn, *Biddle's Bank: The Crucial Years* (New York: Columbia University Press, 1967), 85, 120–121.

15. Richard Rush to NB, December 10, 1828, *CNB* 60.

16. JQA, *MJQA,* 4: 490.

17. Biddle quoted in Thomas Hart Benton, *Thirty Years' View; or, A History of the Workings of the American Government for Thirty Years, from 1820 to 1850,* 2 vols. (New York: D. Appleton, 1886), 1: 159.

18. Jackson quoted in Sean Wilentz, *Andrew Jackson* (New York: Times Books, 2005), 81, emphasis in original.

19. See NB to Thomas Cooper, August 16, 1834, *CNB* 215; NB to Robert Lennox, October 1, 1833, *CNB* 215–216; Hammond, *Banks and Politics in America,* 418–433; and Jacob P. Meerman, "The Climax of the Bank War: Biddle's Contraction, 1833–34," *Journal of Political Economy* 71, no. 4 (August 1963): 379–384.

20. NB to JMe, May 28, 1824, *CNB* 147.

21. NB to Charles Hammond, March 11, 1834, *CNB* 225–226; NB to William Appleton, January 27, 1834, *CNB* 219; and NB to John G. Watmough, February 8, 1834, *CNB* 221.

22. JM, speech of February 8, 1791, *PJM* 13.

23. JM, "Monopolies. Perpetuities. Corporations. Ecclesiastical Endowments," *PJM* Retirement Series 1, emphasis in original.

Chapter Eight: The Vilest of Cheats

1. See F. W. Taussig, *The Tariff History of the United States,* 5th ed. (New York: G. P. Putnam's Sons, 1910), 18–23; and Edward Stanwood, *American Tariff Controversies in the Nineteenth Century,* 2 vols. (Boston: Houghton, Mifflin, 1903), 1: 127–130.

2. JCC, speech of January 31, 1816, *AC* 14: 832–837.

3. See Alexander Dallas, "Tariff of Duties on Imports," *ASP,* 3: 89–91.

4. Taylor, speech of May 4, 1824, *AC* 18: 686.

5. "Memorial of the Citizens of Richmond, South Carolina Against Increase of Duties on Imports," *ASP* 5: 707.

6. JM, *Federalist* 10, *PJM* 10.

7. George Dangerfield, *The Awakening of American Nationalism, 1815–1828* (New York: Harper and Row, 1965), 283.

8. See Hezekiah Niles, "The Woollens Bill," *Niles Weekly Register,* 32: 295.

9. Andrew Jackson to Littleton Coleman, April 26, 1824, in *The Papers of Andrew Jackson,* ed. Sam B. Smith et al. (Knoxville: University of Tennessee Press, 1980–), 5: 398.

10. See Dangerfield, *The Awakening of American Nationalism,* 280; W. M. Hargreaves, *The Presidency of John Quincy Adams* (Lawrence: University Press of Kansas, 1985), 194–196; Stanwood, *American Tariff Controversies in the Nineteenth Century,* 253–270; Taussig, *The Tariff History of the United States,* 72–92; and Charles Wiltese, *John C. Calhoun: Nationalist* (Indianapolis: Bobbs-Merrill, 1944), 355–368.

11. Thomas Mitchell, speech of April 15, 1828, *RD* 20: 2844; John Randolph, speech of April 22, 1828, *RD* 20: 2472; James Buchanan, quoted in Philip S. Klein, *President James Buchanan* (University Park: Pennsylvania State University Press, 1962), 66; HC to Peter B. Porter, March 1, 1828, in *The Papers of Henry Clay,* ed. Donald Jackson et al. (Lexington: University Press of Kentucky, 1959–), 7: 136; HC, speech of February 2–3, 1832, *RD* 22: 264; JCC, speech of February 23, 1837, *RD* 24: 906. Robert Remini argues that Van Buren wanted the measure to pass all along. See Robert Remini, "Martin Van Buren and the Tariff of Abominations," *American Historical Review* 63, no. 4 (July 1958): 903–917.

12. See JQA, Fourth Annual Message, *APP.*

13. Jackson, First Annual Message, *APP.*

14. See Douglas Irwin, "Antebellum Tariff Politics: Regional Coalitions and Shifting Economic Interests," *Journal of Law and Economics* 51, no. 4 (November 2008): 723.

15. JCC, *Selected Writings and Speeches,* ed. H. Lee Clark (Washington, DC: Regnery, 2003), 288; JCC to Tazewell quoted in William Montgomery Meigs, *The Life of John Caldwell Calhoun* (New York: Neale Publishing, 1912), 360; and JCC to James Edward Calhoun quoted in Theodore Dehon Jervey, *Robert Y. Hayne and His Times* (New York: Macmillan, 1909), 212.

16. Aristotle, *Politics,* trans. Ernest Barker (Oxford: Oxford University Press, 1995), 100.

17. JCC, *The Essential Calhoun: Selections from Writings, Speeches, and Letters,* ed. Clyde Norman Wilson (New Brunswick, NJ: Transaction Publishers, 1992), 10 and 33; and JCC to JMe is quoted in Meigs, *The Life of John Caldwell Calhoun,* 360–361.

18. JCC, *The Essential Calhoun,* 35.

19. JM, "Virginia Resolutions," December 21, 1798, *PJM* 17; and AH, *Federalist 26, PAH* 4. See JM, speech of June 8, 1789, *PJM* 12; JM, "The Report of 1800," *PJM* 17; JM to Joseph C. Cabell, September 18, 1828, *PJM* Early Access; JM to Joseph C. Cabell, October 30, 1828, *PJM* Early Access; JM, "On Nullification," *PJM* Early Access; JM to Robert Young Hayne, April 3, 1830, *PJM* Early Access; and JM to Unknown, "Re: Majority Governments," *PJM* Early Access. See also Irving Brant, *James Madison,* 6 vols. (Indianapolis: Bobbs-Merrill, 1941–1961), 5: 468–500; Christoph Fritz, "Interposition and the Heresy of Nullification: James Madison and the Exercise of Sovereign Constitutional Powers," Heritage Foundation, February 21, 2012, www.heritage.org/the-constitution/report/interposition -and-the-heresy-nullification-james-madison-and-the-exercise; Kevin R. Gutzman, "A Troublesome Legacy: James Madison and 'The Principles of '98,'" *Journal of the Early Republic* 15, no. 4 (December 1995): 579; Drew McCoy, *The Last of the Fathers: James Madison and the Republican Legacy* (Cambridge: Cambridge University Press, 1989), 119–170; Adrienne Koch, *Jefferson and Madison* (New York: Knopf, 1950), 174–211; and August O. Spain, *The Political Theory of John C. Calhoun* (New York: Octagon Books, 1968), 184–215.

20. JM, "British Government," *PJM* 14; and JM, "Spirit of Governments," *PJM* 14.

21. Daniel Webster, speech of January 26–27, 1830, *RD* 21: 80. See also William Hart Benton, speech of January 18, 1830, *RD* 21: 22–26; and Robert Hayne, speech of January 19, 1830, *RD* 21: 31–35.

CONCLUSION

1. JM to TJ, May 1, 1791, *PJM* 14.

2. See Richard Franklin Bensel, *The Political Economy of American Industrialization, 1877–1900* (Cambridge: Cambridge University Press, 2000), 457–458; Douglas Irwin, "Tariffs and Growth in Late Nineteenth Century America," National Bureau of Economic Research, working paper 7639, April 2000, www.nber.org/papers/w7639.pdf; and Yeo Joon Yoon, "The Role of Tariffs in U.S. Development, 1870–1913," University of Warwick, October 2013, www2.warwick.ac.uk/fac/soc/economics/staff/yyoon /jobmarket3.pdf.

3. 1892 Democratic Platform, *APP*.

4. See, for instance, Charles W. Calhoun, *Minority Victory: Gilded Age Politics and the Front Porch Campaign of 1888* (Lawrence: University Press of Kansas, 2008), 144–151; and Richard E. Welch Jr., *The Presidencies of Grover Cleveland* (Lawrence: University Press of Kansas, 1988), 83–89.

5. Lincoln Steffens, *The Struggle for Self-Government* (New York: McClure, Phillips, and Co., 1906), 126; and David Graham Phillips, *The Treason of the Senate* (Chicago: Quadrangle Books, 1964), 79.

6. See Jerome L. Sternstein, "Corruption in the Gilded Age Senate: Nelson W. Aldrich and the Sugar Trust," *Capitol Studies* 6, no. 1 (Spring 1978), http://www.starkman.com/hippo/history/aldrich/sterns.html; and Clarence A. Stern, *Republican Heyday: Republicanism Through the McKinley Years* (Ann Arbor, MI: Edwards Brothers, 1962), 22.

7. See, for instance, William Randolph Hearst, "New Standard Oil Letters and Their Lessons," *Hearst's Magazine,* June, July, August 1912.

8. Edmunds quoted in Ray Ginger, *Age of Excess: The United States from 1877 to 1914* (New York: Macmillan, 1975), 104–105.

9. See Sean Dennis Cashman, *America in the Gilded Age: From the Death of Lincoln to the Rise of Theodore Roosevelt* (New York: New York University Press, 1993), 249–252; and Neil Rolde, *Continental Liar from the State of Maine: James G. Blaine* (Gardiner, ME: Tilbury House, 2007), 177–183.

10. See John Steele Gordon, *An Empire of Wealth* (New York: HarperCollins, 2004), 219–220; and Maury Klein, *Union Pacific: Birth of a Railroad, 1862–1893* (Garden City, NY: Doubleday, 1987), 291–302.

11. 1912 Progressive Platform, *APP*. See Herbert Croly, *The Promise of American Life* (New York: Macmillan, 1904), 153.

12. See Kenneth A. Shepsle and Mark A. Bonchak, *Analyzing Politics: Rationality, Behavior, and Institutions* (New York: W. W. Norton, 1997), 274.

13. Cicero, *"On the Commonwealth" and "On the Laws,"* ed. James E. G. Zetzel (Cambridge: Cambridge University Press, 2010), 19; Polybius, *The Histories of Polybius,* ed. and trans. Evelyn S. Shuckburgh, 2 vols. (Cambridge: Cambridge University Press, 2012), 1: 461; and Machiavelli, *The Discourses,* ed. Bernard Crick (New York: Penguin Books, 1998), 109.

14. Machiavelli, *The Discourses,* 385, 386, 390; and JM, "Spirit of Governments," *PJM* 14.

15. JM, speech of June 8, 1789, *PJM* 12.

16. JM, "Spirit of Governments," *PJM* 14.

17. JM, "British Government," *PJM* 14; and JM, "Public Opinion," *PJM* 14.

INDEX

JAY COST IS a contributing editor at the *Weekly Standard* and columnist for the *Pittsburgh Post-Gazette* and *National Review*. He holds a PhD in political science from the University of Chicago. The author of *A Republic No More,* he lives in western Pennsylvania.